THE SEPOY and THE COSSACK

THE SEPOY
and
THE COSSACK

PIERCE G. FREDERICKS

An NAL Book

The World Publishing Company

NEW YORK AND CLEVELAND

For Joan

Devon

Stacey

and

Mariah

with love

Published by The New American Library, Inc.
in association with The World Publishing Company
Published simultaneously in Canada
by Nelson, Foster & Scott Ltd.

First printing—1971

Library of Congress catalog card number: 74-115808

PRINTED IN THE UNITED STATES OF AMERICA

All pictures, except the first three,
are from *The History of India,*
published by Cassel & Co.

WORLD PUBLISHING
TIMES MIRROR

CONTENTS

INTRODUCTION

It was 1876 and Victoria Regina wanted very badly to be Victoria Regina et Imperatrix. "I am an Empress and in common conversation am sometimes called Empress of India," she noted. "Why have I never officially assumed this title? I feel I ought to do so and wish to have preliminary inquiries made."

Her Prime Minister, Mr. Benjamin Disraeli, was thoroughly in favor. To a colleague, he wrote that Her Majesty "demands her imperial crown." She might, of course, have had it in 1858 when the Crown formally took over the rule of India from the Honorable East India Company after the mutiny of the Indian troops in Bengal. At the time, however, it had seemed unwise to ask a people obviously unenthusiastic about any sort of British rule to accept an Empress into the bargain.

In addition to Her Majesty's wishes—which it was never safe to take lightly—there was now a second pressing motive for change. Slowly, steadily, closer to the India border, the Russians were moving southward in Central Asia. When the British first were in India and the Russians gave serious attention to Central Asia, their bases were some four thousand miles apart. By 1876, they were only one thousand miles apart. Mr. Disraeli was not "of that school who view the advances of Russia in Asia with those deep misgivings that some do." On the other hand, if the Queen became Queen-Empress, it would point up "in language which cannot be mistaken that the Parliament of England have resolved to uphold the Empire of India."

Parliament had the impertinence to debate the necessary Royal Titles Bill, the *Times* of London ridiculed the idea, and Her Majesty was "much upset." By May, 1876, however, the thing was done. It remained only to proclaim Her Majesty properly to the people of India.

The man who would do the proclaiming was Edward Robert Bulwer-Lytton—Lord Lytton—whom Disraeli had sent out as Governor-General of India. He was the son of the author of *The Last Days of Pompeii*, and a poet in his own right under the *nom de plume* Owen Meredith. A prominent nose, a heavy black beard, and a vaguely theatrical air made him look much like a road company actor, although he had actually spent twenty-five years in the foreign service and was the British minister at Lisbon when Disraeli persuaded him to go out east.

The prospect of proclaiming his Queen as Empress delighted Lytton. As a later Viceroy who found him "picturesque," "poetic," and "bohemian" wrote, "To such a man the Proclamation of the queen as Empress of India appealed with as much force as it did to the Oriental vision of the Jewish Prime Minister. . . . Lytton addressed himself with ardour to the marshalling of the Imperial Assemblage at Delhi."

Indeed he did. In order for it to be done right and for there to be the best possible weather, the event, he informed London, could not take place before January 1, 1877. At that time, he hoped to create an Indian Privy Council of Great Chiefs, an Indian Peerage, and an Indian Heralds' College. After all, he wrote Disraeli, what was the good of putting the chiefs and princes to the trouble and expense of coming to the Assemblage if it was "unconnected with any practical advantage or benefit to themselves"? The point was well taken. An old India hand estimated that the Assemblage would cost a really first-rate prince like the Nizam of Hyderabad between $350,000 and $400,000. In the event, however, London vetoed the Privy Council and the Indian Peerage, but looked to the advantage and benefit of the princes by giving each an increase in allowance and a silken banner, designed by the Governor-General* himself and with the Prince's own coat of arms on it.

---

* On Victoria's taking the title "Empress," Lytton added the title "Viceroy"—that is, he governed directly in the name of the Queen.

As the new year approached, tent cities circled Delhi.
The British camps were on the ridge north of the city—a
somewhat tactless reminder of the Bengal mutiny when
British troops had occupied the same ground. The British
tents were white, set up in two rows facing one another.
The Indian camps were looser and far more gay with
blue-and-scarlet tents, their tent poles frequently tipped
with golden knobs.

Lytton himself was to arrive in Delhi on Saturday
afternoon, December 23. For the occasion, Indian army
troops and those of the princely states were drawn up
alternately along the line of march from the railway
station to the Viceroy's camp. Among the princely legions
were elephants with steel tips on their tusks, their
howdahs hung with gold and silver embroidery and their
riders wearing the chain mail of another age. The forces
of the Gaekwar of Baroda received special attention,
since their artillery was cast of either gold or silver. The
golden guns had silver wheels and the silver guns golden
ones.

At two o'clock in the afternoon on a bright cool day,
the officials of British India and sixty-three Ruling Chiefs
saw the Governor-General alight from his train and heard
his greeting:

It is with feelings of unusual pleasure that I find
you here assembled from all parts of India to take
part in a ceremonial which I trust, will be the means
of drawing still closer the bonds of union between the
Government of Her Majesty and the Great Allies and
Feudatories of the Empire. . . . Accept my hearty
welcome to Delhi.

The chiefs were introduced and Lytton spoke separately with the most prominent—the Nizam of Hyderabad (a
boy of ten), the Maharaja Sindia, the Maharaja Holkar,
the Maharaja of Kashmir, the Gaekwar of Baroda (a boy
of thirteen), and the Maharaja of Jaipur. He then
mounted his elephant, and the procession began to move
through the packed streets of Delhi. Much of the crowd
had been waiting since early morning.

At the head of the parade rode the 11th Hussars, and it
is worth pausing a moment to examine this prestigious
formation, since it tells a great deal about a world which
seems too long dead to have been quite real less than one

hundred years ago. The 11th was, as befits a crack cavalry regiment, "splendidly mounted." Their tunics were dark blue with gold loops on the breast and gold braid on the sleeves. Cherry-red britches slid into black knee-high boots. The headgear was a black sable busby—by regulation, six and three quarter inches high in front and eight inches at the back. Atop everything was a white ostrich-feather plume fifteen inches high with a small collar of crimson vulture feathers about its base.

This magnificent unit had been in existence since 1715 and found nothing odd in having a German regimental motto—*Treu und Fest* ("Steadfast and Staunch"). It had acquired the motto in 1840 when the Hussars were sent to meet German Prince Albert when he arrived at Dover to wed Victoria and they became "Prince Albert's Own." No really good British regiment is without its oddities of regimental ritual and the 11th was no exception. Its band played a Spanish hymn just before last post each night as a penance for one of the few bad marks on the unit's record: it had sacked a Spanish convent during the Peninsula campaign.* On the brighter side, they had charged with the Light Brigade at Balaklava and come out of that terrible day with the nickname "Lord Cardigan's Bloodhounds."†

As an instrument of war, cavalry was already virtually useless, but as a symbol of the Imperial power beyond the sea, the black water, the 11th Hussars would do very nicely. A little farther down the line of march, the 3d Bombay Cavalry—Indian troopers, British officers—might look equally magnificent in blue and silver uniforms with white headgear, but the presence of the 11th was a reminder that in the Bengal mutiny it was British troops that had prevailed against vastly superior numbers.

On Sunday the Governor-General attended Divine services conducted by the Bishop of Madras, and on Monday he celebrated Christmas with his family. The day was

---

* In the 12th Lancers, they play five Spanish hymns after last post for misdeeds on the Peninsula. One trusts that they do not represent five convents.

† In another war they would win another nickname. They were "the Desert Rats"—the most famous unit of the armored division that chased the Italians across North Africa for General Sir Archibald Wavell. By this time, the 11th Hussars had, of painful necessity, changed from horses to armored cars, but their officers on leave still swanked it around Cairo in cherry-red britches.

marred only by the death of an unfortunate captain of the 9th Lancers who broke his neck playing polo.

At ten o'clock Tuesday morning, Lytton got down to business. Seated in his tent beneath a portrait of Victoria, he received princes and chiefs until seven in the evening. As each advanced through an escort of lancers, cannon fired the appropriate salute and trumpeters set up a flourish which, according to a contemporary account, went "wildly trembling o'er the plain." In all, Lytton received twenty-three visitors that day, another thirty-one on Wednesday, sixteen on Thursday, and the rest on Friday. Each received a gold medal presented in the name of Her Majesty and one of the banners on which Lytton himself had worked so hard. He noted that they were well received in spite of the fact that the brass poles on which they were mounted turned out to be so heavy that it required two Highlanders to carry them.

In general, all went well. The Scindia of Gwalior appeared to be "out of sorts," but the weight of opinion was that he was either ill at ease or wished to show particular respect by remaining silent. There was a flutter when a minor Nawab from Central India announced that he had heard that His Excellency wrote poetry, that he too wrote poetry, and that he proposed to recite some of it. According to the *Times* of India, "His Excellency heard this with something like consternation. . . . The Nawab then went into a history of his studies in literature. . . . When Lord Lytton tried to edge in the final compliment, the eloquent Nawab simply talked faster and louder than ever. . . ." Still orating, the Nawab was backed out the tent door.

Saturday and Sunday were devoted to the more mundane matter of the worst famine of the century in Madras and Bombay. It took five and a half million lives—the population of the city of London—and the Indian press was quite vocal in its conviction that the assemblage expenses might better have been spent on famine relief. Then Proclamation Day arrived—clear and, for India, cool.

The ceremony was to take place on a plain some four miles north of Delhi. Here had been constructed a Throne Pavilion for Lytton—a blue, red, and gold six-sided structure some 240 feet around. Its base was masonry, the upperworks a canopy of conical shape described by one reporter for an Anglo-Indian newspaper thus: "For some distance down, the narrow part of the cone shone as if it were entirely of silver or rather as if it were sheathed in a cloth made of silver thread. Then the design changed to red and gold and became much suffused with flags."

Opposite was a second pavilion for British officials and Indian princes. Done in blue, white, and gold, it stretched for some eight hundred feet. In it "every effort was made to mingle the Ruling Chiefs with European officials, so as to avoid questions of precedence which have excited bitterness and heart-burning in India from the remotest antiquity."

Visiting diplomats and unofficial British had seats on either side of the Throne Pavilion; the general public stood by the larger structure opposite. British troops were drawn up north of the pavilion, Indian troops to the south, and around the entire gathering of 68,000 people there was a solid circle of elephants.

All morning the soldiers had marched into position, the ordinary people of Delhi walking through the fields beside them and the dignitaries following in carriages. At noon, there was a flourish of trumpets and the Governor-General's carriage arrived; he alighted, followed by his wife and two daughters, and took his seat upon the throne. The Chief Herald was commanded to read the proclamation. It was a lengthy one, but the heart of the matter was that Victoria informed her people that she was changing her title from just plain Queen to Queen and Indiae Imperatrix—in English, Empress of India.

The proclamation was repeated in Urdu, and one hundred and one salvos of artillery were fired, plus some *feux de joie* from the surrounding infantry. The assembled bands accompanied this with the National Anthem, then the March from *Tannhäuser*. The elephants stood the artillery, the National Anthem, and *Tannhäuser* pretty well, but the *feux de joie* musketry set them to rushing wildly about, flailing with their trunks and trumpeting. Reports differ as to whether there were any casualties.

The Governor-General and Viceroy rose to speak, and his instructions from home would have challenged a Demosthenes. He was to:

> . . . remember that you have two audiences; one in India, oriental, fond of the warm colors of oratory and pardoning exaggeration more easily than coldness; the other partly in India, mainly in England,

frigid, captious, Quakerish, Philistine, only considering the composition faultless when it has been divested
of all richness and all force. It would be very agreeable to speak entirely for the benefit of one audience
only; a task of appalling difficulty to please both. Yet
it must be attempted.*

Lytton did his best. He assured everyone that though
Her Majesty's possessions took in one seventh of the
earth's surface and three hundred million of its inhabitants, there was no portion of it which she regarded with
deeper interest than India. He further assured them that
the British Crown had been called to its place in India by
Providence—a reference which must have baffled a good
many of the non-Europeans present.

To the "British Administration and Faithful Officers of
the Crown" he offered what consolation he could on a
very sore subject:

The doors of fame are not open to all; but the opportunity of doing good is denied to none who seek
it. Rapid promotion is not often in the power of any
Government to provide for its servants. But I feel assured that, in the service of the British Crown, public
duty and personal devotion will ever have higher in-
centives than the expectation of public honours or
personal emoluments.

The *Times* of India termed the statement "a very
elegant paraphrase, indeed, of the old truth that virtue is
its own reward."

The military was told that Her Majesty viewed them
with pride, the Princes were promised that their traditional rights would be respected, and a great many words
were said on the "burning question of the employment of
natives in the administration of the country." Of the
words, the *Times* said, "A more oracular concatenation of
sounding sentences and promises more explicitly inexplicit
it would be difficult to conceive."

For a finale, the Viceroy declared that Her Majesty
had no desire to annex territories bordering India, and
then took it back by adding, "Her interests and duties,
however, are not confined to her own dominions . . .

* Quoted in Lady Elizabeth Balfour's *Lord Lytton's Indian Administration.*

should [her power] at any time be threatened from
without, The Empress of India will know how to defend
her great inheritance." Everyone present knew precisely
what Lytton meant; they did not need the *Times* to tell
them that "this must be taken as a deliberate menace to
His Highness Sher Ali." His Highness was the Amir of
Kabul, Afghanistan—the nearest thing to a ruler that
strifeful country had, and at the moment under dark
suspicion of being partial to Russia.

The *Times* called it "perhaps the most splendid pageant
ever witnessed in the East." There was a certain amount
of grumbling because there had been "neither balls nor
theatricals nor concerts" and many ladies "had sat discon-
solate upon boxes of the loveliest dresses which they took
with them in the vain hope of balls that were not to be."
The explanation offered was that "balls did not sit well
with gentlemen of the Mahometan persuasion." One correspondent complained that the decorations had been
gaudy and the whole business gay rather than grand. The
press in general complained—as it always does—that it
had difficulty getting news out of government sources.

Her Majesty, however, was pleased. Mr. Disraeli became Lord Beaconsfield and in due course was invited to
dine at Windsor. The Queen, usually a notably plain
dresser, made her satisfaction clear by appearing in "a
mass of Oriental jewelry, most consisting of very large
uncut stones and pearls" which were gifts from the Princes
of India. Disraeli was so tickled that he quite forgot
court etiquette and rose to toast the Empress of India
"with a little speech as flowery as the oration to a Maharaja." Her Majesty responded with a "pretty, smiling
bow."

In India, Lytton had no time for such pleasantries. He
had been sent out with strong instructions:

> The maintenance in Afghanistan of a strong and
> friendly power has at all times been the object of Brit-
> ish policy. The attainment of this object is now to be
> considered with due reference to the situation created
> by the recent and rapid advance of the Russian army
> in Central Asia towards the northern frontiers of
> British India. . . . Her Majesty's government cannot
> view with complete indifference the probable influence
> of that situation upon the uncertain character of an
> Oriental Chief. . . . Sentiments of irritation and alarm

at the advancing power of Russia in Central Asia find frequent expression in the English Press.

In other words, the situation was just what it had always been since the British had become what they liked to call "the paramount power" at the beginning of the century: there was trouble or there seemed to be trouble or there was likely to be trouble on India's northwest frontier.

The British navy stood guarantee that the coasts of India were unassailable. On the northeast frontier there were the Himalayas and, behind them, only the Chinese, who were in no position to invade anyone. But the northwest—had not Napoleon and Czar Alexander plotted an invasion by that route in 1807? Had not a British-Indian army marched that way in 1838, only to be annihilated in the Afghan passes in a war so disastrous that even G. A. Henty* wrote, "Of all the wars in which our troops have taken part, never was one entered upon so recklessly and so unjustifiably. . . . Misfortunes have befallen our arms, but never one so dark and disgraceful as this." Had not Lord Palmerston—then Her Majesty's Foreign Minister— declared in 1840: "It seems pretty clear that sooner or later the Cossak [sic] and the Sepoy, the man from the Baltic and he from the British islands will meet in the center of Asia. It should be our business to take care that the meeting should be as far off from our Indian possessions as may be convenient and advantageous to us. But the meeting will not be avoided by our staying at home to receive the visit."

His was not the first and certainly not the last similar pronouncement. Winston Churchill would say of another generation of English aristocrats that their nerves were stronger than their imaginations. The men who ruled India in the nineteenth century had only to look to the northwest to acquire stronger imaginations than nerves. Otherwise sensible men had envisioned Napoleon marching an army from Paris to Delhi. Even in Lytton's day, the Russians were one thousand miles away, and yet a seemingly endless stream of books, broadsides, and speeches announced that if something was not done, and

---

* George Alfred Henty, the Horatio Alger of British imperialism, wrote some eighty books with titles like *With Kitchener to the Sudan* and *With the Allies to Pekin*. They are very high camp indeed.

promptly, Russia would seize Turkey and/or Persia and/ or Afghanistan and go on from there to take India and/or most of the civilized world.

Looking back, it is possible to see that the two great powers were simply feeling their way toward one another in Asia, their policies often confused by ignorance of one another's intentions. There is some comfort in the knowledge that what follows is the story of a war, widely pronounced to be inevitable, that never happened. There would be middle-size wars, little wars, punitive expeditions, "butcher and bolt" expeditions, and Wilcox's Weekend Wars—but no great-power bloodletting.

CHAPTER

I

The Coming of the Raj—
and the French—and the Russians

Before examining how the British got to the northwest
frontier, it might be well to start with some names.

About two thirds of the way up the west coast of India
is the port of Surat. This is where the British established
their first trading post, or, as it was called at the time,
factory. About halfway up the same coast is the island of
Bombay, which eventually replaced Surat as the chief
British station in the area. On the east side, the first
British foothold was at Madras. Calcutta, which became
the capital of British India, is almost all the way up the
coast in the province of Bengal. The city was founded by
the legendary Job Charnock.*

Of the areas within the country, the Punjab—the country of five rivers—is of greatest interest because at various
times two of its rivers—first the Sutlej, later the Indus—
marked the British boundary with the northwest.

The British arrived in India as a "Company of merchants of London" chartered in 1600 by Queen Elizabeth
to trade "into the East Indies." In February, 1601, four
ships—the largest about one quarter the size of a U.S.
Navy destroyer—set out from England. They carried
lead, iron, and woolens to trade, and pistols, plumes, and
looking glasses as gifts for any local princes they might
encounter. They had no larger end in view than to bring
home a cargo of pepper for the English market—the price

* Very little is known for certain about Charnock, but the stories
about him are wonderful. He is supposed to have married a beautiful Hindu widow whom he rescued by force from her husband's
funeral pyre, set half a city afire with his burning glass, and cut
with one stroke of his sword a heavy chain set to impede his passage along the Hooghly River. He was a rough and ready sort who
was said to have "reigned more absolutely than a Rajah, only
wanted much of their humanity."

19

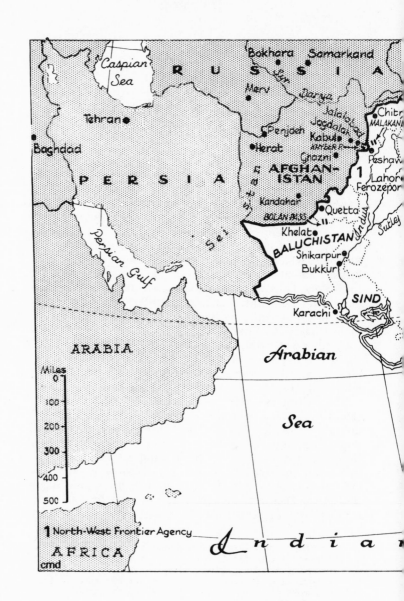

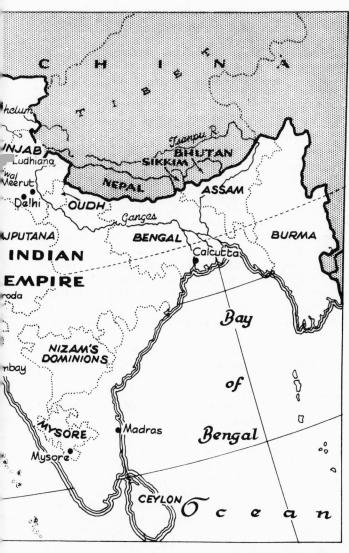

Charles MacDonald

of that commodity having been sent sky-high by the Dutch, who were already trading in the East.

Thus the modest origins of the British East India Company. Far from being part of some grand imperial design, it did not even send its early voyagers to India. Instead, they were sent to Sumatra, where the English woolens found a poor market in the steamy Indonesian heat. A Company agent was dispatched to Surat to see if lighter fabrics more suitable for the spice islands' trade might be purchased. He reported that the Portuguese already trading there were not glad to see him: "I could not peep out of doors for fear of the Portuglas who in troops lay lurking in the byways to give me assault to murther me."

Portuguese influence was strong enough to get the agent expelled, but the situation was not past retrieving. English ships took to stopping the vessels of Surat merchants, Surat got the point, and in 1612 the British were allowed to enter the port. Once in, they did not simply sail home again when the cargo was loaded. The Company's hired help—"servants" was the word preferred—stayed the year round to buy fabrics and indigo when prices were low, or to lead caravans inland when goods were not ready to hand. A young Cornishman left a plaintive record: ". . . I am thrust out alone with little language, having nobody that I can trust or who cares to take any pains to ease me to look after the company's goods. . . ."

The trade grew. By 1700 Company stock was paying a 25 percent dividend and selling for five times its book value. Bombay, Madras, and Calcutta coined their own money, levied taxes, raised troops, and set up courts. Most important, the Company represented a coherent force in a country whose government was rapidly falling to pieces. The Mogul dynasty had been founded by Babur, a Turk from what is now Russian Asia who came down through Afghanistan to seize Delhi. Although his successors included the Great Mogul, Akbar, by 1700 the occupant of the bejeweled Peacock Throne was a sot, befuddled by drink and opium. The Hindu Marathas were in revolt against their Mohammedan rulers, and even some Muslim princes were breaking away from Delhi to set up small states of their own. What Indians call their "Time of Troubles" was at hand, and the power vacuum into which the British would move was beginning to appear.

In 1739 the Persian Nadir Shah raided Delhi and carried off what was left of the treasury and the Peacock Throne. The Marathas were supreme in Central India, and for a second in history it seemed that perhaps here was the new national power, the new occupant of Delhi. Then out of the northwest whence so much had come before came something new. The Afghans, fighting for the first time with a semblance of national unity, raided Delhi, fell back to the Afghan hills, then came again and in 1761 collided with the Marathas fifty miles north of the city. The Marathas were thoroughly whipped. The Afghans looted and went home to Kabul; India was ready to be taken over by the first force with the discipline and the fire power to do the job.

The last thing the Company wanted was fighting in India—it was expensive. Nevertheless, from the first it had raised small bodies of troops to protect the factories and caravans. The story of the Bengal European Regiment is as good an example as any. It was formed in 1652 as a guard of honor and consisted of one officer and thirty men. The officers were appointed by the Company from London, and the only requirements were "good health, courage and common sense." Contrary to later practice, the enlisted men were not Indian, but Europeans kidnapped or picked up drunk by press gangs and shipped out to India. To get some idea of the rigors of the life, note that as punishment for insubordination "they were placed in irons and made to work with the Native Convicts on the roads." A temperature of 120 degrees was not unusual on the roads during much of the year.

By the 1740's, however, there was obviously a need for a little more professionalism in the defense force. The French, though late starters in India, were about ready for a fight to dominate the trade. Out from England came "the Father of the Indian Army"—Stringer Lawrence, an officer with a King's commission and a good deal of European fighting behind him. For the new assignment he was promoted "major in the East Indies only."

It was the French who first decided that it was simpler to use local manpower as enlisted men. Thus, the sepoy, from the Persian *sipahi,* or soldier—drilled, uniformed, and disciplined in the European manner—was born. Lawrence copied them and in the end was victorious in the fighting that went on spasmodically in the Madras area until 1754. The details are of no great concern, but the appearance of Robert Clive is. It is Clive—however unwittingly—who took the first long step toward the Russians. He got the British off the beaches and into India. As a boy in England, Clive had been what today would be called a problem child. His father gave up on the boy and shipped him out to India as a writer or clerk in the employ of the Company. If the change in climate produced no improvement in his conduct, the French war proved better therapy. Commissioned when the fighting started, he came to the notice of Stringer Lawrence, who promoted him captain and sent him off to capture Arcot with a force of 200 Europeans and 300 sepoys. Clive got into the town and promptly found himself besieged by 7,000 Indians and French plus some war elephants who tried to batter down the gates. After fifty days, the besiegers gave up and, twenty-seven years old, Clive went back to England to be hailed as "the heaven-born general."

Promoted lieutenant-colonel, he arrived back in Madras just as the young Nawab of Bengal attacked and captured Calcutta. Most of the British got away in ships; the rest were stuffed into the famous Black Hole.*

Clive retook Calcutta, got the Nawab's signature on a treaty which restored all former privileges and added a few, then found himself in a situation appealing to the most complex set of motives. Taking even the most charitable view, the Nawab was a bad lot, and his most substantial subjects, Hindu bankers, had determined to replace him with one of his generals, Mir Jafar. Clive could not stand neutral and was well advised to be on the side most likely to win. It must be noted, however, that the agreement between Clive and Mir Jafar not only included compensation for European losses during the attack on Calcutta, but also a secret agreement— unknown to the Company—by which Clive got $700,000

*Historians today are inclined to regard the Black Hole incident as one of negligence rather than viciousness. On the evidence of a British officer serving in India at the time, the prisoners were at first allowed the freedom of Calcutta and only confined when some of the soldiers became drunk and abusive. The facts are bad enough—143 prisoners confined in a room so small that only 23 were alive the next morning. In one Victorian version, however, the space is only "20 square feet," or 143 prisoners in a room four by five feet—a job of compression rather beyond even the most ferocious Nawab.

outright and *jagirs,* or tax rights to villages, worth $90,-000 a year.

Under this somewhat mottled banner, Clive led 1,100 Europeans and 2,100 sepoys against 58,000 of the Nawab's forces on the field of Plassey on June 23, 1757. For the first time in Indian history, a royal regiment—the 39th Foot (Dorsetshire)—was part of the British force, and very gay they must have been in their grass-green cuffs, collars, and straps.

Although it is regarded as one of the decisive battles in history, it was more of a confrontation than a fight. In torrents of rain, both sides cannonaded one another at long range. Mir Jafar kept his troops aloof from the proceedings, and when Clive's force finally advanced, the Nawab fled the field. The casualties tell the story: Clive had 23 killed and 49 wounded, the Nawab had some 500 dead.

The Company now ruled Bengal, the richest province in India. When Mir Jafar proved intractable, they replaced him with a rival who paid $600,000 for the post, and when he too proved difficult, Mir Jafar was allowed to buy his way back for $1,300,000.

Back home, Clive was praised and damned as though he alone was responsible for the giant step inland. Subsequent events suggest the contrary. In vain, the Company would send out as Governor-Generals men like Warren Hastings and Charles Cornwallis (of Yorktown fame) with the most rigorous instructions not to waste the Company's money by getting involved in wars and acquiring territory. In the most upright manner, they would try to carry out orders, yet under each of them the Company still edged forward a little. The vacuum was there, and if the Company wished to remain and trade, the Company was going to be sucked into it. And the farther inland they moved, the more they would have to emulate every previous ruler of India and keep a nervous eye on the northwest. As the first Briton to visit that mysterious area and leave a record wrote, "Rumours wafted from the court at Delhi have occasionally agitated our quarter of India and taught us to believe that [the Afghans] with a mighty host had crossed the Indus and were making rapid marches to Delhi to restore the lost authority of the Moghul empire."

The writer was George Forster, a civilian employed by

the Company at Madras. Although the authorities eventually commended his "laudable spirit," there appears to have been little official interest in his expedition at the outset. In any event, he had to pay his own expenses.

Setting out in 1783, he traveled in a variety of disguises through Afghanistan, Persia, Russia, and, finally, home to England. Arriving at Kabul, "I first designed to take the name of a Frenchman, but the wandering temper of that people, who stray into every corner of the earth, made me fear detection . . . I denominated myself a Spaniard."

Kabul did not impress him. Its fortifications struck him as meager and its inhabitants as "a rude, unlettered people." He did mention approvingly that they were not so devoted to the "pleasures of the harem" as the Indians, and that "they avow an abhorrence of that unnatural passion to which many of the Mohamedan sects are addicted."

Nor did the power of Timur Shah, Kabul's ruler, awe him. ". . . the Shah's palace . . . exhibits but a slender testimony to the dignity of its master," he felt, and far from planning to invade India, the Prince struck him as being afraid to leave his own capital. Indeed, Forster doubted that he could invade even if he wanted to. Indian rumor had endowed Timur's predecessor with a revenue of three million pounds a year and a standing army of one hundred thousand men. Forster says dryly that "if such was the state of that prince's power and resources, it hath greatly decreased in the reign of his successor." At best, Forster gave him an army of thirty thousand men and a revenue of a million pounds. In short, there was little to fear from a man of "little enterprize or vigor of mind" with a small army, a scrawny treasury, and rebellious relatives. Very few of the Honorable Company's servants seem to have bothered to read Forster's book.

Timur Shah was only the second ruler—and a shaky one at that—of what might be called the nation of Afghanistan. Situated on the main route between eastern and western Asia, the country had either been ruled by hordes passing through in either direction or fragmented into tribes which British writers are fond of comparing to Scottish clans in the wilder days of the Highlands. Most of the time, the Hindu Kush mountains, which run from east to west across the center of the country, held the migrant hordes in the north. However, though the Hindu

Kush goes up to 24,000 feet, there are passes cutting through at 12,000 to 13,000 feet. Alexander the Great traversed one in 327 B.C. and penetrated as far as modern West Pakistan before withdrawing. Tamerlane came down far enough to sack Delhi.

It was 1747 before it was even remotely possible to talk about Afghanistan as a nation. Ahmed Shah Abdali had commanded a considerable Afghan force serving the country's most recent conquerer, the Persian Nadir Shah. Nadir was assassinated and the Afghans confronted a rare opportunity. Both their powerful neighbors, Persia and India, were temporarily weak. With a unanimity unusual in Afghan politics, the chiefs elected Ahmed Shah king. A good soldier, he conquered as far west as Herat on the Persian frontier, extended his southern border to the Indus River, and, as noted, licked the Marathas outside Delhi.

Timur Shah, as Forster wrote, was a good deal less energetic, and when he died—probably by poisoning—his successor, Zaman Shah, was at first too busy holding on to the throne to trouble anyone. He clapped twenty of his brothers into prison, defeated another in battle, and the twenty-second—Mahmud—fled to Persia, whence he will reappear shortly.

Contemporary accounts rate Zaman Shah "a man by no means remarkable for personal activity and somewhat wanting in courage." Nonetheless, British India and Afghanistan were about to meet.

Richard Colley Wellesley was the eldest son of the Earl of Mornington, and while being eldest son of an earl sounds quite grand, the fact is that Mornington was an Irish peer and Irish peerages are not quite top-drawer. In fact, an Irish peer could not yet sit in the British House of Lords, but only in the House of Commons. Nor were Irish peers necessarily wealthy—when Mornington died, one of the first matters demanding his son's attention was paying off his father's debts. He paid them off, but for the rest of his life paid sharp attention to keeping not only himself but his brothers gainfully employed. Brother Henry proved a successful diplomat and eventually became Baron Cowley; Brother Arthur showed a military talent and is better known as the Duke of Wellington. Both of them had a very helpful leg up from Richard along the way.

Wellesley went out to India as Governor-General in 1797 after four years' experience on the Board of Control for Indian Affairs in London. He was a strongly handsome man, just thirty-seven years old, and distinctly aristocratic in outlook and method. He was in the habit of referring to the Company as "the cheese-mongers of Leadenhall Street," and a successor said of his work habits that "to plan was to execute, with or without sanction."

He brought with him the usual injunctions about getting involved in wars, and nothing was clearer than that if he did, he could expect very little help from home. Napoleon stood on the Channel with fifty thousand men supposedly ready to invade England. A French naval expedition was being outfitted at Toulon and was variously reported aimed at the Channel, Portugal, or Ireland. In India, French officers commanded the army of Hyderabad, and Tippoo Sahib of Mysore was talking with the French about a treaty under which they would loan him ten thousand European troops to help drive the English from India.

In February, 1798, Wellesley, accompanied by brother Henry as private secretary, was sailing around the tip of Africa and, even before taking up his new duties, found himself involved with Zaman Shah. A homeward-bound vessel with dispatches from the Company came by; with "characteristic decision," Wellesley opened them and, after reading, added a letter of his own. ". . . but the most remarkable step which Tippoo has lately taken is his communication with Zaman Shah," he wrote the Secretary at War.* "It is not impossible that the late intercourse between Tippoo and Zaman Shah had for its object, on the part of the former at least, some such plan of joint operation."

He admitted that "it is the fashion to treat the projects of Zaman Shah very lightly" and conceded that the Shah had troubles of his own at home, but concluded, "The result of the examination of these materials upon my mind is a conviction that Zaman Shah has not abandoned his project of invading Hindostan."

His peace of mind was not improved when, less than a month after his arrival in India, Napoleon slipped out of

---

* The Secretary at War was chiefly responsible for getting the army budget through Parliament.

Toulon with his fleet, evaded Nelson's blocking force, and
landed in Egypt. There were those in India who reacted
as though an expedition from Egypt to Calcutta was
nothing more than a hike. In due time, Nelson would
destroy the French fleet in the Battle of the Nile, but for
the moment, Wellesley had Tippoo to the south of him,
Napoleon to the west of him, and Zaman Shah to the
north. To make matters worse, Zaman sent along a letter
which, as Wellesley wrote London, contained "a declaration of his intention to invade Hindostan" and a "peremptory demand for English help against the Mahrattas."
Peremptory demands did not sit well with what his staff
liked to call the "glorious little man."

Actually, the Shah was talking a good deal more
strongly than he felt—and, to a degree, out of both sides
of his mouth. He had advanced to Lahore in the Punjab
two years earlier and found himself unable even to deal
with the rising Sikh power in what was technically still
part of the Afghan empire. Nevertheless, he wrote Tippoo, "We shall soon march with our conquering army to
wage war with the infidels and polytheists and to free
those regions from the contamination of the shameless
tribes with the edge of the sword."

With the British he took a milder tone. It was his
intention to "visit Hindostan," and he was sending an
agent along to find out "who are our friends and who are
our enemies." To Wellesley—even though he admitted his
intelligence of the subject was "defective," "vague," and
"tardy"—it seemed unlikely that the Shah's intentions
were less than to plunder the Punjab and Bengal. When
the Shah's next letter announced that he would regard
anything less than Wellesley's full assistance against the
Mahrattas as an act "of disobedience and enmity," it was
clearly time to see to defenses in the northwest.

When Wellesley looked to his defenses in the northwest,
the prospects were not reassuring. His commander there
felt that the Sikhs would not fight and dismissed the
forces of Oudh, the state just northwest of Bengal, as a
"nullity." Wellesley responded by putting British troops
into Oudh, and London howled. The Governor-General's
defenders replied that he could do as he liked with an
Indian state, since "England stands confessedly in India as
an ascendant power; invested with supremacy in virtue of
European civilization and Anglo-Saxon energy."

Wellesley himself decided to supplement Anglo-Saxon

energy with Anglo-Saxon guile. To Jonathan Duncan, Governor of Bombay, he wrote that it might be a very good idea if one Mehdi Ali Khan, employed as British agent in the Persian Gulf, tried to persuade the Persian government to divert Zaman Shah by an attack from the west. Such an attack would "alarm Zaman Shah for the safety of his hereditary dominions and may recall him from the prosecution of his designs against the tranquillity of India." Wellesley also suggested—correctly as it turned out—that the Shah's brother Mahmud, who had fled to Persia, might be interested in the scheme. To sweeten the package, Duncan was authorized to give the Persians as many cannon and other military stores as he could spare.

Rumors flew—the Shah was across the Indus and at Lahore (true); he would soon advance on Delhi (untrue: he had far too much bad news from home to contemplate such a trip); the French were advancing on Herat. This last was too much for Wellesley's chief military aide, who pointed out that they simply wouldn't have had time to get there from Egypt.

Quite peacefully, 1799 dawned and Wellesley was able to write a gleeful note to Duncan reporting "Zaman Shah commenced his retreat from Lahore on the 4th of February, the principal cause assigned for his retreat is the appearance of Mahmud, the Shah's brother. . . . From a comparison of dates, I think the movement of this Prince may possibly be the work of your agent, Mehdi Ali." There follows an appreciation of the agent's work and the suggestion that he might be rewarded with no less than two lakhs of rupees, or about a hundred thousand dollars.

So the matter was quite settled with no bloodshed except that the good news had not yet reached London— four months being about minimum time for dispatches to arrive from India. London had been doing some serious thinking and sent off the results to Wellesley in the form of a communiqué from Henry Dundas, the Secretary at War.

It was some time ago the fashion in my opinion, too much to undervalue the menaces of Zaman Shah respecting India . . . if the French were ever able to obtain such a footing as to enable them to seriously to distress us, I have long thought that it would be a material point of the plan to obtain the co-operation of Zaman Shah . . . we ought to keep a very watchful eye upon the motions of that Prince, whose talents, military force and pecuniary resources afford to him the means of being a formidable opponent.

Mr. Dundas had based these opinions on reports from Harford Jones, British Resident at Baghdad—and for that reason usually known as "Baghdad" Jones—whose information about the Shah was even more unreliable than Wellesley's. Dundas wanted Persia to keep the pressure on.

Now the Governor-General might refer to the Honorable Company as "cheese-mongers," but the Secretary at War was apparently quite a different matter. On the very day he received Dundas's letter—August 5, 1799—he fired one of his own off to Duncan in Bombay. "The annual menace of Zaman Shah's invasion of Hindostan having recently been renewed. . . ," immediate measures should be taken to check it. Mehdi Ali had done well enough earlier, but now "it is not consistent with the dignity of the British Government to employ any native of this country as its representative at a foreign court, nor could the British interests be with any degree of safety confided to any person of that description. Intrigue, falsehood and collusion are the uniform characteristics of such of the natives of India as aspire to the qualifications of statesmen."

So much for an Indian whose services had only recently been valued at a hundred thousand dollars.

Captain John Malcolm would replace him as head of mission. Depending on whose opinion one accepts, "Boy" Malcolm was either a pure joy of youthful exuberance or a youth of "the most outré egotism." He was one of the numerous Scotsmen who did so well in India that there came to be a saying that "promotion cometh from the north." His story was a fairly typical one—the son of a family of modest means, not particularly good at schoolwork, shipped out to India at fourteen with an appointment secured through a prosperous uncle. He had served in the campaigns against Tippoo, but his chief qualifications for the task assigned were a proficiency in Persian and a powerful belief in the evil designs of Zaman Shah and the French. He himself described the job as designed "to relieve India from the annual alarm of Zaman Shah's invasion . . . [and] to counteract the possible attempts of those villainous, but active democrats the French."

He was to "engage the court of Persia to act vigorously and heartily against the French in the event of their attempting to penetrate to India." In getting the desired treaty, he was to exert himself to the utmost to put "as light a charge as possible to the Company." He could offer three lakhs of rupees ($150,000) for the treaty, raise the ante to four lakhs if he had to, but if the job could be done simply by bribes, so much the better.

Wellesley did not stint him. Malcolm had a retinue of five hundred people and carried presents of such value that they were not only criticized in London, but made life difficult for subsequent British missions who were not so lavishly supplied. He bribed so heavily that the Persians were under the impression that the Indian government had promised him 5 percent of everything he could give away.

The Persians were delighted with Malcolm and even more delighted to accept his presents; in November, 1800, Malcolm was received by the Shah at Tehran. After much present-giving and even more talk, a treaty was signed by which Britain and Persia agreed "to coop- erate against any Afghan domains." If, on the other hand, the Afghans were to invade Persia, the British commit- ment was simply to send as many cannon "as possible." If the French were to invade Persia, both nations would fight them, and as a hedge against any such penetration, no Frenchman would even be allowed to live in Persia.

It all looked perfectly wonderful on paper, but there were two things wrong with it. First off, long before the treaty was ever signed, the dread Zaman Shah was a captive of his brother Mahmud and blinded by the appli- cation of a dagger point to his eyeballs. The Persians had been supporting Mahmud enthusiastically long before the British ever suggested the idea to them. As for the French portions of the document, they lasted only as long as the Persians failed to realize that what they really needed was not protection from the French, who were a long way off, but from the Russians, who were right on their northern border. Having made the discovery, they applied to Bri- tain for aid, failed to get it, and promptly turned to Napoleon for help.

Perhaps the ultimate nonsense on the Zaman Shah menace was spoken in London by a director of the

Company who suggested that what the British really needed to protect themselves against the Shah was an alliance with the Russians. The suggestion was vetoed by a cooler head at the Foreign Office who noted:

> . . . making such a proposal at St. Petersburg . . . would only tend to give that court a persuasion that we are dependent on them in a quarter where nature has separated us by limits more insuperable than the Oceanus dissociabilis which Horace speaks of. If I am wrong . . . set me right . . . but do it, if you please, with a map in your hand and with a calculation of distances, a reference to history and a consideration of the present state of intervening countries between Petersburg and Calcutta.

In truth, there was a good deal more Russian interest in India than the Foreign Office imagined. Barely a year after Zaman Shah turned back, a Russian expedition was ordered to proceed to Delhi.

The fortress of Orenburg was built by the Russians in 1737 as a base for their expansion into the tribal territories of Central Asia. Just south of the Aral Sea is the city-state of Khiva, the prime target of the early expansionists, and to the east, Tashkent and Bokhara, the other two major city-states. To the west is Merv, near to the spot where the Russians and British were finally to collide and the source of one of the worst political puns in history: when the showdown came, the British Foreign Office would variously be said to be "Mervous" or to "suffer from Mervousness." In Afghanistan three cities are worth noting—Kabul, approached from India by the Khyber Pass, Kandahar, reached by the Bolan Pass, and, on the Persian border, Herat, a standing source of trouble between the two countries.

As far back as Peter the Great, the Russians had taken an interest in India, but Peter's interest went no further than the dispatch of an envoy to have a look around. The envoy died en route, and Peter let the matter drop until a Turkoman trader's tales of gold in the Oxus River valley reached St. Petersburg in 1713. A captain of the Imperial Bodyguard, Prince Bekovitch, was sent off with three thousand men to capture Khiva as a base for the gold rush. The Russian infantry was doing well against the headlong rushes of the Khan of Khiva's tribesmen when Bekovitch, a startingly inept commander, accepted an offer from the Khan to negotiate and, worse, accepted the suggestion that his troops be dispersed into six separate camps. The small bodies of soldiers were massacred, Bekovitch was beheaded, and Peter gave up on Khiva as a bad job.

Interest revived in 1793 when the Khan of Khiva asked Catherine the Great for a doctor to attend his uncle, who was going blind. In what must be one of the most venturesome house calls in history, a Dr. Blankenagel made the trip, found he could do nothing for the afflicted man, and barely escaped with his life when the Khivans, apparently feeling let down, tried to kill him. His report to Catherine, however, dealt with a good deal more than the Khivan medical situation. Khiva, he said, had "rich and inexhaustible" gold and silver mines, and five thousand men could easily capture the state.

Catherine died before she could do anything about the reported riches, but she did consider, at least briefly, an expedition not only to Khiva but all the way to India. Her son, Czar Paul, went further.

Paul—in spite of a nasty temper and a taste for having people flogged—was a pitiful figure. He looked like a near-sighted Pekingese, and his mind, never strong, was further unhinged by the not unreasonable fear that Catherine might have him assassinated as she had his father. It further amused his mother to pretend that he was illegitimate.

This unstable mind was attracted by the notion, popular with visionaries of the period, that a Russian army marching from Orenburg could link up with a French force advancing from Egypt or Paris for a joint invasion of India. Initially, indeed, Paul did not even feel the need for French help. In 1800 he sent twenty thousand Cossacks off under Vasili Orloff to do the job alone. His instructions were more hortatory than helpful:

> I am preparing to be beforehand with the English, who intend attacking me by land and sea. I propose to attack them in their most vulnerable part, where they least expect it. It is three months' march . . . the enterprize will cover you with immortal glory, will secure you my goodwill, will load you with riches.

He did regret to have to inform Orloff that "I enclose all the maps I have. My maps only go as far as Khiva and the Oxus. Beyond that, it is your business to get information up to the English settlements." He might also have mentioned that what might be a march of three months in good weather was quite something else in winter. On the steppes, temperatures regularly ran down to thirty below and there were particularly violent snowstorms called *bourans*. As a measure of their ferocity, one, a few years later, was sufficient to kill an estimated 280,000 horses and over a million sheep.

Orloff marched off in January, 1801, and almost immediately lost half a regiment trying to get his men across the Volga on ice floes. Paul himself must have begun to have doubts, for in the same month he opened negotiations with Napoleon for a more elaborate project. Under the new plan, 35,000 French were to come down the Danube, sail across the Caspian Sea, and march to Asterabad, where 35,000 Russians would be waiting for them. All 70,000 men would then march across Afghanistan to India. Planning with customary care, Paul included plans for fireworks displays to impress the Indians. Napoleon, a less impetuous soul, replied to Paul that "supposing they combined to be united at Astrabad; how do you propose that it [the army] should get to India through countries almost barbarous and without resources, having to march a distance of 300 leagues [about 750 miles; actually 1,200 miles would have been more like it] to the frontiers of Hindostan?" Paul told him that caravans did it all the time.

Fortunately for Orloff and his Cossacks, Russian patience with Paul ran out in March. He was strangled by an army officer and the Orloff expedition was recalled. Unfortunately, the dangers of winter campaigning on the steppes were quite lost on the Russians; there would be a far more dreadful disaster before the lesson got home.*

So end the first moves by either side. The British made one error which would haunt northwest frontier policy for the next hundred years: they vastly overestimated the ability of a major power—in this case the French, later

---

* British India apparently never knew of the Orloff expedition. In Wellesley's very extensive dispatches—five thick volumes—there are a few offhand references to danger from Russia, but nothing specific.

the Russians—to move large bodies of troops through the deserts and mountains of Central Asia to attack India. For overestimating Zaman Shah, it is somewhat easier to forgive Wellesley. It was barely fifty years since a successful invasion had come from the northwest, and, as an apologist wrote, "Kabul in those days was associated with the invasions of Timur, Nadir Shah and Ahmed Shah." Nor did Zaman Shah's letters announcing his arrival help matters.

There would shortly be something much more substantial to worry about. In 1802 a French envoy appeared in Persia to suggest substituting a French alliance for the British. He was turned down, but in 1804 another envoy appeared with a much more attractive proposition—a French-Persian treaty directed against Russia. Russia had just taken Georgia away from the Persians, and the Shah was extremely anxious to get it back. On the other hand, he viewed with a good deal of suspicion representatives of a government which had come to power by cutting a king's head off. The British were asked if *they* would like to help the Shah get Georgia back and they procrastinated. They could hardly do otherwise, since at the moment they were allied with the Russians against Napoleon—a matter considerably more important than any Persian treaty.

Left without much choice, Persia signed with France in 1807. Far more important than the treaty itself, however, was the arrival of a French military mission of some seventy officers and noncoms under General Claude-Mathieu de Gardanne to train the Persian army. Gardanne had the authority to offer the Shah six French infantry battalions, three artillery companies, and supplies if he would go to war with Russia. For an expedition against India, twenty thousand Frenchmen would be made available and Gardanne was instructed to investigate routes to India.

Even more distressing news for Calcutta would be along shortly. Wellesley had departed and the Governor-General's chair was now occupied by Gilbert (to his friends, Gibby) Elliot, Lord Minto. London had not been happy with Wellesley. As Lady Minto said, "While he was engaged in creating an empire, his masters in Leadenhall Street were learning to their dismay that the process was not a paying one." In Minto, Leadenhall Street thought they had found their man. He had inveighed against expansionism in India. He had pronounced himself one with Edmund Burke, who during the debate on the Indian Bill of 1783 had spoken feelingly of "the indignation with which he saw the interests of the native princes and people trafficked away by the servants of a trading Company."

Minto had scarcely arrived in India when all prospects of a quiet regime devoted to budget balancing went out the window. Napoleon thumped Czar Alexander in the battle of Friedland, and in July, 1807, the two met on a raft in the Nieman River near the town of Tilsit in what is today Russian territory and signed the Treaty of Tilsit. Under its secret clauses, which did not remain secret very long, Alexander committed himself to declaring war on England, and an elaborate set of coercive measures was set up to bring most of the rest of Europe into the fight. As a young man in India wrote:

> What an unexampled and surprising picture the state of Europe now presents: France, Russia, Austria, Prussia, Germany, Holland, Spain, Portugal, Denmark, Italy, Turkey—all Europe save little Sweden—combined against our country. . . . Although this is a state of things which no one could have wished to see, I confess that I feel a pride in it— Hurrah for the tight little Island!

Actually, nothing was said about India in the Treaty of Tilsit, but most of Calcutta thought an invasion certain in the spring of 1808. One pamphleteer—signing himself "A Late Resident of Bhagulpore"—fired what may have been the very first shot in a long, long debate by proposing that the line of the Indus River was India's proper defense. The subject would be endlessly argued in the years ahead.

Minto himself was at first dubious; the French, he felt, would try instead to "unsettle the minds" of the native princes. As 1808 came in, however, he was hearing rumors of a French army advancing through Persia* and writing London that it was desirable to send ambassadors to India's border states to awake them to a sense "of common danger." Malcolm was to return to Persia to try to repair the old alliance, and if he found a French army

---

* Napoleon mentioned an India expedition to Alexander, but not very seriously.

there, Minto would send up twenty-five thousand men to meet them at the frontier. Young Charles Metcalfe—only twenty-three years old, but already a political officer of seven years' experience—would go the Punjab to the Sikh ruler Runjeet Singh and, for the first time, a British official would visit the ruler of the Kingdom of Kabul.

The man selected was the Honorable Montstuart Elphinstone. He was the son of a Scottish peer, but one of very modest means, and at sixteen the boy had been shipped out to India as a cadet in the Bengal cavalry. Since, as Elphinstone wrote in his *Account of the Kingdom of Caubul*, the Afghans "were known to be haughty, and supposed to entertain a mean opinion of the European nations, it was determined that the mission should be in a style of great magnificence . . ." and so it was. When Elphinstone departed Calcutta in October, 1808, he was accompanied by three civilians, a surgeon, two surveyors, eight officers for the military escort which consisted of 200 cavalry and 200 infantry, and some 600 camels to carry supplies. As was usual with Europeans in India, they marched chiefly at night, loading up at two or three in the afternoon and stopping sometime between midnight and dawn. With a trumpeter in the lead and a drummer banging away in the rear, they were able to cover between fifteen and twenty-five miles a day. The news of their purpose preceded them; when they stopped with the Rajah of Bikaner, "He showed a knowledge of our relation with France and one of the company asked whether my mission was not owing to our wars with that nation."

At the crossing of the Indus River, they encountered Indians less well informed; there were rumors that the British carried cannon packed in trunks, that they had mysterious small boxes which could explode and kill half a dozen men, and that they could raise the dead.

The object of the mission, Shah Shujah, was not an easy man to locate. Mahmud, who had replaced Zaman Shah, had been overthrown in turn by Shah Shujah, who now found himself fighting to hold the throne against Mahmud and some other brothers. Elphinstone paused outside Peshawar, the gateway to the Khyber, heard that the Shah was at Kandahar, and was about to start in that direction when further intelligence put His Majesty at Kabul and about to start for Peshawar. In due time, an envoy appeared at Elphinstone's camp, made arrangements for his entry into the city, and then "in the evening

I went to a tent pitched about one hundred yards from my camp, to receive a dress of honor sent me from the King. . . . I was instructed to bow to the dress, and was afterwards invested with a large flowing robe of gold cloth, lined with satin, which I was told the King himself had worn; a shawl was wound around my hat. . . . The dress was rich and the shawls costly."

The streets were crowded as the British rode to court— an oblong room lined on three sides with triple lines of the Shah's guards and with a pond and fountains in the middle. The Shah himself sat "on a very large throne of gold or gilding. . . . His appearance was magnificent and royal, his crown and all his dress was a blaze of jewels. . . . On coming in sight of the King, we all pulled off our hats, and made a low bow; we then held up our hands to heaven as if praying for the King." A herald (who had prudently asked Elphinstone to have each of the British whisper their names) announced them and concluded, "They have come from Europe as ambassadors to your Majesty." His Majesty replied, "They are welcome."

The Shah was then about thirty, a handsome man with a heavy black beard. Elphinstone's first impression was that he was wearing an "armour of jewels," but on closer inspection it turned out to be a green tunic embroidered with gold and precious stones. Over it was a breastplate of diamonds, and in one of his bracelets the envoy spotted the Kohinoor—"known to be one of the largest diamonds in the world." In due time, the Kohinoor would become the property of the Queen of England.

Elphinstone liked the man: "It was scarcely to be believed of an Eastern monarch how much he had the manners of a gentleman, or how well he preserved his dignity, while he seemed only anxious to please." Some of the Shah's entourage he found less attractive. When the presents the mission had brought arrived, the officers put in charge wanted to keep the camels carrying them as well, stripped the elephant drivers of their livery, and pretended to think that two English servants in the company were part of the gift. For the Shah's part, he was most pleased by a pair of pistols, an organ, and the British officers' silk stockings. The mission was promptly ransacked to get him some more.

After so sparkling a beginning, it is sad to report that the negotiations themselves came to very little. Shah Shujah had only a very vague impression of the French, but felt quite certain that any invasion by them would unite Afghanistan and equally certain that a united Afghanistan could whip any army sent against it. Moreover, it seemed to him distinctly one-sided for the British to ask him for help against their enemies while they refused to help him against Mahmud. Elphinstone tried to talk his way around it by making out that the British had not come to ask for a treaty, but simply to warn the Shah of the danger he was in and to offer help.

In the end, Elphinstone got a treaty of sorts; one gets the impression that the Shah signed it to be rid of him and get back to fighting Mahmud. The Afghans agreed to resist a French invasion if one came, and the British agreed to pay any expenses involved. There were the usual formalities about eternal friendship between the two states and finally a recognition that British India had taken a long step toward Afghanistan. Between the two states, said the treaty, "the veil of separation shall be lifted up."

In June Elphinstone headed south, and he may have felt he didn't have much of a treaty, because he was badly afflicted by what he called "blue devils" and solaced himself with a quote from Aristotle: "All who have become eminent, either in philosophy, politics, poetry or the arts appear to have been subject to the blue devils." In any event, a treaty with Shah Shujah would not have been worth a great deal. That unfortunate man lost his battle with his brothers, took refuge with the Sikhs at Ludhiana, and had to turn his Kohinoor diamond over to their leader, Runjeet Singh. There he stayed for thirty years and then emerged to join the British in a disastrous intervention in Afghan affairs.

Elphinstone could console himself that neither of Minto's other two envoys had had much better luck in whipping up alliances against the French. In Persia, Malcolm had been turned down flatly, and then there was a terrible row in Bombay when London sent out Baghdad Jones, "created a baronet for the occasion," to try his hand. Minto, who had no taste for London's attempts to conduct his Persian policy, first tried to keep Jones from going to Tehran and when he did manage to get away, announced that he would refuse to honor a treaty if he got one.

Jones arrived at Tehran to find that the Persians had given up trying to get French help against the Russians and had sent Gardanne packing, but were nevertheless unenthusiastic about a new British treaty. The minister negotiating for Persia accused Jones of trying to cheat him. Jones, an unusual diplomat, replied by calling the man a blockhead and threatening to pound him against the wall. Then, apparently carried away by the idea, he did push him against the wall "with a slight degree of violence," kicked over the candles with which the room was illuminated, and stalked out. Surprisingly, he got his treaty and Minto had to swallow his pride while Malcolm fumed about "fools at home" who had called off a military expedition with which he had intended to chastise the Persians.

Communication was easier for Metcalfe in the Punjab. Because he knew almost from the first that the Persian-Napoleonic menace to India had vanished, he spent the time trying to persuade Runjeet Singh not to lay violent hands on Indian states lying south of the Sutlej River. Since Runjeet did as he was asked, Metcalfe can be called successful—but the advance of British troops to the Sutlej must also be thrown into the balance.

From here on, the French menace—which never was very real anyway—recedes to the vanishing point. The British under Arthur Wellesley—whom Napoleon liked to deride as "the Sepoy general"—gave the Emperor's armies a bad knock in Portugal. Then came the fateful campaign in Russia, abdication, the return, and finally Waterloo in 1815. In Afghanistan assorted claimants to the throne were far too busy fighting one another to menace anyone else. For the moment, the British could regard the northwest frontier with a quiet mind.

A great deal had happened in India since Clive had made Bengal secure at Plassey. The Honorable East India Company was no longer a merchant organization buying goods in India for sale in England and in the process giving the Exchequer tremors over an unfavorable trade balance. Now the process was reversed; factory-loomed cloth from England dominated the Indian market to a degree that caused Governor-General William Bentinck to remind London of the fate of the Indian cottage weavers: ". . . the misery hardly finds a parallel in the history of commerce. The bones of the cotton weavers are bleaching the plains of India." In all that follows, the desire to make

Central Asia a similar market for British goods is never far from the minds of the men in London.

As the Honorable Company had grown, it had lost control of its own affairs. In business matters it was still its own master, but the military, political, and financial decisions for India were now made by a new department of the British government—the Board of Control. The Chairman of the Board had Cabinet rank and in time the title changed to Secretary of State for India.

In the old days, merchants who went out from England, if they did not die from the fever or from drinking far, far too much, returned home with a fortune, bought a seat in Parliament, and revolted their neighbors by their ostentation. The process was known as "shaking the pagoda tree"—an elaborate pun based on the fact that there is in India a pagoda tree and also a coin of the same name. The pagoda-tree shakers were largely men who made personal deals and took bribes from local rulers when they were supposed to be working for Leadenhall Street. Under the Governor-Generals immediately preceding and including Wellesley the looting was stopped. Company servants were put on decent salaries, schools provided for their proper training, and quite a different sort of man became attracted to the Indian service.

As is the case with so many highly desirable reforms, the professionalization of the army and civil service had a few undesirable side effects. An ordinary officer in the Indian army could sweat out his entire life in cantonments, drilling Indian troops and putting his hopes of advancement in the stock toast of junior officers: "To a bloody war and a sickly season." Getting rich Clive-style was out of order. A more enterprising young man might, however, get himself posted to the political branch. It was hard work. It meant learning Indian languages, and the British themselves are the first to admit that most of them were never very good at it. It meant living with the contempt of the army (including military officers assigned political duties). But a political officer did have prospects.

Once an Indian state was conquered, the army went back to cantonments, but assorted politicals remained and for all practical purposes were the real rulers of the state. A man who did well at it had a great deal to look forward to. Although it was against policy to draw Governor-Generals from the ranks of the Company's servants, most of the important Indian posts below that august figure went to politicals.

Thus policy was made in that murky area where sound measures and personal ambition tend to become confused. A man was apt to think of a number of good reasons for taking over a state when there was a very decent chance that he might wind up as Resident. By 1818 all India south of the Sutlej River was British, and the eyes of the adventuresome and ambitious had to turn north. Directly over the river was the Sikh power with an excellent army trained by French veterans of the Napoleonic wars and a formidable train of artillery. Beyond the Sikhs lay the Afghans and Central Asia, and Elphinstone's treaty said there was a veil of separation to be raised.

Elphinstone himself had left a string of Indian intelligence agents—"newswriters" as they were called—along the frontier. For the most part they remain unknown, but there is a record of one Mir Izzet Ullah who, in 1812–13, went from Kashmir to Bokhara, then doubled back through Kabul to India. The first Englishman since Forster to get to the Hindu Kush was William Moorcroft, an imaginative veterinarian in the Company's service. In 1811 he went through the Himalayas into Chinese Tibet. In 1819 he set out again and for the remaining five years of his life ranged the western borders of China, became the first Englishman from India to visit Bokhara, and sent back to India inflammatory reports that the whole of Central Asia was swarming with Russian agents.

Actually, the only identifiable Russian agent in the area at the time was a Captain Muravieff, who in 1819 explored along the eastern shores of the Caspian Sea, then pushed on to Khiva where the Khan promptly put him in jail. The chief priest of the city favored burying him alive, but the Khan told the priest, "If I should kill him, his master, the White Czar, will come next year to steal the women of my harem." Accordingly, Muravieff was simply sent packing. Back in Russia, he pronounced Khiva a bar to trade in Central Asia and stirred considerable public sentiment by reporting that Russians picked up along the border were held there as slaves.

If Calcutta paid little attention to Moorcroft's stories about Russians in Asia (men only a few years after his time in India speak of him as "almost legendary"), it was alarmed by Russia's successful extensions southward at the expense of Persia. The explorers of the ground between the great powers cease to be civilians and become officers of the Indian army. First in the field was shy, deeply religious young Arthur Conolly who had been more or less pushed into the Bengal cavalry by his family. Sent home to England on sick leave, he returned to India by an overland route which began at St. Petersburg; he went to Moscow, then to Tehran, thence eastward across Persia and through as much of Afghanistan as he could manage. By the time he reached the Indian frontier in 1831, he had seen enough to have some strong opinions about the Russian threat. If they could take Khiva—and it was the talk of every bazaar in Central Asia that they intended to—they could then descend upon India by crossing the Hindu Kush and pushing down through Kabul and the Khyber Pass, or they could move down along the Persian border and approach via Herat and Kandahar. A cooler head than a good many of his seniors, Conolly was not disposed to overrate the danger. The Russians were not established in Khiva and, in his judgment, "Many years will be requisite to bring their plans to maturity there." He thought it more likely that they might march across Persia and then down through Afghanistan. It could, he felt, be done, in spite of enormous problems of supply, disease, and the shortage of water Russian troops would face in a strange climate, if one condition held: the Afghans had to cooperate.

> If the Afghans, as a nation, were determined to resist Russian invasion of India, the difficulties of the march would be rendered well nigh insurmountable; for though Afghanistan is a country through which an unopposed European army could without great difficulty move, its natural advantages are so many that the resolute people occupying its fastness could greatly check, if not altogether prevent it.

On this basis, Conolly proceeded to set out a coherent Afghan policy for the Indian government. A strong and united Afghanistan was the best defense for the northwest frontier. The threat of Afghan invasion was unreal; those who argued that the country should be kept in its "pastoral and distracted state" were wrong, since "the rulers of petty Afghan states cannot have the motives to oppose foreign invasion of India that would be felt by a monarch whose dignity and interests would in many ways be associated with ours."

There was, he conceded, a conflict between an Afghan alliance and the Persian alliance. He was firmly for letting the Persian alliance go by the boards. For one thing "they are neither the most resolute nor constant people in the world," but, more important, Russia sat directly on Persia's northern border, and if she chose to march in, there was very little the British could do about it.

Conolly did not take his case to the public in book form until sometime later, but his paper "Overland Invasion of India" was offered to the government as soon as he returned to Calcutta; since his cousin, William Macnaghten, was Political Secretary to the Governor-General, it seems unlikely that it went unread. Indeed, in his final summing up of the military situation, Sir William Bentinck adopted Conolly's view that the Russian danger would come through Persia and Herat. He himself, however, was less a "forward policy" man and was inclined to meet the danger on the Indus River rather than meddle in Afghan affairs.

At the very least, Bentinck seems to have learned enough from Conolly to make him want to know more, and as he considered who might be sent north, his attention turned to Lt. Alexander Burnes, another young Scotsman packed off to India to make his fortune. He arrived in 1821, was posted to the 11th Regiment of Native Infantry, and set about the study of Indian languages with a good deal more than the usual diligence. From the first, "I ordered my servants to address me in Hinostanee." Two years later, he could write in his diary, "I reckon three more years will make me a Persian scholar and five more give me a tolerable knowledge of Arabic." There were powerful drives in the man. He felt himself "the only illiterate man in my family"—his brothers were all in the professions—and he was haunted by the expectation of a short life. He frequently made a poor impression on others. He quarreled with superiors, and one of the most fair-minded observers of Indian personalities of the time wrote later, "He is a man of inordinate ambition, but of average ability and shallow acquirements, sanguine in temperament and wanting in self-control."

Burnes got his first chance in 1830 when London decided on a not particularly ingenious scheme for exploring the Indus River, which the Company was anxious to open to commerce. Most of the Indus flowed through Runjeet Singh's Punjab, and that wily man can scarcely have been taken in when informed that the Company wished to present him with a handsome team of horses and an ornate coach—and that since the coach might be damaged by overland travel, it would be brought by boat up the Indus. Captain Claude Wade, who had been posted at Ludhiana for the dual purpose of keeping an eye on Shah Shujah and dealing with the Sikhs, finally persuaded Runjeet to accept the gift. Wade had a reputation for special influence with the Sikhs, but one need look no further than their nickname for him to discover the source of it—he was the "bakshi Sahib," the money man.

The lower portion and the mouths of the Indus, however, were in Sind, and though there were also presents for the Mirs (chiefs) of that state, they were not in the least anxious to receive them. They had observed that where the British came to visit they usually came to stay. First they refused to admit Burnes, then refused to sell him food; they only gave in after protracted negotiations.

In the Punjab, thanks to Wade, his reception was better. He presented his gifts, stayed a month, then went to the Simla* hill station to report to Bentinck.

As noted, Bentinck was looking for a man to make a trip. In his mind, Afghanistan was presently "no cause for alarm"; indeed, it should be strengthened as a barrier between India and Persia—the Conolly position. Persia itself was "distracted," but Sir William found himself imagining that a Russian army of twenty thousand could cross Persia's northern border, settle the Persian civil war, and then combine with the Persians to take Herat, "the key to Kabul." With soldierly precision, he toted up the mileage from the Russo-Persian border to Herat, came out with 1,189 miles, and pronounced such a trip short and easy.

From Herat to the Indus River was only another 1,032 miles, and by that time Sir William decided that the

---

* Simla was just emerging as the summer capital of India. From this time on, the government spent the warm weather at the hill settlement 170 miles north of Delhi and 7,000 feet up in the Himalayan foothills. The temperature hovered around a decent 75 degrees as against 110 or so on the plains. There was no Simla before the British; it all started when an army officer built himself a summer cottage on the site in 1819.

Afghans would have thrown in with the enemy and India would be faced with twenty thousand Russian regulars plus a hundred thousand Persian and Afghan cavalry.

In this frame of mind, it is not surprising that Sir William sympathized with Burnes's desire to explore in Central Asia, particularly since there were rumors of a Russian fort building somewhere between the Caspian Sea and Khiva. Burnes wanted to go to Kabul and Bokhara. Sir William felt that a Russian advance along that line was "a very distant speculation"; nevertheless, intelligence from the area would be welcome. Burnes was given a party of three. The other European, Dr. Gerard, had explored on his own in the Himalayas, and Indian experience had shown that doctors were always welcome in eastern courts. In addition there was a surveyor, Mahomed Ali, and a Kashmiri, Mohun Lal, who would remain with Burnes for the rest of his life as his *munshi,* or secretary.

The party traveled in Indian dress but carried government credentials to be presented to the rulers of the states through which they passed. For the first time, a British official had come to Kabul, and when Burnes was presented to its ruler, Dost Mohammed Khan, he was struck by his "knowledge, intelligence and curiosity" and can scarcely have imagined that only six years later he would help lead an army against him. From Kabul, the party went north to Bokhara, where they were well received in spite of the ferocious reputation of the ruler of that city, thence westward to the Caspian, south to Tehran, on to the Persian Gulf, and back to Bombay by boat.

Burnes's account of his trip, having been thoroughly scoured by the Secret Department of India House in London, is a mild travelogue of no political interest of any sort. His reports to Bentinck, however, were sufficiently impressive for the Governor-General to send him to London to report in person. "Bokhara" Burnes was the lion of the London season. It was all fine, but the young man of vast ambition went back to India with the same old appointment he had had before he became a hero— Assistant Resident for Cutch. Cutch is in west-central India and it is notably dry, barren, and hot. Burnes must have simmered even above the temperature induced by the heat.

Burnes was to have another chance, and the occasion of that chance would be Dost Mohammed Khan. The Dost's story properly begins in 1816 when Shah Shujah became a British pensioner at Ludhiana. His brother and conquerer, Mahmud, ruled at Herat, and Mahmud's chief ally, Futteh Khan, sat as Mahmud's man at Kabul. Dost Mohammed was a very junior brother of Futteh Khan, but already known as a hard drinker and a very apt man with a knife.

Afghan clannishness being what it was, no alliance between Mahmud, who was a Sadozais, and Futteh Khan, who was a Barukzais, was likely to be particularly long lived. Futteh Khan felt that he and his clansmen had less influence with Mahmud than they should have had. It was also alleged that Mahmud was a weak and dissipated ruler, but it is difficult for an impartial observer to find him that much more dissipated than the men against him. Probably the most important fact was that Herat controlled the richest part of the country, Mahmud was embroiled in a fight with the Persians, and it must have seemed a good time to take Herat away from him.

Dost Mohammed led Futteh Khan's assault on Herat, took the city, then had to run for his life when Mahmud turned from the Persians and chased his late allies. It is said that before departing, the Dost gave particular offense to Mahmud by tearing a jeweled waistband off one of the wives of the royal princes. Mohun Lal, who wrote the life of the Dost and who is inclined to be a little franker in these matters than Victorian historians, adds that he "treated her rudely in other ways."

Dost Mohammed got away to Kashmir; Futteh Khan was less fortunate. At first, Mahmud was content to put out his eyes with the point of a dagger and scalp him. Later, he ordered him to command his brothers to surrender, and when he refused, further steps were taken. The price of failure in Afghan politics was considerable:

> Futteh Khan was brought into a tent . . . in which sat a circle of his mortal foes. They commenced by each in turn accusing him . . . Atta Mahmoud Khan then stepped up to him and seizing one of his ears, cut it off with a knife. . . . Shahugaussie Newaub cut off the other ear. Each, as he wreaked this unmanly vengeance upon the victim . . . named the wrong of which it was the recompense. . . . Another of the

barbarians cut off his nose; Khana Moola Khan severed his right hand; Khalook Dad Khan his left hand, the blood gushing copiously from each new wound. Summurdar Khan cut off his beard saying "This is for dishonouring my wife." Hitherto the high spirited chief had borne his sufferings without either weakness or any ebullition of his excitable temper. He had only once condescended in a calm voice, to beg them to hasten his death. The mutilation of ears and nose . . . had not been able to shake his fortitude; but the beard of a Mohammedan is a member so sacred that honor itself becomes confounded with it; and he who had borne himself with the constancy of a hero . . . burst into a passion of tears. His torments were drawing to a close. Gool Mahommed Khan, with a blow of his sabre, cut off his right foot and a man of the Populzye tribe severed the left. Atta Mohammed Khan finished his torments by cutting his throat.*

Revenge for the death of a clansman is a great responsibility for an Afghan. Dost Mohammed offered to raise an army in Kashmir for the job. An older brother, Azim Khan, was less precipitous about family responsibilities but willing to lend the necessary money. The Dost retook Kabul, drove Mahmud back to Ghazni, and then lost most of what he had won when Azim Khan seated himself at Kabul and paid the Dost off with Ghazni. Five years later, the Dost evened the score. Azim launched an army against Runjeet Singh; the Dost took a bribe from the Sikhs and let Azim take a beating. Azim died and the Dost ruled at Kabul—facing only his own envious brothers at Kandahar and Mahmud at Herat.

To Claude Wade at Ludhiana in 1832, the situation looked sufficiently messy to warrant a try at putting Shah Shujah back on the throne. He may have believed that a British-sponsored ruler at Kabul would be a firmer guarantee against the Persians and Russians, but taking Wade's record as a whole it would appear that he was out to do a little private empire building. In any event, the Shah was more than willing; he was convinced that his people wanted him back. First an attempt was made to raise the necessary money from Runjeet Singh, but the

* Mohun Lal, *Life of Dost Mohammed Khan.*

Sikh was not optimistic about the Shah's chances and set too high a price.

Next the Shah sent a letter via Wade to the Governor-General. Bentinck gave him a curious reply. After the usual remarks dating back to Wellesley about the British unwillingness to interfere with the internal affairs of their neighbors, he added, "Your Majesty is, of course, master of your own actions." Wade felt sufficiently encouraged by the reply to write Macnaghten and ask if the Shah might have three months' allowance in advance to finance the try. Macnaghten's answer was so genial that Wade raised the ante to six months' allowance. They compromised on four months, and in January, 1833, Shah Shujah marched north. The affair was going to be a fiasco, but both Wade and Macnaghten would still be on hand to advise the next Governor-General when the question arose anew of putting the Shah on the throne at Kabul.

Dost Mohammed wrote Wade to ask if the British were supporting the venture and was told that the British were not involved, but that they wished the Shah well. It is hard to imagine a reply calculated to create so much ill will and at the same time be of no help whatsoever to the Shah. The Dost hurried his army to Kandahar, where the Shah, the Dost's Kandahar brothers, and his own troops all had to be watched with about equal suspicion. In the battle—fought by men chiefly concerned over who would offer them the largest bribe—only the Dost's cavalry led by his son Akbar fought with any particular dash. Defeated, the Shah fell back to Ludhiana, leaving in his baggage letters which the Dost must have read with some interest. They were from Wade to various Afghan chiefs apprising them that any assistance they could give Shah Shujah would be much appreciated by the British.

To make things worse, while the Dost was busy at Kandahar, Runjeet Singh took the opportunity to snatch Peshawar from him. When, later, the Dost made British help in retrieving Peshawar the condition of an alliance, it must have been very much on his mind that except for Claude Wade he might not have lost the city in the first place. Not surprisingly, the Dost began to look elsewhere for help against the "wicked Sikhs." A letter to the Shah of Persia combined a request with a threat:

> I shall persist in contending with the Sikhs as long
> as I am able, but should it prove that I be unable to

resist that diabolical tribe, then I have no choice, and must connect myself with the English, who will thus obtain a complete authority over the whole of Afghanistan; and it remains to be seen hereafter to what places, and what extent the flame of the violence of this nation may be carried.

To the Russians, he wrote that without their help against the Sikhs he could not prevent a British commercial penetration of Afghanistan, which would ruin the trade with Russia. Neither nation appeared in the least anxious to rush to his help, but Calcutta knew of the letters and worried accordingly.

II

The Promenade in Afghanistan

While the Dost worried about Peshawar, a straight hard stare in London was slowly turned toward the east. The owner of the stare was Henry John Temple, Lord Palmerston. Until he became Foreign Secretary in 1830, his public life had been spent in the backwater post of Secretary at War, and he was considerably better known for his interest in boxing, horse racing, and ladies than he was for his diplomacy. His talent with ladies was in fact so marked that even the London *Times* referred to him as "Lord Cupid." At one point, he had as mistresses Dorothea Lieven, who was the wife of the Russian ambassador, and Caroline Lamb, who was not only the wife of Lord Cowper but the sister of the Prime Minister under whom Palmerston served, Lord Melbourne. There is indeed suspicion that some of the little Cowpers may actually have been little Palmerstons.

The Eastern Question to which Palmerston now addressed his obviously considerable energies was simply what was to be done about the collapsing government of Turkey. To Palmerston, it seemed quite clear that if it did collapse, Russia, as the nearest great power, was likely to grab the most and that that grab might well include control of the Bosphorus and the Dardanelles. Through these the Russian Black Sea fleet could get into the Mediterranean—and since Napoleon, the British navy had regarded the Mediterranean as a more or less private pond.

Considering all this made Palmerston think very darkly about the Russians—the more so since he had a high regard for a navy as a means of diplomacy. As he said, "Diplomats and protocols are very good things, but there are no better peace-keepers than well appointed three deckers." Russia seemed likely to require some peace-keeping; to Palmerston it seemed that she was "pursuing a policy of universal aggression on all sides, partly from the personal character of the Emperor, partly from the permanent system of her government." Even the Prime Minister entertained the notion that the Russians might send a fleet into the English Channel.

As early as 1835, Palmerston thought he divined Russian intentions against India. To a new English ambassador to St. Petersburg, he wrote that the Russians "once in possession of Khiva . . . command the Oxus which is navigable till you come very near the spot where the Indus is navigable, and this would be the route they would take to attack or threaten our Indian possessions."*

The Chairman of the Board of Control for Indian Affairs in the administration was John Cam Hobhouse. He was altogether without previous experience in Indian affairs (a not unusual state—few of his predecessors were better qualified) but he was under the firmest instructions to look out for India: "I had an audience with the King, who urged the necessity of watching the western frontier of India. . . . 'Now' continued the King 'this is a fine country; but it is nothing without its Colonial possessions, especially India.' "

The Governor-General Palmerston and Hobhouse selected to watch the northwest and thwart the Russians was George Eden, Lord Auckland. A nephew of Gibby Elliot and of the same family which produced Anthony Eden in our own time, he had been a satisfactory, if unspectacular, First Lord of the Admiralty. Like Hobhouse, he was innocent of Indian matters, and a contemporary found him ". . . a man without shining qualities or showy accomplishments, austere and almost forbidding in manner, silent and reserved in society, unpretending both in public and private life." At fifty-one, he was still single and would be accompanied on his mission by two adoring sisters, Emily and Fanny.

His mission did not begin with particular promise. The vessel with the Auckland party ran aground while being towed up the Hooghly River to Calcutta and was prompt-

* The ambassador, Lord Durham, generally took a milder view of the Russians than Palmerston did. In this matter, however, he agreed fully that the Russians intended a commercial penetration of Central Asia. An invasion of India he regarded as "improbable," but nonetheless real enough to warrant efforts in Persia and Afghanistan (George Reid, *Life and Letters of Lord Durham*).

ly rammed by another vessel following close astern. Once ashore, Auckland was presented with a memorandum by Sir William Bentinck confirming that the Russians were indeed building a fort between the Caspian Sea and Khiva, going over the matter of a Persian-Russian advance via Herat, and concluding with Sir William's familiar computations about a Russian-Persian-Afghan advance to the Indus.

Eden's immediate staff consisted of Macnaghten, the fine linguist and experienced India hand carried over from Bentinck, and two new men, John Colvin and Henry Torrens.

In the spring of 1836 Auckland had a letter from his northern neighbor, the Dost. The Dost had not been fond of Bentinck, whom he held responsible for Shah Shujah's abortive invasion and the loss of Peshawar. Indeed, when he thought about Bentinck, he was, as Charles Masson* wrote, "very wroth." Now, at the suggestion of both Claude Wade and Masson, he determined to try his luck with the new man. In his letter the Dost referred to his ties "of friendship and affection with the British government," then mentioned the "field of his hopes," which under Bentinck had "been chilled by the cold blast of wintry times," but now hopefully would become "the envy of Paradise."

These Oriental effusions having been gotten out of the way, the Dost got down to the business of the "reckless and misguided Sikhs" who had taken Peshawar and desired Auckland communicate to him "whatever may suggest itself to your wisdom for the settlement of the affairs of this country."

Auckland can hardly be accused of rushing into an involvement with Kabul. He received some more letters in the same vein, but it was August before he even got around to answering the Dost. His Lordship's wish was that the Afghans should be a "flourishing and united nation," and in his view the best way to bring this about was to stop quarreling with the Sikhs and improve commerce. To that end, he planned to send a commercial mission to Kabul. The note closed with the usual form: "My friend, you are aware that it is not the practice of

---

* Masson was a newswriter employed at Kabul by Claude Wade. He was a deserter from the British army and a gifted archaeologist and linguist. His opinions on British officials are rarely charitable.

the British government to interfere with the affairs of other independent states."*

For the moment, however, Auckland was a good deal more worried about the Persians than he was about the Dost. Russian influence at Tehran was sky-high, and Ellis the British Minister there, was writing home, "It is unsatisfactory to know, that the Shah has very extended schemes of conquest in the direction of Afghanistan—and is much sutained . . . by the suggestions of Colonel Borowski."

Two months later, Ellis was reporting to Palmerston that since the Russian envoy, Count Simonich, was urging the Shah to go ahead with the Herat expedition and even offering his own services as military adviser, Ellis had felt it necessary to explain to Simonich the position of his government. "I commenced by stating that Afghanistan must be considered as frontier to our Indian Empire; . . . that accordingly I could not conceive that the British Government would view, otherwise than with jealousy, any interference, direct or indirect, in the affairs of Afghanistan."

Nevertheless, the Persian advance seemed about to start, and Auckland had an "apprehension of our being at no distant date involved in political and possibly in military operations upon or beyond our western frontier." Shortly there came instructions from Hobhouse in London. Hobhouse had information which he regarded as reliable that the Dost was negotiating with Persia for the partition of Herat. Since Persia was simply a Russian puppet in Hobhouse's view, any such arrangement tarred the Dost with the same brush and Auckland was to prevent anything which would seat the Russians firmly in Afghanistan looking down on the northwest frontier.

The instructions for dealing with "this very important question" were so vague as to give a much stronger-minded man than Auckland the willies. He might send an agent to Kabul simply to keep an eye on events, he might establish commercial or political relations, and he might adopt other measures "that may appear to you to be desirable in order to counteract the Russian influence." If

---

* Even in British circles such formulations were something of a joke. As Emily Eden wrote a friend about a similar affair: "It is not actually any business of our's, but . . . it is obvious that it might at last furnish one of those pretences for interference England delights in, and when once we begin, I know (don't you?) what becomes of the country we assist—swallowed up whole."

the Russians appeared to be gaining ground, he might "interfere decidedly in the affairs of Afghanistan."

For information on how the Russians were doing, he was to rely heavily on the new Chief of Mission in Persia, Dr. John McNeill. There can have been little doubt in Auckland's mind about the sort of advice he would get from McNeill. He was a card-carrying Russian hater, a disciple of the extraordinary David Urquhart,* and had that very year produced a pamphlet entitled "Progress and Present Position of Russia in the East." He foresaw dire events in Persia. "It is there ... that the danger to British interests is greatest and most imminent. ... It signifies little to object that the Russian troops are not even yet at Herat. ... The Moscow Gazette threatens to dictate at Calcutta the next peace with England." His finale was a rouser:

> The only nation in Europe that attempts to aggrandize itself at the expense of its neighbors is Russia. The only state whose preponderance and ambitions threaten to disturb the general tranquillity is Russia. The only power that seeks to put down an existing government is Russia. All nations except Russia wish to maintain the independence of other countries—to preserve things as they are and to build up rather than pull down—Russia alone threatens to overturn thrones, to subvert empires, and subdue nations hitherto independent. ... The integrity and independence of Persia is necessary to the security of India and Europe; and any attempt to subvert the one is a blow at the other—unequivocal act of hostility to England.

Both Auckland and Macnaghten thought it "madness" to expect any help from the Afghans against the Persians unless they took the Afghan side against the Sikhs, and they told Hobhouse so. Nevertheless, London continued to press, and McNeill sent up alarm flares from Persia as the advance on Herat drew nearer. Auckland decided on

* Urquhart was a sort of messiah type for whom no one was anti-Russian enough—even Palmerston seemed to him soft on the subject. Insofar as it is possible to explain him, he seems to have hated the Russians so much because he loved the Turks, with whom the Russians had recently been at war, so much. He introduced the Turkish bath to Britain and also kept a harem. His propaganda contributed considerably to British Russophobia.

one of the mildest of the courses suggested by London: a commercial mission would go to Kabul.

Alexander Burnes was recalled from Sind and its 135-degree temperatures for a journey to discuss with the Dost "the best means of promoting the interests and commerce and facilitating the intercourse of traders between India and Afghanistan." There have probably been very few missions which set out with so small a chance of success. Burnes was empowered to offer nothing but vague future commercial advantage, and as Masson wrote him from Kabul, "I have no idea that the Amir, or any one here, fully appreciates the advantage of a strictly commercial treaty ... all, no doubt, look forward to some political advantages."

Moreover, although Burnes was told to take gifts, they would be nothing like those Elphinstone had brought in 1809. His instructions for selecting gifts read: "They ought not to be of a costly nature and they should be chosen particularly with a view to exhibiting the superiority of British manufactures."*

Nor did it help that Claude Wade, who thought he should have been given the assignment, wrote the Dost that he, rather than Burnes, should have been sent, since he, Wade, could do more for the Afghans because of his influence with Runjeet Singh. The final millstone to be hung around Burnes's neck came in the form of a letter from John Colvin only a few days before the mission arrived in Kabul: "It must be nearly needless to say that you are in a position in which you should regulate your conduct marking the firm maintainance of our old alliance and friendship with Runjeet Singh as the avowed first principle of your duty and policy of bringing Dost Mohammed to his senses and to a just measure of his most hazardous position."

---

* Even in this he was not spectacularly successful. Among the gifts for the ladies of the Dost's *zenana,* or harem, was a toy accordion which one of the children promptly broke. It was turned over to Josiah Harlan, an American serving the Dost, for repairs, but he failed. Harlan was a venturesome soul who first came to India as a doctor—although there is no evidence that he had any training—and served with the British army. Taking service with Shah Shujah, he went in native dress to Kabul as a spy, switched allegiance to Runjeet Singh, then served the Dost as a drillmaster. After the Dost's fall, he returned to America, commanded a cavalry regiment during the Civil War, and retired from the strenuous life to practice medicine in San Francisco.

In other words, the best offer Burnes could make was that the British would prevent the Sikhs or Shah Shujah from attacking Kabul. The Sikhs hadn't the slightest intention of risking troops in the Afghan passes and the Dost knew it.

There was a good deal of disagreement about just what the trip was supposed to accomplish. Macnaghten—whom Emily Eden liked to call "our Lord Palmerston"—wrote that "he [Auckland] is satisfied that there is yet no adequate motive for the interposition of the British power in the contests of the Sikhs and Afghans; and he does not anticipate any further result from the present mission of Captain Burnes than the collection of accurate information."

From Persia, however, McNeill was exhorting Burnes and Auckland to do whatever necessary to get the Dost to march to Herat and help hold it against the Persian. ". . . with a little aid from us, [he] could be put in possession of both Kandahar and Herat." At Ludhiana, Claude Wade saw it just the other way: "Such an experiment on the part of our government would be to play into the hands of our rivals." In his view, any attempt by the Dost on Herat would simply throw the Heratis into the arms of the Persians.

Nevertheless, Burnes—in the customary portrait he is in Oriental regalia complete with turban and looks like nothing so much as someone's slightly overweight child costumed for the school production of *Ali Baba*—let his hopes run high. As he saw it, "A stirring time for political action has arrived ... I shall have to show what my government is made of ... at Kandahar, a Russian letter to the chiefs and presents from the Czar. Why, zounds! This is carrying the fire to our door with a vengeance."

He was well received. A force from Kabul escorted him through the Khyber, and on September 10, 1837, he entered the city atop an elephant. The Dost, however, listened politely to Burnes's remarks on the desirability of commerce and then got down to asking embarrassing questions about what the British would do to help him recover Peshawar. The Dost was willing to make concessions—if he were allowed to hold the city, he would pay tribute to Runjeet Singh. Burnes countered with a proposal which he had no authority to make: Would the Dost agree if Runjeet let the Dost's brother Mahomed hold the city? The Dost, who had enough trouble with his Kanda-

har brothers without elevating another one, replied that
he'd rather let the Sikhs have the place.

Somehow Burnes could still manage to write that the
Dost "has fallen into all our views," that he had the
Peshawar matter about settled, and that save for his
fortunate presence the Russian-Persian influence would be
paramount at Kabul. In fact, they were not far away. In
November the Persians finally laid seige to Herat, and a
Captain Vikovitch,* a messenger from Count Simonich,
was on his way to Kabul. He arrived "with a pair of
black kid gloves, a French translation of Burnes' travels,
and a long Persian epistle, well powdered with gold leaf,
purporting to be from the Emperor of Russia."†

The replies he brought to the Dost's request for Russian aid against the Sikhs, however, were not encouraging. The Czar's letter, which may or may not have been
genuine, said that it was nice to hear from him and that
he hoped Afghan-Russian commerce would continue to
prosper. A letter from Simonich introducing Vikovitch
simply urged the Dost to "trust him with your secrets"
and listed some presents which would be along as soon as
transportation could be found.

The Dost showed Burnes the letters, and in spite of
their lack of content the envoy panicked. He was "in a
mess," Herat might fall, Vikovitch had been sent by the
Czar "to offer Dost Mohammed money to fight Runjeet
Singh!!!!!," it was now "neck and neck" between Russia
and Britain. Auckland must do no less than send agents to
Bokhara, Herat, Kandahar, and Sind. To Auckland he
wrote again to support the Dost's claims on Peshawar,
and to the chiefs at Kandahar he promised a good deal
more British help against the Persians than his instructions authorized.

Auckland was angry with his envoy. Macnaghten wrote
back that the Governor-General attached "little immediate importance to the mission of the Russian agent," and
suggested that Burnes tell the Dost to give Vikovitch his
walking papers and warn the Afghans that if they did not
do as they were told they could expect no help from the

---

* Vikovitch was a Pole, born Jean Witkiwicz. He was exiled to
Central Asia for helping a Polish patriotic society against the Russians and eventually won a Cossack commission. Returning to St.
Petersburg after the Kabul mission, he was found shot and his
papers destroyed.

† Masson, quoted in H. M. Durand, *Sir Henry Durand*.

British in their difficulties with the Sikhs. As for Burnes himself, "it is with great pain" that His Lordship reminded him that he had exceeded his instructions.

Small wonder that Burnes, according to Masson, "bound his head with wet towels and handkerchiefs and took to the smelling bottle." He kept trying; in February Calcutta was still telling him that they were "sorry to see" that he was still trying to give the Dost some share of Peshawar. Claude Wade did not make the task easier by assuring Auckland that the Dost was unpopular with his own people, that his army was unreliable, and that Wade's old candidate Shah Shujah could be put back on the throne by the "simple appearance" of a single British officer. Every writer on the first Afghan War has his particular villain—Palmerston, Auckland, Auckland's secretaries. Wade's role is an interesting one. As early as June, 1837, he suggested to Macnaghten that the Sikhs be unleashed against the Afghans. In August he repeated the suggestion and added that Shah Shujah should go along. No Englishman in all of India knew better than Wade that the Sikhs would not go into Afghanistan alone. If they went at all, it would only be with extensive British support, and it is impossible to escape the suspicion that Claude Wade sensed there would be something good for Claude Wade in such an undertaking.

His hand—what there had ever been of it—played out, Burnes headed south in April, 1838, and at Peshawar found orders to report to Macnaghten, who'd gone up to visit Runjeet Singh at Lahore.

In the same month matters were moving toward a climax at Herat. The city sat in a pleasant valley surrounded by orchards and smaller settlements. It had 45,-000 inhabitants and was divided into four quarters by four long bazaars, arched over, which met in a covered quadrangle in the center of town. When Arthur Conolly had passed through a few years earlier, he thought the place must be "one of the dirtiest in the world." The streets were odorous with garbage, dead dogs, cats, and horses. The locals seemed impervious to it; as one said to Conolly, "If dirt killed people, where would the Afghans be?" Conolly, however, thought the place well fortified. In November, 1837, when the Persian artillery first opened fire on it, another young British officer thought differently:

"It was a very disheartening sight to see the breaches they
made in the rotten parapets."

The observer was Lt. Eldred Pottinger of the Bombay
artillery. In due time, he would become famous as "the
hero of Herat," and if the facts do not bear out the
contention of the day that he conducted the defense virtually single-handed, he comes through as an attractive,
steady youngster of great good sense.

The boy had come out to Bombay at sixteen under the
patronage of his uncle, Col. Henry Pottinger, himself a
famous explorer of the Indian-Persian borderlands. The
colonel dispatched his nephew, disguised as a horse trader, to Afghanistan to see what he could pick up in the
way of information. Pottinger was not a total success as a
Muslim horse trader, being notably weak on points of
religious ritual. He muddled through, however, by claiming to be either a recent convert or a bad student who
was bound for the city of Meshed to study hard and make
up his deficiencies.

When he arrived at Herat in August, Mahmud's son
Kamram had succeeded his father as its ruler, but the
real power lay with his chief Minister, Yar Mahommed.
The British considered Yar Mahommed able but "unscru-
pulous," a circumspect way of saying that he was adroit
at playing the various contenders for Herat off against
one another. He received Pottinger cordially, the lieutenant was able to discard his horse trader disguise, and
once the siege began, he sat back to watch.

In his opinion the Persians should have taken the city
in twenty-four hours, but their chiefs held back, each
anxious to let someone else lose his men in the assault.
The Afghans contented themselves with sorties from the
city at night—chiefly to bring back for reward the heads
or ears of their enemies. If no Persians were available,
some of the gallants were not above bringing in the ears
of another member of the sortie party.

In February Pottinger first took part in the languid
siege when he carried messages to the Persians from
Kamram asking them if they'd care to join him in an
attack on Kabul. The Persians declined and the siege
dragged on. Then, in April, John McNeill came blunder-
ing up to the front from Tehran with the notion that he
could arrange a truce. He not only failed, but made
matters worse. If the English ambassador to Persia was at
the front, the Russian ambassador could hardly be else-

where. Simonich came to the front and as McNeill wrote London, "the siege was prosecuted with renewed activity" as Simonich lent one of his officers to the Persian artillery and furnished the Shah with money to pay his troops. McNeill growled to the Shah about the British government "having recourse to measures which it would resort to with extreme reluctance," but neither his growling nor Simonich's urgings to the attack changed the stalemate.

As McNeill arrived at Herat, Auckland arrived at Simla after a five-month passage through India which had begun at Calcutta the previous October. It had been an extraordinary cavalcade of troops, servants, and diplomats with His Lordship and the Misses Eden riding near the head of the procession to be out of the clouds of dust their passage raised. Emily Eden found Simla "a beautiful place. . . . Views only too lovely, deep valleys on the drawing room side to the west and the snowy range on the dining room side . . . now I come back to air again I remember all about it."

In this refreshing atmosphere, Auckland sat down to consider what was to be done about his northwest frontier. Burnes had failed at Kabul and Vikovitch appeared to have succeeded. At Herat, by which London set great store, it seemed likely the Persians and Russians must sooner or later take the place. Still Auckland thought ahead with caution. "I would not commit myself, now, to any course of action," he wrote Hobhouse. "But we must Shah Shujah. . . . The third course would appear to be the first, to confine our defensive measures to the line of the Indus and leave Afghanistan to its fate; the second, to attempt to save Kabul by granting succour to the existing Chiefships of Kabul and Kandahar; the third, to permit or to encourage the Advance of Runjeet Singh's armies upon Kabul under counsel and restriction and (as subsidiary to his advance) to organize an expedition headed by Shah Shujah. . . . The third course would appear to be the most expedient . . . [I am] very strongly in favor of it." Clearly, Auckland had been reading the letters Claude Wade sent.

He was quite clear about how much British participation he intended. It was to consist of ". . . some contributions in money, and the presence of an accredited agent of the government, and of a sufficient number of officers for the direction of the Shah's army." It may be argued that Auckland was new in India and actually thought

Runjeet Singh would buy the package, but it would be hard to demonstrate that Macnaghten didn't know better.

Moreover, far simpler measures than an invasion of Afghanistan were at hand to relieve Herat. Palmerston sent McNeill a good stiff note to wave under the Shah's nose. Auckland himself—on McNeill's advice—sent a small force up the Persian Gulf to seize the island of Kharg, and it could not have been lost on the Shah that the island made a splendid base for an invasion of Persia.

The Persians themselves apparently sensed that it was now or never. On June 24 they put in a determined attack which fell on a Herat garrison so accustomed to peace and quiet that most of it was asleep. The assault came at five points; at four it was pushed back, but at the fifth the Persians got into a breach in the wall made by their artillery. According to the generally accepted version of the story, it was Pottinger who dragged Yar Mahommed to the threatened point and exhorted him until he pushed his men into a successful counterattack. In his own version, Pottinger says only that "people about" Yar Mahommed did the dragging, but his biographer assures us that the manuscript copy clearly shows the word "I" erased and "people about" substituted.

Auckland did not wait for London to react to his letter about the three options. Instead, three days after he wrote the paper, Torrens was drawing up instructions for Macnaghten, whose task it was to visit Runjeet Singh and bring him into the plan. For the first time, British troops are mentioned—Torrens made a brief reference to a British division occupying the city of Shikarpur, which stands on the north side of the Indus River and guards the entrance to the Bolan Pass much as Peshawar guards the Khyber.

There was no lack, either in India or in England, of prestigious opinion against pushing British troops so far to the northwest. Sir Charles Metcalfe had written as early as 1835, "You may depend on it, that the surest way to draw Russia upon us will be by our meddling with any of the states beyond the Indus." Sir Henry Fane, Commander-in-Chief of the Indian army, was of the opinion that "every advance you might make beyond the Sutlej to the northwest ... adds to your military weakness. ... If you want your empire to expand, expand it over Oude or over Gwalior and the remains of the Mahratta empire. . . . But let alone the far west!" Among older India hands, Wellington had warned that an advance across the Indus into Afghanistan would wind up "a perennial march into that country" and Elphinstone had even opposed a commercial agent at Kabul.

In May, though, Macnaghten crossed the Sutlej River, which divided the British dominions from the Sikh, and was presented to Runjeet Singh. In almost unbearable heat, the two parties approached one another on some seventy elephants and finally met beneath the trees of a mango grove. A British officer present thought "the Lion of the Punjab" to be "a very small, infirm looking old man of fifty-five (looking ten years older)," whose single eye was "bleared and bloodshot" and whose speech was so impaired by a stroke that all his remarks had to be repeated. By local standards, he was conservatively dressed in a green turban, coat, and gloves, with a rope of pearls around his neck and a string of diamonds wrapped around one arm. Some of his entourage were considerably dressier, one of them ". . . literally one mass of jewels, his neck, arms and legs were covered with necklaces, armlets and bangles, formed of pearls, diamonds and rubies . . . so thick that it was difficult to discover anything between them."

Macnaghten's instructions called for him to offer Runjeet alternative plans. Under one, the restoration of Shah Shujah would have both Sikh and British support, the British contribution being money for the Shah to raise an army and British officers to train it. Under the second plan, Runjeet would take on the entire task himself and Macnaghten was to tell him—presumably with a straight face—that the British considered the second plan best. Under the table, Runjeet was also to be informed that the British intended to restore the Shah even if the Sikhs stayed out and the British had to do the entire job themselves. The language employed was diplomatic; it went: ". . . the possibility that might occur of our being compelled, in self defense, to take our own measures to ward off approaching danger, and use our own troops to restore Shah Shujah to the throne."

Unsurprisingly, Runjeet saw no profit in taking on the Afghans by himself, but considered that the first plan calling for British assistance would be adding "sugar to milk." He then went on to inquire about the number of British troops to be used, and Macnaghten's vague answers about the division to be sent to Shikarpur did not in the least satisfy him. He squirmed, raised new questions, made new demands—while the British kept sharpening the threat to do the job alone if necessary. Runjeet did not relish the prospect of being odd man out with British India on one side and a British-supported ruler of Afghanistan on the other. In the end there was nothing to it but to give lip service, and on June 26, 1838, a treaty was signed. It was simply one of alliance and friendship, with only vague references to an Afghan expedition, and committing Shah Shujah, although he had not been a party to the talks, to various annual payments to the Sikhs. Runjeet's signature having been obtained, Macnaghten proceeded to Ludhiana to get the Shah's.

A traveler who saw Shah Shujah about this time recalled him as a man about fifty, medium-size, and "looking more like a gentleman who had lost an estate, than a monarch who had lost his kingdom." For a man who held very poor cards, he took a stiffish position. He objected strenuously to payment of tribute to the Sikhs, but Macnaghten finally wore him down on the point. He was adamant about his own authority being absolute both over the army to be raised for him and over the people of Afghanistan. Macnaghten reassured him on both matters. Two days after reaching Ludhiana, Macnaghten was on his way back to Simla to deliver his treaty to Auckland.

Incredibly, Auckland—at this point—seems to have honestly believed that the job could be done without the significant use of British troops. Nor was he without authorities. He had Wade's assurances. He had a letter from Burnes in June which, although it made a last eloquent plea for the Dost, included the fatal lines: "As for Shah Shujah ... the British Government have only to send him to Peshawar with an agent, and two of its own regiments as an honorary escort, and an avowal to the Afghans that we have taken up his cause, to ensure his being fixed for ever on the throne." When he wrote this, Burnes knew an expedition was in the wind, and it is a fair surmise that so ambitious a man was determined not to be left out of it even if he would have preferred some other solution to the problem.

There has been an enormous amount of debate about how British troops came to be committed in strength to the first Afghan campaign. The usual villains are Auckland's secretaries, who "induced him to sanction an enterprise of a magnitude commensurate with the bold and ambitious views of his irresponsible advisers." Masson even repeats a story which has Burnes arriving at Simla, and "Torrens and Colvin came running to him and prayed him to say nothing to unsettle his Lordship; that they had all the troubles in the world to get him into the business, and that even now he would be glad of any pretext to retire from it."

There is no need for mystification. The only wonder is that plans for the expedition had gone so far *without* British troops being committed. The raw levies being raised for Shah Shujah might do to lay some sort of a patina of power on him, but no one could have expected much fighting from them. Runjeet Singh himself had expressed the most serious doubts about whether his own troops would go to Afghanistan. Most important of all, it was gospel in India that an expedition once undertaken must be made strong enough so that it could not fail, since one failure at arms would send all India into a revolt too vast for the Company's army to put down. As a slightly earlier writer had put it, "The country hangs by a thread. The slightest reverse would set the whole into a flame."

In short, once the expedition was definite the involvement of the Indian army was inevitable. Auckland was only making it official when he wrote London in August that he would

> . . . give the direct and powerful assistance of the British Government to the enterprise of Shah Shujah, in a degree which was not in the first instance contemplated by me, from a conviction, confirmed in the most decided manner by every opinion of authority on the subject, that the measure could not be trusted mainly to the support of the Sikh ruler and army without imminent hazard of failure, and of serious detriment to the reputation of the British name among the Afghan people.

In a reply which did not reach India until after war was declared, Hobhouse said that while London was "disposed to concur" with Wade's opinion that a "comparatively insignificant effort" could put the Shah back on the throne, it wanted to take no risks. "If . . . any effort so decisive is to be made means should be adopted to prevent almost the possibility of failure. A considerable force, composed partly of British troops, should be assembled on your Northwest frontier . . . and prepared for an advance into Afghanistan."

Certainly the government made no effort to hold Auckland back. Palmerston wrote to his ambassador at St. Petersburg of a meeting which the Prime Minister himself had attended. "Auckland has been told to take Afghanistan in hand and make it a British dependency and there is no doubt of his being able to accomplish that object. We have long declined to meddle with the Afghan and have purposely left them independent, but if the Russians try to make them Russian we must take care that they become British." The Prime Minister called the move "decisive" and admitted that it might bring on "great events," but that the question was no less than "Who is to be master of Central Asia?"

On September 10 the army was directed to assemble. Some of the officers thought they were going to fight the Russians, and none of them knew that four days earlier the chief ostensible reason for the expedition had vanished.

The force Auckland had sent up the Persian Gulf to the island of Kharg had established itself, and on August 11 Col. Charles Stoddart arrived at the Persian camp outside Herat to suggest personally to the Shah that he was in danger of invasion. He made his point with sufficient clarity for the Shah to say, "The fact is, if I don't leave Herat, there will be war, is not that it?" Stoddart assured him that that was about it. Though the Shah dawdled a bit, at 8:00 A.M. on September 9 Stoddart was able to write, "I have the honor to report that the Persian army has marched from this place and His Majesty the Shah is about to mount." At 10:26 he added in a postscript that His Majesty had in fact mounted and was headed for Tehran.

Since the chief reason advanced for replacing Dost Mohammed was that he was under Persian and Russian influence, what reason now existed when the Persians and their Russian advisers were in retreat? In his Simla Manifesto, in which the Afghan expedition was announced to the public, Auckland had stressed heavily that the Persian threat was the reason "we should have on our western frontier an ally who is interested in resisting aggression."

The manifesto was issued before Auckland knew of the retreat at Herat, but when he did receive word from Stoddart, his only reaction was to issue an order saying that while the retreat was a "just cause for congratulation," the expedition would go ahead to establish "a permanent barrier against schemes of aggression upon our Northwest frontier."

The thing had simply gone too far to stop. As a veteran India watcher said, "In India every war is more or less popular." There hadn't been a good one in years, and even the English press at home was enthusiastic about the prospects. In a long, approving editorial the *Times* of London mentioned the need for "barriers against Russian aggression," called the state of affairs in Afghanistan "as unsatisfactory as possible," and quoted approvingly from a pamphlet which said, "Of our right to aid Shah Shujah in resuming his sovereignty no doubt can be entertained." Even Palmerston was not anti-Russian enough for the mood of the moment. The editorial concluded, "With such men as Lord Palmerston at Whitehall ... need we wonder that Russia has been permitted quietly to sap the British power throughout the vast territories which extend from her own dominions to the Indus."

The Army of the Indus was to consist of one force from Bengal and another from Bombay. The Bengal detachment contained the 16th—the Scarlet-Lancers, the 13th—the Somerset Light-Infantry which would become very famous indeed before the war was over, and the 3d Buffs—actually the Royal East Kents—so nicknamed because of the buff facings on their uniforms. In addition came the Company's European Regiment plus two regiments of Indian cavalry—one of which would disgrace itself—and twelve regiments of Indian infantry. In the Bombay section were the 4th Dragoons,* the 17th Leicestershire Infantry variously nicknamed Green Tigers or Bengal Tigers, and the 2d West Surrey Regiment. One regiment of Indian infantry completed the force.

The Indian regiments involved largely ceased to exist after the mutiny, when the non-European portion of the Indian army was increasingly recruited from Sikhs, Pa-

---

* Renamed the 4th Hussars, they held the line during the first gas attack of World War I.

thans, and Gurkhas and less from other parts of India. Of all the regiments on the Indian army list at the beginning of World War II only five claim even remote connections with units which marched to Afghanistan in 1838: the 7th Rajput Infantry, the 9th Jat Infantry, Skinner's Horse, the Poona Horse, and the 13th Duke of Connaught's Own Lancers. The 35th Bengal Native Infantry, for example, which with the Somersets became "the illustrious garrison" of Jalalabad, vanished when it joined the mutineers of 1857.

Of the men raised for Shah Shujah's army, no one had any great opinion. As an English officer who observed them said, "Time did not allow the selection to be very good; and, from what I have lately seen, I fear it will be many a day before these troops will be much use either to their master or anyone else." He had further fears based on the fact that the men knew "that they were destined to fight against a race celebrated through the East for their bravery and fanaticism," and, finally, he speculated— accurately as it turned out—that men used to the heat of the Indian plains would do badly in the rigors of an Afghan winter.*

The Bengal section of the army was brought together at Ferozepore near the Sutlej River. The Governor-General joined his forces on November 27 and two days later met Runjeet Singh at a reception which very nearly turned into a riot. At 9:30 in the morning the "clangor of a band of indescribable musicians" heralded the approach of the great Sikh. Dressed in red silk, Runjeet came mounted on an elephant, with the elephants of his chiefs lined out to either side. The English rode out to meet him on their elephants in two columns. An officer present observed that "the crowd was what one might expect from the meeting of upwards of one hundred elephants with the space of as many yards wide; . . . elephants trumpeting, gentlemen swearing and each one trying how he could poke out his neighbor's eye with the corner of his howdah."

The confusion was not lessened by the cannon firing salutes, the band playing the British national anthem, miscellaneous Sikhs galloping in and out of the crowd in "wild disorder," and British officers trying to push into

* Sir Henry Fane in his *Five Years in India.*

the durbar (council) tent. The crush became so bad that
Runjeet was nearly trampled and probably would have
been had not Sir Henry Fane almost carried him inside.
Eventually, two companies of infantry were brought up
to clear a passage.

Once seated inside, the Maharajah was presented with
gifts including a portrait of Queen Victoria which Emily
Eden had painted especially for the occasion. By her own
admission, the likeness was not exact, but she calculated
that the Sikhs were not likely to know what the Queen
looked like anyway. The dress she had gotten quite right,
she felt, from descriptions she had read in papers from
home. She was pleased to note that Runjeet Singh studied
the painting for five minutes. An officer commented, "I
do not think he quite understood, but seemed to think her
Majesty made a very decent Nautch girl."

The next day the whole thing had to be turned around
and the British rode off to visit Runjeet at state pace, or
what an officer called "a snail's gallop," in 110-degree
heat. The entire British force was marched out for the
Sikhs' inspection, and in the evening Runjeet gave the first
of several parties which brightened the affair. Although
one guest complained that the Sikh liquor would "kill
most people in a week," he could not but have been
impressed by the dancing girls, who were not only bejeweled but sprinkled with silver dust. Miss Eden, who
thought Runjeet looked "exactly like an old mouse with
grey whiskers and one eye," did not particularly care for
the affair; it was "all those satraps in a row and these
screaming girls and crowds of long bearded attendants
and the old tyrant drinking in the middle."

At Ferozepore, Auckland made his only concession to
the relief of Herat. He ordered that the size of the force
going to Afghanistan be reduced and Sir Henry Fane
ticked off the Buffs and five Indian infantry regiments to
stay behind. He then resigned himself. From the first he
had been against an expedition to a land "so distant and
which hardly produces sufficient food for a very scanty
population." His son, who was his aide at the time, later
represented him as feeling that the whole thing was simply
a product of Auckland's ambition and that, moreover,
altogether too much power had been given Macnaghten.

The departure left the Bengal force under command of
Sir Willoughby Cotton, but, by virtue of his seniority, the

whole expedition now came under Sir John Keane, the Bombay commander. Bengal was nettled. Since they were supplying most of the troops, they felt they deserved the commander, too, and besides they considered Keane a "Peninsula general"—that is, antiquated.

The Bombay force sailed up the western coast of India intending to disembark at Karachi in what is now West Pakistan. It was a quiet voyage—so much so that one of the voyagers was moved to note in his diary that there was not "any threatened approach of that abdominal mutiny and revulsion . . . to which my frail inward man is most painfully liable."

Things were not to remain quite so calm. Plans called for the Army of the Indus to enter Afghanistan by the Bolan Pass. This was the long way round, but the Bolan was somewhat easier going than the Khyber; moreover, going through the Khyber meant going through Sikh country, and Runjeet Singh regarded the idea of large bodies of British troops marching through his territories with profound distaste. A much smaller Sikh-British force under Claude Wade would go by way of the Khyber.

Accordingly, the Bengal force would march down the Sutlej to the point where it joined the Indus, then follow the south bank of the Indus until it came to the crossing point—the spot where the great island-fortress of Bukkur sits in mid-river. In this arrangement there was one difficulty. Bukkur was in the territories of the Amirs of Sind. The Amirs were not enthusiastic about Shah Shujah, who openly regarded them as Afghan subjects behind in their tax payments. Nor did the Amirs like one British army marching through from Karachi while another marched in from the north. Finally, they did not like being told that they had to cede the Bukkur fortress to the British for the duration of the expedition. Even on the British side of the fence there was some feeling that the demand was a bit high-handed, and one British officer wrote that "one cannot but think well" of the Amirs for rejecting the demand.

For most of the army, however, the rejection was simply a splendid excuse to thrash the Amirs and then loot Hyderabad, their capital. Cotton marched his men past Bukkur, but the Amirs gave in and he had to retrace his steps lootless. On March 4, 1839, the Bombay contingent joined up and the Army of the Indus was complete. A thoughtful observer delivered himself of the following:

> Oh, blind to the future, if drum and sword
> Be all that your vision contemplate!
> May the warning voice not remain unheard
> Till the warning voice shall be heard too late.

The army consisted of 9,500 men from Bengal, 5,600 from Bombay, plus the auxiliary force of 6,000 men raised for the Shah. European and Indian infantry wore the same uniform. At the top was worn a rather dress-parade-looking tall black shako made of black cloth pulled over a wire or wicker frame. It had a black leather visor, and the regimental badge was worn on the front surface of the shako. Over this, most regiments wore a plume or pompon. The whole was held in place by a chin strap which must have chafed abominably.

The scarlet jacket, or "coatee," buttoned to the throat in front and was swallow-tailed in back. The cuffs and the collar were in the regimental facings—white, sky-blue, pearl-gray, grass-green, or what-have-you. A white cross belt going from the right shoulder to the left side supported the sword and bayonet, while another from over the left shoulder supported the ammunition pouch. The rest of the man's gear was in a knapsack on his back. To the top of the knapsack, the rolled greatcoat was strapped. White duck trousers—at that time "trowsers"—completed the outfit.

The infantry weapon was the Brown Bess musket, which had not changed since the Battle of Waterloo twenty-five years earlier. It was a muzzle loader, effective to only 150 yards, and a good man could get off a maximum of two rounds a minute. By comparison, the Afghan *jezail,* though awkwardly long, was reputed to be effective at eight hundred yards when fired from a rest, and an artillery officer, accustomed to estimating ranges, saw one kill a horse at six hundred yards. The origin of the term "Brown Bess" is in dispute, but the most widely held theory is that it is a result of the Duke of Wellington's order that the musket barrels be painted brown lest enemy attention be drawn to troop movements by sunlight glinting on silvery musket barrels.

If it seems remarkable that the firearms had not changed since Waterloo, it must be borne in mind that the

Waterloo commander was still in command and he took a dim view of innovation. The army ought not to "hastily" adopt improved weapons, since "it was ridiculous to suppose that two armies could fight at a distance of five hundred or six hundred yards."

The European portion of the force was not at this time known as Tommy Atkins. The nickname came into being only in 1847, when a soldier's record book—his "small book"—was issued and the sample form made out to an imaginary Thomas Atkins. Unlike the Indian army man of an earlier day, the enlisted man had probably joined up more or less of his own free will. Some came for adventure, some for the uniform—they were said to have "caught the scarlet fever"—and some because men in court for minor offenses were offered the alternative of enlisting rather than going to jail.

Well over half the lot were illiterate, and it was the army's intention that they should remain that way. Among Wellington's other conservative convictions was the notion that teaching a soldier to read would undermine discipline and open the way for revolutionary propaganda. Discipline was not at this moment maintained by the lash in the Indian army. Bentinck had abolished it in 1835 and it was not reintroduced until 1843. There was a limitation of two hundred lashes at the time, although fifty seems to have been more than enough to tear a man's back to pieces.

The officers of the force left a great deal to be desired. In Royal regiments, commissions were still purchased and many of the purchasers exemplified a saying of the period that the first four rules of arithmetic were enough for a young officer and that fractions was "going a little too far." European officers in Indian regiments came from poorer stock but were equally deficient save for what they picked up in the field—and the army had long been at peace. Though Indian regiments had a cadre of Indian officers, they had virtually no authority and, since they were promoted entirely by seniority, were likely to be men of advanced years. The exceptions were the so-called irregular cavalry units like Skinner's Horse, where British officers were fewer and Indians a functioning part of the chain of command.

At Bukkur, a bridge of boats had been laid across the Indus. Nineteen boats with planks laid over them covered the distance from the shore to the island, and fifty-five more from the island to the northern bank of the river. Besides the army, there was a cloud of camp followers waiting to cross—38,000 of them in all—servants, animal handlers, and what were euphemistically referred to as bazaar girls. Some thirty thousand camels carried the force's gear and made day and night hideous with their caterwauling. A man who had to put up with it concluded that "there is scarcely a more disagreeable sound than that of the camel's outraged feelings with which he groans and grumbles and resents every fresh addition to his load . . . it conveys a distinct idea of reproach and remonstrance, and it is uttered in such loud and discordant tones that a camel man must have a heart of stone to be able to endure it."*

The horde of camels carried a good deal more than the sinews of war. A British officer campaigned in comfort with half a dozen servants, glass, crockery, and silverplate for his table, a wine chest, and a portable bathtub. Sir Willoughby Cotton required no less than 260 camels for his own and his servants' equipment and traveled himself in a buggy. The Bombay forces claimed that some of their medical stores had to be left behind to make room for officers' luxuries, and one disgusted officer thought the excess equipment "as useful or desirable to men in our situation as a horse to a sailor on his quarter-deck."

On February 23 the Bengal troops crossed the river, to be followed in a few days by the Shah's contingent and then the Bombay men. At first the country was pleasant enough with yellow-blossomed acacias and tamarisks of "dingy, dusky hue." The day began at midnight when the camp woke to bugles and packed by the light of brushwood fires. The march began before dawn, while the quartermaster general hurried ahead to mark out the next campsite. When the men came up to it, they marched to their allotted places and, on a bugle signal, pitched their tents. There were sixteen men in tents fourteen feet square—which works out to a space about six feet long and two feet wide per man, or very close quarters.

North of Shikarpur, the land turned desert—not sandy, but a "boundless level plain of indurated clay of a dull dry earthy color." The camels, who from shortages of

* Richard Kennedy, *Narrative of the Campaign of the Army of the Indus.*

food and water had already been dying at such a rate that one officer counted twenty corpses in a space of four miles, now began going down in even larger numbers. The army began to spread out, partly from bad march discipline, partly because there were few campsites with wells sufficient for the entire force. The Beluchis—very fierce-looking fighters with long black curls and twenty-eight-inch knives—took to raiding in the night to cut off stragglers and carry off camels. The cavalry was sent after them, but with no great success. A squadron of the 16th Lancers was ordered out ". . . and were kept out half the night, going at full gallop with drawn swords over watercourses, and bad ground of all sorts; during which no less than four men had falls, horses and all, and one was seriously hurt. This proceeding gave no little cause for grumbling."*

By March 11 the entire advance—men and animals—was on half rations, and the horses struggled along with "tuck-up bellies and high bones." In the Lancers the men were leading their horses more than they were riding them. The Indian cart drivers and animal men began to crack under the Beluchi sniping, took to running away, and were thoroughly flogged when they could be caught. To add to everyone's discomfort, there was an abundance of scorpions—light green ones about the size of a small frog and larger black ones. The sting made the area swell ferociously, turn black, and pain damnably.

In mid-March the advance entered the Bolan Pass—sixty miles long—and if there was now plenty of water there was even less forage for the animals. An officer in the advance thought the entrance to the pass "grand"—walls 500 feet high on either side, no road, but only a little river running through and the floor of the pass varying from 500 yards wide to 70 yards or less.

The artillery horses were now so weak that it took eight to move a gun. Even then a rest was necessary every half hour. The Beluchis peppered the columns from the sides of the pass, and the Bombay column was not heartened by passing the bodies of men and camels from the Bengal troops ahead of them. Sir John Keane, whose temper was not improved by the suspicion that Cotton was deliberately keeping his Bengal men out in front to avoid falling under Keane's command, took to dealing out

* Fane, op. cit.

fierce justice to the Beluchis. His chief medical officer
passed a spot where

> ten Beluchis had been summarily executed by Col.
> Wandwith . . . under written orders from Sir John
> Keane. . . . The first order was a verbal one, but Col-
> onel Wandwith, not liking it, required a written one,
> and received it on half a sheet of note paper. . . . The
> poor wretches had their elbows secured, and were
> made to sit on the ground; then each had a bullet
> sent through his brain from a carbine. Lt. Loch, the
> officer who superintended the execution, spoke very
> feelingly of what he had been no willing agent in.
> Some of them, he said, sat quietly down and sub-
> mitted to their fate; some resisted, and, to keep them
> quiet, the execution party fastened their heads together
> by their long, luxuriant hair. . . . Two young lads
> seemed horrified to bewilderment by their fears and
> implored mercy, seizing the feet and knees of the su-
> perintending officer, but they were made to sit down.
> Ere the fatal volley exploded they were endeavouring
> to embrace, leaning their heads against each other,
> weeping bitterly their last farewell.*

The medical officer found himself wondering whether a
good flogging wouldn't have done just as well.

An officer who went over the ground later thought it
"extraordinary" that the force ever got through, and an
officer with them thought they looked more like an army
retreating after a disaster than advancing conquerers. By
the end of March, however, the advance staggered clear
of the northern end of the pass, although the last ten
miles were very bad going with the narrow gorge winding
"zigzag like the teeth of a saw" between cliffs a thousand
feet high. The men thought the town of Quetta a
"wretched place," but the country around was pure joy
after the desert and the pass. There was water, there was
forage, there were peach and apricot orchards, and the
plain was quilted with wild flowers—scarlet and yellow
tulips, daisies, and wild thyme that scented the air. The
locals called the place "Unhappy Valley," but the British
were quite content with it.

On April 6 Sir John Keane came up with the Bombay

---

* Kennedy, op. cit.

column and for the first time since Bukkur had his entire
army united. He had mismanaged his supply problem so
badly, however, that the troops had to go on half rations
and the camp followers on quarter rations. It would be
three months before they got back on full rations again.
Macnaghten was writing Auckland that "the troops and
camp followers are nearly in a state of mutiny for food."

There was worse to come as they continued the march
north. The country turned bad again. It was almost totally devoid of water; one account goes so far as to say that
"in the evening a few drops of water could not be
obtained even to mix with the medicines of the sick."
Horses dropped, were prodded with lances, and still refused to rise. Men had to be put on drag ropes to move
the guns. The trail rose again, this time into the Khojak
Pass, which was not so long as the Bolan but very steep
and very narrow. At night the mountaineers sniped or
rolled boulders down into the camp. A frustrated officer
grumbled into his diary about the "blackguards not standing out" to receive the "thrashing they so richly
deserved." Once over the pass, the march continued across
a desolate plain of sandy earth where the only vegetation
was tufts of herbs or wild grass, each tuft some two or
three yards from its neighbor. When water was sighted,
discipline broke down altogether: "The moment the
horses saw the water they made a sudden rush into the
river as if mad; both men and horses drank till they
nearly burst themselves."

The more militant were briefly cheered by a rumor that
the Kandahar chiefs would come out and make a fight of
it. Burnes's aide Mohun Lal bribed them so thoroughly,
however, that although one officer was moved to remark
that "the campaign promised to be more severe on the
Company's purse than on anything else," there was no
battle. Conditions in fact were judged to be so safe that
the Shah and his badly drilled troops were allowed to lead
the advance.

On April 26 the head of the British column—having
marched, in the case of the Bengal units, 1,005 miles—
sighted Kandahar "seated in an open plain of corn field
and meadows, intersected by water-courses—a mass of
buildings, worthy of the title of city, surrounded by a
quadrangular wall."

The Shah himself had entered the city the day before,
and Macnaghten was so pleased with the crowd that

turned out that he wrote Auckland, "The Shah made a grand public entry ... and was received with feelings nearly amounting to adoration." Macnaghten and the Shah took up residence in the palace of one of the departed chiefs, and a cynical officer observed that "they talked very patriotically at one time of giving this up for a hospital, but finding it hot outside they took care of No. 1 and left the sick to their fate."

If the crowd had been good for the Shah's arrival, the turnout for his official enthronement as Shah of Afghanistan was considerably less impressive. At dawn on May 8 the entire Army of the Indus was drawn up north of the city. As the Shah rode down the line there was a general salute, and as he ascended the throne which had been set up on a platform on the plain a 101-gun salute was fired. It was a splendid spectacle, but various observers felt it lacked something. A young lieutenant wrote home, "The concourse of Afghans was much less than I had anticipated, and no symptom of loyal enthusiasm was to be discovered." Another man felt that "all the national enthusiasm of the scene was entirely confined to his Majesty's immediate retainers." A third raised the more general objection that "everyone is surprised at the misinformation given us regarding the roads and resources of this country, and the disposition of its inhabitants towards Shah Shujah."

Nevertheless, the Army of the Indus had accomplished what it had come to do, and after the review, Alexander Burnes invited its officers to a breakfast which seems to have consisted chiefly of iced champagne and claret. In the evening there was a dinner which went on until the very small hours and resulted in "some of the party being placed on camels, and sent home in a state of utter unconsciousness."

Waiting for provisions kept the army at Kandahar for two months, and the longer it sat, the unhappier it got. It was difficult to keep enlisted men from looting in the city; forty of them were punished in one day for the offense. The sepoys were homesick and, in the opinion of one of their officers, the Europeans equally so. The Afghans did a lively trade by stealing the army's camels and then selling them back. Occasionally, there was more serious crime; two lieutenants of the 16th Lancers were ambushed returning from a fishing trip. One was killed, the other managed to fight his way out.

Nor were the leaders of the force in any particular harmony. Before moving on to Kabul, Macnaghten wanted to leave the Bombay column at Kandahar to ease the supply problem, and he had actually brought Keane around to his position when Thomson, the force's engineering officer, reminded the general that at some point the Afghans were likely to make a fight of it and swung him back the other way. Keane did decide that his heavy artillery which had been so painfully dragged over the Bolan and the Khojak was more trouble than it was worth and left it behind. Only outrageously good luck saved him from regretting the decision.

On June 27 the army marched off for Kabul; although food was still short, water was not and the going was easier. In a little less than a month, the force was approaching the fortress town of Ghazni and its journey had been hampered only by sniping from Ghilzai tribesmen. Such Ghilzai snipers as he could catch, the Shah had blown from cannons. The process was described thus: ". . . the only one I saw executed, being blown to shivers in a second, his legs and head both severed from his trunk being the only portions we could recognize afterwards . . . the wretch was tied, standing on the ground with his back to the mouth of the cannon and met his end with the philosophy most natives evince on those occasions."

When Sir John Keane looked at Ghazni—walls sixty feet high, a moat or "wet ditch" all around, and perched on the side of a mountain—he must have wondered whether he had done well to leave his heavy artillery at Kandahar. The heaviest pieces he had with him were nine-pounders—useful for anti-personnel work, but no good for breaching a wall. Some of his officers thought it might be best to leave a force covering the city and march straight on for Kabul. Kabul, however, was at the very least a week's march, and no one knew better than Keane that he had supplies for, at the most, three days.

If the walls could not be breached there was, however, another possibility. The enterprising Mohun Lal bribed a nephew of Dost Mohammed's to desert, and for a paltry five hundred rupees, or about $250, the British were in possession of the fact that while the Kandahar gate of Ghazni had been bricked up to prevent its being blown in, the Kabul gate on the other side of town was not so reinforced.

On July 22 Keane moved his men around to the Kabul

side of town, and during the day the army got its first
look at the green and white banner of Islam. A reconnaissance force of the Dost's cavalry appeared and was
easily driven off; fifty prisoners were taken. The prisoners
gave testimony to local enthusiasm for the Shah by curs-
ing him and stabbing one of his servants. In what become known later as the Ghazni massacre, the Shah had
the lot of them beheaded.

Shortly after midnight—it was cold, dark, and windy—
the troops were assembled in silence, moved onto a low
ridge near the city, and ordered to lie down until the gate
was blown. The storming party was to consist of Gen. Sir
Robert ("Fighting Bob") Sale's 13th Infantry—the advance which was to rush the gate as soon as it was blown
to be commanded by Col. William Dennie.

The man who was actually going to blow the gate was
a young lieutenant named Henry Durand and he was
feeling extremely dubious about his ability to get the job
done. He was weak with jaundice and not at all sure how
long he could keep his feet. In the event that he couldn't
manage, he gave both his sergeants strict instructions to
get on with the job by themselves if necessary.

Dawn was just breaking as the party moved out. Six
men from the 13th formed a light advance guard, then
came twelve Indian sappers carrying the powder, then six
more sappers to replace any casualties. By the book, 60
to 120 pounds of powder was sufficient to blow the gate,
but Chief Engineer Thomson, intent on a thorough job, had
ordered Durand to use 300 pounds. The order was going
to turn out to be an excellent illustration of the dangers
of overdoing a good thing.

To get to the gate, Durand and his men had to cross a
bridge over the wet ditch, pass some low outworks which
he hoped prayerfully were not manned, and then do their
work at the foot of two large towers on either side of the
gate. The gate itself was twenty feet wide and might more
properly be called a tunnel, since it remained twenty feet
wide and roofed over until it opened out 150 feet later in
the Ghazni town square.

Just before they crossed the bridge, the party was
spotted from the walls, and to Durand's dismay the "blue
lights" came on, "brilliantly illuminating" the gate area.
British artillery and infantry promptly opened fire on the
walls, the sappers laid the powder bags at the base of the
gate, and Durand and a sergeant who called himself

Robertson* paid out the fuse and tried to light it. Twice the attempt failed. Durand ordered Robertson to retire, intending to blow the powder with a pistol shot—an effort which certainly would have blown him up along with the gate. Robertson pleaded to have one more try. This time the fuse caught, and Durand and Robertson threw themselves into a depression in the ground as the gate blew up with a dull roar which barely made itself heard over the rushing wind.

Engineer Thomson's extra-large powder charge had the first of its unfortunate results; the force of the explosion knocked Captain Peat, who was to signal Dennie to advance when the gate was clear, silly. Durand, getting weaker by the minute with his jaundice, staggered back to try to bring up the infantry. The first officer he found was a lieutenant who promptly refused to take orders from him. Fortunately, his next encounter was with Lt. William Broadfoot of the Bengal Europeans, who hurried back to bring Dennie up while Durand collapsed, unable to move another step.

In the minutes lost, the Afghans were able to assemble a force in the gate and Dennie's stormers found it very hard going. The Afghans made a very good fight of it, taking the British bayonets on their shields and stabbing under the shields with their own swords. Moreover, Thomson's powder charge had made further trouble. Instead of blowing just the gate, it had blown the whole end of the tunnel, filling it with debris hard to get over and giving the Afghans a sort of barricade to fight from.

Word got back to Sale that the gate could not be forced, and a bugler sounded retreat; then Sale reversed himself, the bugler sounded the advance, and the 13th went forward with Sale himself in the van. He had hardly reached the gate when he was knocked down by a saber blow in the face, but his opponent lost his footing in the wreckage and "Britain and Afghan rolled together amongst the fractured timbers." Sale grabbed for his opponent's sword, got it by the blade, and promptly let go again. A Captain Kershaw ran his bayonet through the Afghan's body, and if the stroke did not disable the man it did distract him sufficiently for Sale to get in a cut with

---

* No one knew Robertson's real name, but he was commonly supposed to be a gentleman who had gotten himself into trouble and joined the army as an enlisted man.

his own saber, which split his opponent's head down to
the eyebrows. According to another officer present: "The
Mohammedan once shouted 'Ne Ullah!' (Oh, God!) and
never moved or spoke again."

There was a moment of panic at the gate, the cry
"Back, back!" went up, then the stormers rallied and
pushed through. As they came out the end of the tunnel,
they found themselves in Ghazni's main square, some 150
yards across, with houses on three sides and the citadel
facing them on the fourth. There was some brisk fighting
in the narrow streets between the houses with the Afghans maintaining a fire from the upper stories of the
buildings, but shortly word came back with the wounded:
"We have done 'em." There were 500 Afghan dead and
1,500 prisoners; in return the Afghans had exacted a
"tolerable butcher's bill" of 200 British and Indian casualties.

The troops promptly turned to looting. One officer
thought it would have been a good deal worse if the men
hadn't been forced to go into action sober because the
rum ration had run out, but it seems to have been bad
enough. The men had "Cashmere shawls, ermine dresses
and ladies' inexpressibles over the bloodstained uniforms,"
and a lieutenant wrote home, "I shall not try to describe
the cruelties and action I saw committed that day, as I
am sure it would only disgust you with mankind." To add
to the nightmare quality, fifteen hundred Afghan horses
broke loose and careened around the square until they
were shot down.

The strongest fortress in his kingdom fallen, and aware
that his chiefs had been subjected to Macnaghten's "judicious negotiations" (the phrase is Mohun Lal's), Dost
Mohammed sent his brother to the British camp to see if
there was room for compromise. The best British offer
was a pension in India. The Dost's brother turned it down
and left Macnaghten with the warning: "If Shah Shujah is
really a king, and come to the kingdom of his ancestors,
what is the use of your army and name? You have
brought him by your money and arms into Afghanistan,
and you have behaved toward him in a friendly and
liberal manner in every way. Leave him now to us Afghans and let him rule us if he can."

If there could be no compromise, there was nothing for
it but to fight, and the Dost came out from Kabul with a
respectable force of 13,000 men and 30 guns. The "judi-

cious negotiations" had gone well, however. Many of the
Dost's men were deserting and some of the rest plotting to
turn him over to the Shah. Koran in hand, he appealed
for just one charge against the unbelievers so that he
could die with honor. Either the response was feeble or
the Dost had second thoughts about dying; in any event
he fled north with his family and 2,000 cavalry. A handful of British officers with 500 cavalry from the Shah's
forces dashed off in pursuit, but never caught up—and
considering what the Dost's 2,000 would have done to the
Shah's 500, probably saved their lives as a result.

On August 6 the army was before Kabul. On August 7
Shah Shujah, escorted by Macnaghten and a cavalry detachment, reentered the city after an absence of thirty
years. He made a splendid picture ". . . very superbly
dressed in a long coat of dark cloth covered with jewels, his
waist surrounded with embroidered bullet cases and powder horns and his head covered with a kind of three cor-
nered cap, from one corner of which hung a large
emerald." There were large crowds which duly rose as
their new ruler passed, but one observer "neither heard
nor saw any enthusiasm," while another thought the
crowds "very orderly."

No matter; the mission was complete, the friendly
power was installed at Kabul. The victory had been won
far more by Macnaghten's bribes than by anyone's valor—
indeed one officer judged most of the country through
which they had passed to be "totally impracticable for an
army if properly defended by an enemy"—but at least the
thing was done. The troops settled down to a routine
familiar to all armies of occupation. Less than a week
after their arrival, an order that troops were not to be
allowed into the city without a pass had to be modified by
another cutting down the number of passes because of
"irregularities."

And yet the very specter the friendly power at Kabul
was designed to lay was suddenly quite audibly moving
about on the other side of the Hindu Kush. In August,
Eldred Pottinger wrote from Herat that a Russian force
was being assembled at Orenburg for an advance on
Khiva.

In the Russian view British industry, "exclusive and
jealous," was trying to force Russian commerce "to disap-
pear from all the markets of Central Asia." Their ambas-

sador to London was instructed to tell Palmerston that Russia wanted "fair competition" in the "commercial advantages of Asia." Commercial advantages aside, the Russians felt particularly strongly about Khiva because of the slave trade Muravieff had reported. He had estimated a thousand Russian slaves there, and the Khan of Khiva was informed that Khivan merchants would be detained at Orenburg until the slaves were sent home. Instead of a thousand—and the estimate was probably high—the Khan sent back twenty-five. General V. A. Perovski, the Governor of Orenburg and a long-time enthusiast for an invasion of India, was instructed to prepare an expedition the object of which was "to renew and strengthen the influence of Russia in Central Asia, which had been weakened by the long impunity of the Khivese, and especially by the constant efforts of the English to extend their influence in those lands to the prejudice of our commerce and trade."*

The preparations were scarcely precipitous. The original order was known to Auckland in India as early as February, 1837, but it was not until March, 1839—when the British were moving through the Bolan Pass—that the committee appointed to consider the matter came to some conclusions. The conclusions were that the launching of the expedition should be held off until the English-Afghan war was settled, but that in the meantime the expedition was to be prepared. The English were to be told that it was of a scientific nature. If the English were not out of Afghanistan by early 1840, the expedition would move anyway and Perovski would select a suitable candidate for the throne at Khiva. The British, reasoned the committee, could not possibly object since they had just done precisely the same thing at Kabul.

The Perovski force was to consist of three and a half battalions of infantry, twenty-two guns, four rocket carriages, and three regiments of cavalry—in all, some 4,500 troops, 2,000 horses, and over 10,000 camels. In some details, the planning was magnificently precise. Perovski had fifty Crosses of St. George with him in order that gallantry might not go unrewarded while the troops were on the road. Special camel carts with extra-large wheels and broad treads were built for getting across the steppes. Supply dumps were established 200 and 400 miles out

* Quoted in Alexis Krausse, *Russia in Asia.*

along the 800-mile route. In addition, ten supply ships were to sail down the Caspian to cooperate with the advancing troops.

Other aspects of the planning were less felicitous. The army was a mix of exiled Poles, criminals, and raw recruits. Worse, Perovski had determined to solve Bekovitch's problems with water supply by crossing the steppe in winter, when there would be plenty of snow to be melted. In the event, there did turn out to be plenty of snow.

In June—while the British were en route from Kandahar to Ghazni—the force moved a hundred miles south of Orenburg and then camped until fall while they gathered additional camels. On November 14 it marched again, accompanied by a proclamation announcing that His Majesty the Emperor had ordered the expedition against Khiva "to secure the rights and interests of Russian subjects for the future, to put an end to pillage and violence, to deliver our captives who languish in Khiva, to inspire a proper esteem for the Russian name, and to strengthen that influence which incontestably belongs to Russia."*

On November 22 the temperature went to 13 degrees below zero; the next day it went to 22 below. Out of the first thirty-two days of marching there were only three days when it got as high as 10 degrees above zero at noon. On eleven others, it was between zero and 13 below, on twelve more from 13 to 26 below, and on six from 26 to 40 below. In spite of the cold and the deep snow, the column made a creditable two hundred miles.

Perovski now paused to consider an assortment of depressing facts. His force had 652 men sick and 32 dead, and it was short on fuel. The camels were sickening in alarming numbers. The Kirghiz tribesmen of the steppes had made an attack—unsuccessful it is true—on his supply base. Of the ten supply ships on the Caspian, five had turned back and the other five had gotten themselves frozen in, to the delight of the steppe tribesmen who were busily plundering them. It is small wonder that as Perovski prepared to move again at the end of December he sent an unhappy message to the Minister of Foreign Affairs: ". . . the deep snows render marching difficult and exhausts the camels from want of food. The column which departed four days ago has traversed only 20 versts

* Krausse, op. cit.

[13 miles]. . . . Obstacles which no foresight can take
account of run counter to the success of this expedition,
but we shall advance with complete trust in God and with
a firm resolve to carry out the will of the emperor."

The exhausted camels were struggling ahead through
snow up to their bellies, and three hundred of their
Kirghiz drivers who shared neither Perovski's trust in God
nor his devotion to the Emperor resolved to desert.
Perovski begged them not to; they replied by urging the
other camel drivers to join them. Perovski surrounded
them with troops, but the ringleaders announced that they
would rather die than go farther. The general ordered one
of the men shot, and when that had no perceptible effect,
he shot another and informed them that he was quite
prepared to continue shooting until the survivors went
back to their camels. They went back to work.

By February 1 they had covered four hundred miles—
about half the distance to Khiva—but they were hand-
dragging their cannon, all forage for the animals was
deep under the snow which Perovski had counted on for
water, and there were only five thousand of the original
ten thousand camels left. Perovski told the troops, "However painful it may be to renounce our conquests we must
retire," and messaged the Minister of War, "I cannot
conceal from your excellency that our retreat will be no
less arduous than our advance."

Nor was it. When the column finally struggled into
Orenburg on June 8, 1840, it had left a thousand dead on
the steppe and brought in another six hundred men so
badly used up as to require hospitalization. It would be
another thirty-three years before the Russians finally captured Khiva.

From St. Petersburg, the British ambassador informed
London that he could detect no real threat to India in the
effort against Khiva, and on the whole, Palmerston took
the news calmly. He made his remark about "the cossack
and the sepoy" eventually meeting in Central Asia. He
pronounced firmly that he did not want Russians in Khiva
and that that state should be ". . . a non-conducting body
interposed between Russia and British India." On the other
hand, he conceded that with the British at Kabul, one had
to expect the Russians to react.

At Kabul, the mood was a good deal less calm.
Macnaghten wanted to send a force north of the Hindu

Kush to intercept the Russians. Sir John Keane differed with him—or as one of Keane's officers wrote, "The insanity of the scheme appears to have struck the Commander-in-Chief vividly." Macnaghten, who insisted that "we had better be up and doing," compromised by sending a small troop of horse artillery and infantry north into Bamian, presumably to send up alarm rockets if they saw any Russians.

Alexander Burnes, who was Macnaghten's second in command, cannot have made his chief feel easier about the situation. As an officer who was subjected to his estimates of the situation wrote later, ". . . had we been satisfied with the tales of Sir Alexander's agents, we should have now believed the Russians 300,000 strong and to be within a short distance [a few marches] of Kabul."

Neither man paid much attention to the fact that there were troubles a great deal closer than the Russians. Shah Shujah went through the motions of ruling and he was obviously not up to the job. His chief minister was an ancient crony from the days of Indian exile, but the poor old man was so senile that he was unable to remember anyone he met from one day to the next. The Shah himself indulged a taste for head-of-state formalities—his favorite was keeping people waiting—to a point where not only his own chiefs but the British were thoroughly fed up with him. Even Auckland, who was "anxiously desirous" to pull the Army of the Indus out of Afghanistan because of the expense involved in keeping it there, realized that the man he had put on the throne was unable to sit there by himself. Much as he wanted to bring the troops home, such a return would be "ill attained at the price of leaving unaccomplished the great purposes with which the expedition to Kabul was undertaken."

Moreover, the troops were not particularly popular in Kabul. They drank in public and thereby, in Mohun Lal's words, "excited the religious hates of the people against us." Worse, both officers and men made out very well with the Afghan women,* and if the women don't seem to have minded, their men did very much. In all, there was

* Colonel Sir Robert Warburton, who commanded the Khyber Rifles, was the son of a British officer who married a niece of Dost Mohammed's.

an ugly mood in the city, and when Sir John Keane departed for India in October, 1839, he told a friend that he was leaving a country where, "Mark my words, it will not be long before there is here some signal catastrophe."

It was late spring in 1840 when word of the Russian failure at Khiva finally reached Kabul. Relieved of the menace, Macnaghten promptly set about selling Auckland on an expedition to bring Herat under the Shah's rule. Considering that his force had been reduced by the withdrawal of the Bombay forces for economy reasons, that the Ghilzais were raising a very lively rebellion, and that the tribesman of the Khyber and Bolan were making his only two links with India exceedingly precarious, one might reasonably conclude that he had no need of further distraction. But as Burnes said of him, he was a man whose eyes were always on the horizon and he was accordingly apt to miss what was under his nose.

In 1840, Sir William Hay Macnaghten was forty-seven years old and he had served in India for thirty years. He had made his reputation first as a linguist—he could handle Hindustani, Persian, Tamil, Telugu, Canarese, and Marathi—and then as chief of the sensitive Secret and Political Department under Bentinck. Auckland kept him on in the same post until he sent him to Kabul as senior political officer.

It can (and has been) argued *ad infinitum* who was responsible for the first Afghan War, but that the fate of the Kabul garrison is primarily Macnaghten's responsibility—although he was assisted by some spectacular blunderers—would be difficult to deny. It can be argued that his task was impossible, but it was Macnaghten himself who insisted the contrary. He could assure Auckland that the Shah "was the best and ablest man in his kingdom." The country was "in as prosperous a condition as could have been expected." If Burnes said otherwise, ". . . Sir A., of course, wishes to prove the contrary, since by doing so, when he succeeds me, his failures would thus find excuse and his success additional credit." If, from time to time, he complained of his "overwhelming difficulties," his favorite shorthand for reporting conditions to his superiors was that all was *"couleur de rose."*

Over and over he pressed the Herat project on Auckland; when the Governor-General turned him down, he fumed, "Oh, for a Wellesley or a Hastings at this juncture," and dismissed the arguments against the plan as "driveling . . . beneath contempt."

An overwhelming argument against the project appeared in September, 1840, when the news reached Kabul that Dost Mohammed was moving south with a force of unknown size. Macnaghten was sure that everything north of Kabul was about to go up in rebellion and felt none too sure of the city itself. The 35th Native Infantry of Sale's Brigade was sent into Bamian to supplement the small force sent north the year before, and in its first encounter with the Dost got good work from its artillery and sent him tumbling back. Macnaghten spoke of "this glorious success," but the Dost was still at large and Sale himself went north with the rest of the brigade to join the 35th.

On November 2 they caught up with the Dost. He was seen "retreating along the rugged face of a mountain. . . . He had about 80 ill mounted troopers who were leading their horses."* It was a fine fall morning, the air fresh and the leaves of the trees bright yellow. The 2nd Bengal Cavalry was ordered to charge and cut off the Dost's retreat.

The regulations were quite specific: Indian cavalry was to walk at four miles an hour, trot at eight, and charge at eleven. The 2nd Bengals walked at four, and when the Dost promptly charged them at the head of his eighty motley horsemen, instead of charging at eleven they broke back toward their own start line. Three of their officers were killed and two badly wounded trying to stem the rout. Burnes, who was with the expedition, panicked and messaged Macnaghten to withdraw the entire force to Kabul. Dost Mohammed, however, beat him to it. His honor satisfied, he rode into Kabul the next evening and surrendered to Macnaghten. The Envoy sent him down to India with a note which included the suggestion that he be "treated with liberality."

As 1841 came in, the position of the Kabul garrison was not improved by the arrival of a new military commander. The departing general, Sir Willoughby Cotton, had shown no signs of genius, and he was a good deal too portly to sit a horse for more than brief ceremonial purposes. He had, however, served in India since 1821

---

* Charles Low, *Major General Augustus Abbott.*

and was in reasonably good health. His successor, Sir William Elphinstone, although a man with a decent Napoleonic war record, had never been in India prior to 1839 and had not commanded troops in the previous eighteen years. He was, moreover, in such miserable health that he begged Auckland to spare him the appointment. Emily Eden, who had known him before India, wrote in her diary that she would never have recognized him: "He is in a shocking state of gout, poor man!—one arm in a sling and very lame. . . . He hates being here." Nevertheless, seniority—"the integrity of the roster"—demanded that he go to Kabul. Macnaghten was going to have to face a year of dreadful crisis with a near invalid for a general.

The crisis arose as the bribe money ran out. Macnaghten had bribed his way to Kabul and maintained his uneasy peace by seeing to it that the tribal chiefs were well paid. In London, the Honorable East India Company did some arithmetic and came to the conclusion that it was costing the Indian treasury six million dollars a year to keep Shah Shujah teetering on the throne of Afghanistan. In March, 1841, Auckland and his Council seriously debated abandoning the occupation but, in spite of the fact that the Commander-in-Chief of India, Sir Jasper Nicolls, was strongly for pulling out, decided to stay put. Sir Jasper made a gloomy diary entry:

> . . . the whole thing will break down. We cannot afford the heavy, yet increasing drain upon us. Nine thousand troops between Quetta and Karachi; at least 16,000 of our army and the Shah's to the north of Quetta. The King's expenses to bear in part— twenty-eight political officers to pay, besides Macnaghten—Dost Mohammed's allowance—barracks— a fort or two to build. . . . To me it is alarming.

To some in Afghanistan, the situation seemed equally alarming. In spite of their bribes, some tribes— particularly the Ghilzais—were raiding and cutting up supply parties. Major Henry Rawlinson, political officer with the garrison that had been left at Kandahar, warned Macnaghten that there was worse to come. The Envoy wrote back that he was taking "an unwarrantably gloomy view" and added, "We have enough of difficulties and of croakers without adding to the number needlessly. I have just seen a letter from Mr. Dallas to Captain Johnson in which he says the state of the country is becoming worse and worse every day. These idle statements may cause much mischief, and, often repeated as they are, they neutralize my protestations to the contrary."

For a little while longer, Macnaghten was able to make his protestations stand up. The troops stayed in the field throughout the spring and summer and by September the tribes were quiet again. The Envoy wrote that "everything has a favorable aspect for us" and that "our prospects in this country are brightening in every direction." Indeed, for Macnaghten himself the prospects had brightened spectacularly. His services had been recognized, the lucrative and comfortable appointment as governor of Bombay was his, and in a matter of weeks he would put Afghanistan behind him. Eldred Pottinger might report from north of Kabul in Kohistan that there were rumors "of the formation of an extensive conspiracy," but Macnaghten saw no reason to take him seriously.

He did realize that he faced financial problems. The Melbourne-Palmerston Whig government had lost a vote in the House of Commons in May and done badly in the general election that followed; in August, Melbourne resigned. The Tories were back under Robert Peel, and Tory views on Afghanistan were well known. The Duke of Wellington had pronounced against the war and any number of lesser lights had denounced the expense. Whoever the new government sent out to replace Auckland was certain to be less enthusiastic about the Afghan venture than his predecessor. Macnaghten was worried. "Rumors are rife as to the intentions of the Tories towards this country," he wrote in September. "If they deprive the Shah altogether of our support, I have no hesitation in saying . . . they will commit an unparalleled political atrocity." The same letter concludes with assurances that he is making "great reduction in our political expenditure" and expresses the hope that the job will shortly cost only a million and a half dollars a year rather than six million.

He had been instructed to retrench in two ways. One brigade—half his force at Kabul—was to be returned to India and the subsidies to the tribes were to be reduced. No one pointed out that this amounted to reducing both the carrot and the stick simultaneously. Instead, when the Ghilzais promptly began "kicking up a row about some deductions which have been made from their pay," Macnaghten announced that he intended to "settle their hash" on his way south with Sale's brigade, which had been selected for the return to India.

Two days later, on October 9, the Ghilzais were occupying the Khoord-Kabul Pass only fifteen miles from Kabul. Macnaghten muttered about the "impudence of the rascals" and concluded that something had better be done about them before he himself headed south. Colonel Monteith with a Native Infantry regiment of Sale's brigade was ordered out with some cavalry and two pieces of light artillery.

The circumstances of the departure of this force afford an excellent sampling of the state of command in Kabul in October, 1841. George Broadfoot, who had been ordered to accompany Monteith with a small group of engineers, went to the Colonel for instructions and found him in a rage. "He spoke bitterly of sending officers and men on wild-goose chases, bringing them into scrapes and letting them get out if they could." In the Colonel's opinion, if things went right, Macnaghten took the credit; if they went wrong, the man in the field had it put on his record. Broadfoot, an excellent young officer, went to Elphinstone himself in search of more light and less heat. He found the general so poorly that by the time he had been assisted from his bed to his sitting room he was so weak that it took him half an hour to get down to business. Even then, he was little help; he claimed to know no more than Monteith and to have done no more than supply the number of men requested by Macnaghten. He was, in fact ". . . much hurt . . . and complained bitterly of the way he was deprived of all authority and reduced to a mere cypher." As Broadfoot left, the older man made a last pathetic request that ". . . if anything occur and in case you have to go out, for God's sake clear the passes quickly so that I may get away. For if anything turn up, I am unfit for it, done up body and mind, and I have told Lord Auckland so."*

Young Broadfoot went diligently along to Macnaghten himself. The Envoy was irritated, announced that everyone expected him to be a prophet, and said he could not predict whether there would be any hostilities or not. Monteith was to make a "demonstration" and Broadfoot

* Major W. Broadfoot, *The Career of Major George Broadfoot.*

noted wryly that a demonstration was a "military operation in great favor with political officers." Macnaghten did assure him that there was little to worry about since the Ghilzais were "contemptable."

Thus instructed and comforted, the force marched off, camped the first night scarcely out of sight of Kabul, and took twenty-four casualties when the Ghilzais raided them in the dark. Next day, Sale was ordered out with the rest of the brigade and, though it cost him serious casualties, cleared the Khoord-Kabul Pass. He then pushed on into Ghilzai country, where the accompanying political officer thought he had the chiefs' agreement to a new treaty whereby they got their old subsidies back and, in return, kept the peace. Macnaghten was not happy to spend the money but, as he wrote Rawlinson, "We are positively unable to compete with these mountaineers and their jezails." So much for tribesmen described only a few days earlier as "contemptable".

Sale no sooner began marching his brigade back to Kabul than he discovered that the competition was still on. He had to fight his way through one pass, and his rear guard nearly collapsed under Ghilzai pressure. On October 30 the brigade encamped near the village of Gandamak. Sale thought he was pausing to rest his men and accumulate supplies. Actually, he was as far back on the road to Kabul as he was going to get.

CHAPTER

III

Disasters Unparalleled

November 1 was the date Macnaghten had set himself for departure from Kabul. As it drew near, he wrote that he hoped the events of the past few days were the "expiring efforts" of the Ghilzais, but on the same day he expressed anxiety about new warnings of a rising coming from Pottinger and concluded, "I don't know when I can get away from Kabul, for I am very unwilling to leave affairs in an unsettled state." He had less than two months to live, and most of the rest of the garrison very little more.

Elphinstone finally had Auckland's permission to come south with Macnaghten, but no replacement had been provided. Nott at Kandahar was the best man immediately available, but Macnaghten had quarreled with him—and Nott was an easy man to quarrel with—because he persisted in telling the Envoy unpleasant military truths. In particular, he had no faith whatever in the forces raised for the Shah and he was about to be proved quite correct. General Abraham Roberts,* who had commanded the Shah's contingent, was a good sound man, but he too had fallen victim to Macnaghten's distaste for facts and been replaced. The command was scheduled to devolve on Brigadier John Shelton, a quarrelsome, one-armed veteran who thoroughly disliked Indian troops. Lady Vincentia Sale, Sir Robert's wife, has left an unforgettable picture of him. During staff meetings, it was Shelton's habit to lie on the floor pretending to be asleep as "a resource against replying to disagreeable questions."

* The father of Field Marshal Sir Frederick Roberts, the highly successful British commander during the Second Afghan War. In his autobiography, the Field Marshal credits no small part of his success to stories his father told him about mismanagement in the first campaign.

The situation of the troops was not a great deal better. Engineers had consistently urged that they be put in the Bala Hissar, the walled fortress overlooking Kabul. The Shah, however, felt it undermined his dignity to have them in a citadel which also contained his palace, and Macnaghten gave in. Instead, the men were stationed in a cantonment north of the city which had the double disadvantage of walls too low for protection and too extensive to be properly manned with the force available. Incredibly, supplies for the garrison were kept in a small fort outside the cantonment which the Afghans had very little trouble cutting off once trouble started.

The Ghilzai rising, Pottinger's warnings, the knowledge that the ordinary people of Kabul were discontented because the occupation had driven prices up, the plain fact that four British officers had been assassinated in October alone—none of it seems to have established any sense of clear and present danger. Lady Sale, who had more brains than a good many of the men present, made a diary entry on October 31 in which she talks about going south shortly to rejoin her husband. Most of the rest of the entry is a charming dissertation on Afghan fruits and vegetables.

On November 1, the day Macnaghten had planned to start south, thirty or forty chiefs met to determine the step which would set off the rising in Kabul. The decision was to attack Burnes's house, which was inside the city and well away from aid from the cantonment. Two informers warned Burnes, another told Mohun Lal, and the munshi hurried around with the warning. Burnes rose from his chair, sighed, and observed, "The time is arrived that we must leave this country."

Burnes rejected a suggestion from the Shah that he come into the Bala Hissar, sent a messenger to the cantonment requesting help, and then went to an upper balcony of his house to look at a crowd—it began with about thirty men and rapidly grew to three hundred—in the street below. With him were his brother Charles and Lt. William Broadfoot.

From 6 A.M., the British outside the city could hear gunfire and see smoke from burning buildings; as some of their servants came out of the city they also heard that shops were being looted and the houses of British officers attacked. At 7:30, Macnaghten went to Elphinstone to offer the opinion that nothing very serious was going on and that, to use a word popular early in the rising, it was merely a "commotion." At 8 A.M., Burnes's request for help reached both men. Macnaghten's reaction can scarcely be called precipitous. He didn't want to take any action without first consulting the Shah, and for all his dismissing the affair as a commotion he told Elphinstone that it was "impracticable" to send troops into the center of the city.

The decision was, in any event, academic. While Burnes was haranguing the crowd from his balcony, Broadfoot was shot dead. Shortly afterward, Burnes and his brother descended into the street. Accounts are confused; some hold that he hoped to escape in disguise, others that he hoped to bribe his way out. The crowd promptly hacked both men to pieces.

It was 9:30 before Shelton got orders to take two regiments to the Bala Hissar. The orders were then countermanded when Macnaghten got word that the Shah had sent one of his own regiments to deal with the trouble. Predictably, the regiment did badly and Shelton got fresh orders to move. He made it to the Bala Hissar about noon—just in time to cover the retreat of the Shah's troops back into the fortress.

Neither Macnaghten nor Elphinstone showed any greater gumption on the second day. Sale was ordered to bring his force in, and a messenger was hurried off to Kandahar to tell Nott to send two regiments up; but when the Afghans moved up around the commissary fort—three hundred yards from the cantonment—no troops were sent out to oppose them. The fort was held by one officer and a hundred sepoys, and on November 4 Elphinstone took the incredible step of ordering troops out—not to help defend the fort and its supplies but to bring back the men who were there. His commissary officer managed to talk him out of the order at the last minute, but during the night the men at the fort came in anyway with a sorry tale about being too weak to hold out against an attack.

On November 5 the British could see the Afghans coming and going from the fort "ladened with the provisions upon which had depended our ability to make a protracted defence." Lt. Vincent Eyre, Elphinstone's artillery officer, urged an attack on another small fort which commanded the commissary and offered to lead it himself. Elphinstone—although he was already urging Macnaghten to "consider what chance there is of making terms"—consented, and a mixed force of fifty Europeans and two hundred sepoys went out. Eyre smothered the fort with two of his guns, but the infantry held back when it should have swarmed forward, Eyre ran out of ammunition and the attack collapsed. An attempt the next day carried the fort, but fighting swayed back and forth in a nearby walled garden and the way to the commissary was still blocked. The troops went on half rations and commissary officers made do by buying what they could from villages north of the cantonment which were staying neutral until they were more certain of how things were going to come out.

Macnaghten began to consider whether he might not be able to get out of his predicament the same way he had gotten into it—by bribery. A messenger went to Mohun Lal, who was hiding in Kabul, authorizing him to promise the Ghilzais $100,000 if they came over to the British side. At the same time there were other letters to Mohun Lal, not from Macnaghten but from his aide and cousin John Conolly. On November 5 Conolly wrote, "You can promise one lakh of rupees to Khan Shereen on the condition of his killing and seizing the rebels." In a postscript, he was even more specific: "I promise 10,000 rupees for the head of each of the principal rebel leaders." A letter of November 11 repeated the offer.

Some efforts have been made to show that whatever his failings Macnaghten was too honorable a man to be party to an assassination attempt, but there is a letter over the Envoy's own signature to Khan Shereen in which he says that if he "did not bring in the head of Abdoolah Khan" he would not look on him as a friend. There is another to Mohun Lal, who had written Conolly of the arrangements he had made to have Abdoolah Khan and another chief murdered, in which he says, "I have received your letter of this morning and highly approve of all you have done." Murder cannot be proved, but both chiefs died shortly thereafter.

On November 9 Shelton brought his men back from the Bala Hissar, and even those who disliked him felt he was bound to be an improvement on Elphinstone, "who vacillates on every point." Shelton, whom Lady Sale suspected of simply being hell-bent to get back to India, recommended an immediate retreat to Jalalabad. Macnaghten was flatly against the plan, and though Elphinstone was for it, he and Shelton were on such bad terms that he didn't support him particularly strongly. Elphinstone found Shelton insubordinate, Shelton felt his chief gave him insufficient authority, and the feul did nothing to raise the morale of the force. As Eyre wrote, "The number of croakers in the garrison became perfectly frightful; lugubrious looks and dismal prophecies being encountered everywhere."

On November 10 the Afghans occupied a fort to the north of the cantonment and long-term planning had to give way to immediate problems: the fort was in comfortable jezail range and the cantonment was being liberally peppered. Elphinstone ordered an attack, then—typically—countermanded the order, then finally ordered it again on Macnaghten's urging. As might have been expected, the vacillation communicated itself to the rank and file of the 44th Foot, which was to do the attacking. "The Little Fighting Fours" went off without much dash, broke badly when they were charged by Afghan cavalry, and were only rallied by the exertions of Shelton himself. Even Lady Sale conceded that Shelton "proved a trump," and Eyre noted, "Let me here do Brigadier Shelton justice; his acknowledged courage redeemed the day." The fort was taken and a garrison left there.

A dog belonging to an officer of Sale's brigade wandered into camp on November 11 and the garrison allowed itself to hope that the brigade itself might not be far behind. In fact, the very same day Sale made his decision that a return to Kabul was impossible and turned his men south toward Jalalabad. When the word reached Kabul, Shelton ungraciously told Lady Sale that her husband was acting on the principle, "Being out of a scrape, keep so."

With the hope of additional troops gone, the debate on removing to the Bala Hissar was resumed, produced a great deal of wrangling, and was finally solved by a pronouncement from Macnaghten that it was unnecessary because winter was coming on and the Afghans would doubtless go away. Far from going away, the Afghans were completing their circle around the cantonment. On November 22 they occupied heights north of the camp, and Macnaghten knew well enough that if the position was held, the foraging parties which kept the camp supplied could no longer operate. There was a conference that night, and at 2 A.M. on the morning of November 23, Shelton took a force out to clear the heights. Eyre called it later the day that "decided the fate of the Kabul force."

The men were in bad shape. The sepoys hated the cold and what they heard from their officers must have dispirited both Briton and Indian. Lady Sale called it ". . . more than shocking, it is shameful, to hear the way that officers go on croaking before the men; it is sufficient to dispirit them and prevent them from fighting for us." Even Shelton argued that his force was too exhausted and half starved for the job at hand.

Nevertheless, they went off, supported by only a single piece of artillery. As they came up the heights, the jezail sharpshooters did good work and the shorter range British musket was unable to reply. Finally, a horde of infantry and cavalry—perhaps ten thousand in all—poured out of Kabul itself. The small British force ran "very much like a flock of sheep with a wolf at their heels." Shelton rallied them once, but the Afghans came on again and they came pell-mell off the heights with the Afghan cavalry so furiously in among them with sabers that it seemed briefly as though no one would get back to the cantonment. Those who did, owed their lives partly to cavalry which came out of the camp, even more to Afghan astonishment which led them to fail to press the pursuit home.

The next day, Macnaghten had a message from the Kabul chiefs urging him to accept the fact that he was defeated, to evacuate the country, and to leave the Afghans to "govern it according to their own rules and with a king of their own choosing." Macnaghten was ready to dicker, but before doing so he needed an explanation which would stand up when he got home. From Elphinstone he requested a statement in writing as to whether it was any longer possible to remain in Afghanistan. He could not have doubted the answer and the decrepit general did not disappoint. After alluding to the food shortage, the state of the troops, the sick and wounded, and the lack of hope for reenforcements, he said flatly, "I am of the opinion that it is not feasible any longer to maintain our position in this country, and that you ought to avail yourself of the offer to negotiate which has been made to you."

Thus covered, Macnaghten met with two chiefs at the east gate of the cantonment and found their terms altogether too hard to swallow. What they came down to was unconditional surrender, abandonment of the Shah, and departure from Afghanistan with a promise never to return. There are various versions of the Envoy's reply— that he preferred death to dishonor, that he would leave the result to the God of battles, that they would all meet at the Day of Judgment. Whatever the precise statement, the first round of negotiations was over.

A few days later, the noose was pulled in a little tighter. Akbar Khan, the Dost's tough, capable son, rode in from Kohistan with six thousand men and almost his first act was to terrorize the villages from which the British commissary officers had been buying food. One village complained, and he burned every house in it. The commissary urged Macnaghten to march for Jalalabad while they still had the supplies to do it, but he opted for a two-day delay on the grounds that "something may turn up."

On December 8 the commissary officers put it in writing that not "the smallest quantity of grain or forage" was to be obtained, and Macnaghten covered himself again by writing Elphinstone, "I have to request that you will be so good as to state, for my information, whether or no I am right in considering it your opinion that any further attempt to hold out against the enemy would merely have the effect of sacrificing both His Majesty and ourselves." Elphinstone obliged and this time his letter carried the additional endorsements: "I concur in the above opinions."—J. Shelton, Brigadier; "In a military point of view, I concur in the above."—W. Anquetil, Brigadier, Commanding Shah Shujah's Forces; "I also concur."—R. Chambers, Lt.-Col., Commanding Cavalry. On December 11, with just a day's food left for his force, Macnaghten went out again to treat with the Afghans, this time led by Akbar Khan.

Macnaghten had prepared a draft treaty, and this remarkable document is worth quoting at some length. It began: "Whereas it has become apparent from recent events that the continuance of the British army in Afghanistan ... is displeasing to the great majority of the Afghan nation; and whereas the British Government had no other object in sending troops to this country than the integrity, happiness and welfare of the Afghans, and, therefore, it can have no wish to remain when that object is defeated by its presence ..." and then went on to set out the British terms.

The British troops, assisted and supplied by the Af-

ghans, would return to India. The Shah could accompany them or not as he chose. When the British reached
Peshawar safely, Dost Mohammed would be returned
to Afghanistan. Four British officers would be left at Kabul
as hostages for the return of the Dost. No matter how it
was worded, it was still a capitulation and Macnaghten
was bitter. In a letter written at the same time he talks of
"a contemptible enemy" and the "cowardice of our
troops" and is still hoping that help may come up from
Kandahar.

The events of the next twelve days take place in a
murk of uncertain motives. The chiefs agreed to
Macnaghten's terms, although Akbar Khan was insistent
that the British receive no supplies until they were actually out of the cantonments. Nor was he unreasonably
suspicious. The camp was full of spies and he must have
known that Macnaghten was still trying to buy the
Ghilzais over. It was agreed that the British would march
south in three days time.

The first snow of the season—a heavy five-inch fall—
came down to make the march ahead an even bleaker
prospect. There were rumors that the retreating force was
to be attacked as it went down the passes. All in all, even
Macnaghten cannot have been in any very optimistic
frame of mind when, on the evening of December 22, he
received a message from Akbar Khan. It was an invitation to join Akbar in a plot, and that it was a trap
designed to scotch once and for all Macnaghten's negotiations with the Ghilzais never seems to have crossed the
Envoy's mind. He was to meet with Akbar and the
Ghilzai chiefs the next morning outside the cantonment.
At a signal, the Ghilzai chiefs would be seized by Akbar's
men, one British regiment would rush out to assist, and
another would occupy the Bala Hissar. The rising thus
ended, Shah Shujah would remain on the throne. Akbar
would be rewarded with the position of chief minister, an
immediate gift of thirty lakhs of rupees, and an annuity
of four lakhs for life. The British would save face by
remaining in Afghanistan until warm weather and then
march south comfortably, as though of their own accord.

Macnaghten reacted with an uncritical enthusiasm
which suggested to an officer with him that he was
beginning to crack under the strain. The facts suggest that
the observer was right. Macnaghten went to the im-
prudent extreme of setting out an agreement to the plan

in his own handwriting and talked exultantly about the opportunity it provided for the British and the Russians to arrive at a treaty defining boundaries for each in Central Asia.

At noon on December 23 he rode out of the cantonment with three officers—Captains Trevor, Lawrence, and MacKensie—and a small cavalry escort. For the first time, he told his staff of the plot. One of them warned him that it was a trap and he replied, "A plot! let me alone for that, trust me for that!" When the warning was pressed, he dismissed the dangers with the remark that he would rather die a hundred deaths than live the last six weeks over again.

Five hundred yards east of the cantonment, the party waited for Akbar Khan, who arrived with a considerable force. Blankets were spread on the snow and the four officers dismounted. Trevor seated himself beside Macnaghten. Lawrence, possibly sensing trouble, knelt on one knee and MacKensie drew aside to talk to an Afghan he had known in Kabul. Akbar asked whether Macnaghten was ready to go ahead with the plan and received the reply "Why not?" Both Lawrence and MacKensie protested that too many Afghans were crowding in around them. The chiefs went through the motions of driving the men back with whips and then there was a shout from Akbar Khan: "Begeer! Begeer!" (Seize! Seize!).

The last glimpse we have of Macnaghten comes from MacKensie, who saw Akbar Khan take the Envoy's left hand, heard the unfortunate man cry out "For God's sake!" and saw on his face an expression "full of horror and astonishment." Beyond reasonable doubt, it was Akbar's original intention to seize the four British officers and hold them as hostages for the British departure and the return of the Dost. However, Macnaghten struggled, Akbar shot him with a pistol, and the crowd closed in with knives. Trevor slipped from the back of a horse onto which he had been pulled and came to the same bloody end. MacKensie and Lawrence were hurried into a small fort nearby and the best evidence of Afghan intentions is that both of them would have been killed by the mob if the chiefs themselves had not defended them.

Macnaghten's body—or what was left of it, the head and limbs having been hacked off—was hung in the Kabul bazaar. Lady Sale—although at the time she made the diary entry she thought him a prisoner rather than dead—

wrote him a bitter epitaph: "There is a general opinion in cantonments that faith has been broke on both sides and that the Afghans have made the cleverest chupao" [a raid or surprise].

On the day before Christmas the chiefs sent a new draft treaty into the cantonment and it raised the price of a safe passage to India considerably. The most important new demands were that any money in the treasury be left there, that all but six pieces of artillery be turned over to the Afghans, and that married men and their families should be left behind as hostages. The British sent back a message agreeing to the first and refusing the other two terms. The Afghans countered with an offer to settle for six pieces of artillery and four married officers and their families. They also threw in a new demand on a point which had galled them throughout the occupation: "If any of the Frank [European] gentlemen have taken a Mussulman wife, she shall be given up."

Through a gloomy Christmas day, Eldred Pottinger, who had taken over as chief political officer, argued with Elphinstone and Shelton that they should either retire to the Bala Hissar or abandon all baggage and attempt to fight their way out. The council of war voted him down and there was nothing for it but for Pottinger to sign a treaty in which he himself had not an iota of faith. The only concession he won from the chiefs was that no women or children were to be left as hostages.

The artillery pieces were turned over. The sick and wounded were sent into Kabul and two doctors detailed to remain behind with them. The end of 1841 drew near, and there are a series of monotonous lines at the end of each of Lady Sale's diary entries: "Snow all day."

On January 5 word went out that the army would march the next morning. The engineers set about making a breach in the ramparts since the gates were too small to pass the whole force handily. Rumors were plentiful that there would be a massacre in the passes, and poor Shah Shujah sent a message complaining that not only would none of the officers of his force remain behind with him, but that even the troops raised for him were being taken back to India.

The force that prepared to march the next morning consisted of 4,500 fighting men. Of these, 690 were Europeans—the 44th Foot and one horse artillery troop. Most of the Indians were Company sepoys, only some 1,300 men remaining from the Shah's force. In addition to the soldiers, however, there were the camp followers. Eyre estimated them at 12,000 men plus an undetermined number of women and children. Incredible as the figure is, it is not unreasonable for an Indian army of the time. The baggage for this cavalcade traveled on two thousand animals—camels and small Afghan ponies called yaboos.

It is ninety miles from Kabul to Jalalabad, and at about 9 A.M. on January 6 the advance, led by the 44th Foot, moved out. If the chiefs who were to escort them south in safety did not appear, the force could console itself that no other Afghans did either.

Almost from the first there was no real order of march —only a mob of soldiers, camp followers, and baggage animals all scrambled together. It was evening before the last of it was clear of the cantonment, and in its rear the Afghans were looting by the light of burning buildings. What began as desultory jezail fire developed into a brisk fight which cost the British one officer and fifty men. It was 2 A.M. on a bitterly cold night before the rear straggled into camp at Bygram—a scant five miles from where it started. Already the line of march was dotted with figures who had dropped out to die in the snow, and during the night 850 of the Shah's men deserted—some drifting away, about 400 returning to Kabul in a body.

Lady Sale shared a tent with her daughter, Mrs. Sturt. Trying to sleep seated in a chair with her legs tucked up under her and covered with a sheepskin, she was haunted by a verse she had read before the force left cantonments:

> Few, few shall part where many meet,
> The snow shall be their winding-sheet;
> And every turf beneath their feet
> Shall be a soldier's sepulchre.

"Heaven forbid," she wrote, "that our fears should be realized."

Through snow a foot deep, the mob lurched ahead again the next morning. About half the sepoys were already unfit for duty either because of frostbite or because they'd simply fallen out of ranks to straggle along with the camp followers. Small bodies of Afghan horse and foot hung around the flanks of the force and in mid-morning chupao'd the rear guard and captured two guns. The force had supplies for only five and a half days, hence it was important that it get on quickly, but by 1 P.M. Elphinstone, warned that his rear guard was likely to be altogether cut off, called a halt at the entrance of the Khoord-Kabul Pass and sent his advance back to help out. It got back just in time to prevent the Afghans from occupying the high ground on either side of the road. Night came on; the marchers had made only ten miles in two days and Eyre found the confusion "indescribable . . . 14,000 to 16,000 men, with several hundred cavalry horses and baggage cattle were closely jammed together in one monstrous, unmanageable, jumbling mass. Night again closed over us, with its attendant train of horrors— starvation, cold, exhaustion, death."

There was a great deal worse to come. They rose in the morning so nearly paralyzed from cold that a brandy ration was ordered for the men and tumblers of sherry— an amount Lady Sale felt would have made her "very unladylike" at any other time—issued to the women and children. Ahead of them was the Khoord-Kabul Pass, five miles long, a "mountain torrent" crisscrossing its floor, the rest covered with snow and ice and the sides so steep that "the sun at this season could dart but a momentary ray." Ghilzai tribesmen were high on the walls of the pass— they had "crowned the heights," to use the military term of the day—and the force was under heavy jezail fire from the moment it moved into the pass. Lady Sale got a bullet through her arm and three others went through her cloak. Three other soldiers' wives simply vanished. Ghilzai fire was heaviest against the rear guard—the 44th Foot and the 54th Native Infantry. The 54th was so numb with cold that it slogged ahead, not returning the jezail fire and taking heavy losses. The 44th returned fire until its ammunition began to run out and then suddenly the entire Kabul force—officers, men, and civilians—was running for its life through the terrible pass with the Ghilzais continuing to pour in fire from the heights. When the force stopped on the far side of the pass to make what camp it could in the snow there were only four tents remaining and the day's casualty count was 500 soldiers and 2,500 camp followers.

The news was just beginning to leak down to India, but the Bengal *Herald* made a shrewd guess at the outcome in an editorial which concluded, "The fate of troops in Kabul is now, we fear, almost certainly decided; for unless some special intervention of Providence relieves them from the dilemma in which they are placed, human aid is all unavailing. . . . God help our poor fellows, for they are indeed in a critical position."

Curiously, the nearest thing to a special intervention of Providence around at the moment was Akbar Khan. Even the British conceded that his men had done what they could to restrain the Ghilzais during the day. The next morning, he sent along the suggestion that all women and children be turned over to him for their protection and with a promise of eventual safe conduct to India. Elphinstone agreed, and the column, now almost without provisions, sat in the snow the entire day while the transfer was made. Next morning they marched again, and the Ghilzais kept at them, now working at long range with jezails, now rushing in to do the job with swords. The force that halted in Tezeen Valley late in the afternoon consisted of 50 artillerymen with one gun and 70 infantrymen of the 44th and 150 cavalry. There were still some 4,000 camp followers. The officers concluded that whatever faint hopes they might have lay in a night march to Jagdalak and an attempt to get through the pass there before the Ghilzais were set to receive them.

It was a forlorn hope at best, and dawn found them still ten miles short. By afternoon, forward progress was impossible and they halted on a small hill with a ruined wall which offered some cover. At 5 P.M. a message from Akbar Khan demanded Elphinstone's presence at a conference and the delivery of Shelton and a Captain Johnson as additional hostages. The three men rode to spend the night in Akbar's camp; the move saved their lives.

Throughout the daylight of January 12, what was left of the column held to its ruined wall and took its losses from long-range fire. At dark, they left the sick and wounded and moved into the pass. There was a strongly made barrier of tree branches at the summit of the pass; by the time they had fought their way through it there were only twenty officers and forty-five men left.

They pushed on to Gandamak, and by the time they reached it there were only twenty muskets left, most of them with only two or three rounds of ammunition apiece. The tribesmen picked them off at long range, then finished the job with knives. A handful beat clear and their story is best told by the only man who survived to reach Sale's brigade at Jalalabad. A week after he got there, Dr. William Brydon wrote his brother:

My Dear Tom:

Here I am at this place, all safe, but not all sound, having received three wounds on the head, left hand and knee. I have lost everything I had in the world; but my life has been saved in a most wonderful manner, and I am the only European who has escaped from the Kabul army (although we have heard of two having been taken by the enemy, it is very doubtful that they will be spared). Two natives only have reached this place, making with myself three persons out of an army of 13,000.

I got on very well till within about 50 miles of this, with the exception of losing all my baggage. I then lost the horse on which I was riding. Having taken one of my servants, who was wounded, up behind me, we fell rather too far in the rear, when he was pulled off from behind, and I fell with him. I was instantly felled to the earth with the blow of a large knife, which wounded me in the head. I, however, managed to avert the second blow, by receiving my enemy's hand on the edge of my sword, by which his hand was somewhat damaged, and he dropped his knife and made off as fast as he could, and I, following his good example, managed to reach the main body minus my horse, cap and shoe, which last I lost in the snow. I was then trudging along holding fast by the tail of another officer's horse, when a native, who was riding close by, said that he could ride no further, and told me to take his horse, which I did without delay. I do not know who the man was, as it was quite dark at the time, but the saddle must have belonged to an Afghan. I now got to the front, where I found a number of officers who determined to push on, as the men would obey no orders, and were halting every minute. We traveled slowly all night, fired at occasionally from the sides of the hills and found ourselves at daybreak about 30 miles from this, our party consisting of only seven officers, five European soldiers and myself, the rest having lost us in the dark and gone by some other road.

At about 10 A.M. we were attacked and surrounded on all sides by horsemen; three officers and the five

Europeans were killed.* One of the officers was Lieutenant Bird, of the Madras army who fell close to my
side. I with the remaining four got clear of the horsemen and pushed on; three of our party being well
mounted left the fourth and myself far in the rear
when he, coming on some way, said his horse was
done up, that he would hide until dark, for which purpose he left me about four miles from this. He was
taken and killed.

I proceeded slowly for a short time when I saw a
great many people running towards me in all directions. I waited until they got pretty close and then
pushed my horse into a gallop and ran the gauntlet
for about two miles under a shower of large stones,
sticks and a few shots, in which I had my sword
broken by a stone, my horse shot in the spine close
to the tail and my body bruised all over by the stones.
I was now attacked by a horseman who left a party
of about six . . . he wounded me in the knee and hand,
when seeing me stoop down he galloped away as fast
as he could, thinking, I suppose that I was looking for
a pistol. I now proceeded unmolested, and arrived
here about 1 o'clock, quite done up, as was also my
poor horse who lost the use of his hind legs next day
and died two days after without ever getting up after
his arrival. If you receive this, let them know at home
that I am alive, as I have not been able to write since
October 1, and perhaps we shall not have the road
open when the next overland starts. Since arriving I
have had three shirts, three pair of socks, a jacket and
a pair of trousers given to me. A very fine stock, you
will say; however, it must do until I can get another
outfit. Write to me and let me know the news from
home.

Your affectionate brother . . .

What had been called "the military promenade in Afghanistan" was over.

When the news that there was serious trouble at Kabul
reached Auckland, he was not optimistic about his ability
to rectify the situation. In December he was writing Sir
Jasper Nicolls that ". . . there are already more regiments
beyond the frontier than we can feed or easily pay . . ."

* They were at Futtahabad. The text of this letter appeared in the
London *Times*.

and informing Macnaghten by native messenger that "I would have you share in the feeling which is growing strongly upon me that the maintenance of the position, which we have attempted in Afghanistan, is no longer to be looked to. It will be for you and for this government to consider in what manner all that belongs to India may be most immediately and most honourably withdrawn from the country."

Nicolls, who had been against the venture from the beginning, told Auckland flatly that he doubted the ability of a relief force to get through the Khyber and that if snow had fallen the effort was foredoomed. Moreover, a new Governor-General—Lord Ellenborough—was on his way out from England, and Auckland was reluctant to take any steps he might regard as "rash, impolitic and ruinous." Accordingly, he contented himself with a proclamation on January 31, 1842, which sounded a good deal more vigorous than any measures actually taken justified. He noted that the Kabul army had suffered "extreme disasters" and said that "powerful reenforcements" were being hurried to the frontier. He mentioned a "faithless enemy," lamented the "loss of the brave officers and men," and wound up finding "this partial reverse only . . . a new occasion for displaying the stability and vigour of the British power and the admirable spirit and valour of the British-Indian Army."

The news took longer to reach London, but when it did there was much less talk about "admirable spirit and valour." The *Times* broke the story on February 7 under the headline "INDIA—EXPRESS FROM MARSEILLES" in the largest type that journal permitted itself. Rather than deliver the unhappy facts straight to its readers, it prepared them with a little lead-in: "We regret to announce that the intelligence which this express has brought us is . . . so far of the most disastrous and melancholy nature." It then gave the facts and wound up:

> . . . our worst fears regarding the Afghanistan expedition have been justified. . . . God pray that next month we may have more favourable intelligence to communicate, our prospects at present are gloomy enough, but, under Providence, the shattered bark will right itself . . . much of the evil which is now befalling us, we have cut out for ourselves and it is

probable that the country, under a wiser Administration, may yet be reduced to—a Roman peace.

In the same edition, however, a letter from an Indian correspondent set out the line of policy ahead. It was his opinion that "to withdraw a man from Afghanistan, to give up one step of our policy now . . . is impossible. Our power, our name, our influence must be maintained there at every risk, to every end. If we withdraw with . . . the eyes of every disaffected man in this country [India] upon us, it is not too much to say that we shall have to fight for our very existence as a political power." Thus an early, though certainly not the earliest, proponent of the domino theory.

The *Times* then thought about the matter for five more days, decided in a lead editorial that the Afghan troubles were "somewhat exaggerated," and then went into the background of the matter. It noted that as early as 1836 Mr. Ellis in Persia had warned that any Russian influence in Afghanistan would bring them "to the very threshold of our empire." It noted that Russian agents "in disguise" were exploring all the countries of Asia and "examining with the greatest care the passes of the Hindu Kush." It quoted at length from an alleged letter of Dost Mohammed to the Czar in which he asked to be taken, like Persia, under Russian protection.

Had not Burnes, "the keenest antagonist of the Russian agents," been the first to die? Was not the rising well organized? "Is there any other cause so efficient and so probable as that Power whose growing influence amongst those tribes first called for our interference?"

As Lord Durham had written a few years earlier when he was the ambassador at St. Petersburg, "The very changes of the winds of the heavens are laid to Russian influence."

John Cam Hobhouse, Chairman of the Board of Control for Indian Affairs, started by talking of "small reverses" which were to be expected and assuring a friend that "matters in India will come right at last." As the bad news piled up, however, the search for a scapegoat began. The *Times* indulged itself in a lengthy editorial berating poor Elphinstone, and Hobhouse noted in his diary that Wellington considered "as everyone else did" that the disaster proceeded from "the neglect and misconduct of General Elphinstone." Gossip was still being exchanged among Palmerston's lady friends, and Lady Cowper wrote Dorothea Lieven, "Lord Auckland will arrive here soon; it is sad for him to have to defend himself after such a period of brilliant success.... All blame will fall upon the army chiefs for their foolish sense of security and carelessness—they believed that it was possible to trust savages and took not the smallest precaution to defend themselves against treachery—it is incredible."

The man on whom would fall the burden of making it right was already at sea on his way to India when the trouble began. Edward Law, Lord Ellenborough, who was to succeed Auckland, had considerably more experience than was usual for Indian Governor-Generals. He had been President of the Board of Control for Indian Affairs three times, and though the new Prime Minister, Peel, worried over "a tendency to precipitation and over-activity," he was confident of "his integrity in the administration of patronage, and in his desire to curtail expence, and place the revenue of India on a satisfactory footing."*

At the traditional farewell dinner, Ellenborough announced that it was his policy to "bring peace to India," but when his ship arrived off Madras in February, 1842, he learned by signal from the beach what had happened. The same day, he wrote Peel that "the honour of our arms must be re-established in Afghanistan." A week later, he went ashore at Calcutta, and even as the salutes of welcome were being fired, the departing Auckland was enduring a farewell affair of which a journalist said, "The speeches were only remarkable for their indifferent style and mistaken matter.... There was a great deal of very fulsome stuff uttered about his Lordship's Afghan policy

* Although it has no bearing on the events under consideration, there is a lurid episode in Ellenborough's private life which it seems a shame to pass up. Five years after the death of his first wife, he married a Miss Jane Digby, a seventeen-year-old half his age. Whether Ellenborough was simply too busy to attend to the young lady or, as some alleged, impotent, is a matter of debate. In any event, she shortly presented him with a son generally believed to have been fathered by a young man working at the British Museum. From there, she went on to a notorious relationship with an Austrian diplomat, which led to her divorce by act of Parliament. She then followed the Austrian to Paris, had an affair with Balzac, moved on to Ludwig of Bavaria, then to a Bavarian baron, a Greek count, and an Albanian general. The trail finally ends when Miss Digby married a Syrian sheik with whom she seems to have spent the rest of her days in great contentment.

which had far better not been mentioned." The same writer predicted that once back in England, Auckland would promptly be returned to private life. He was altogether wrong; as soon as the Whigs came back to power in 1846 they made Auckland First Lord of the Admiralty.

In early December, a single brigade had been ordered up to Peshawar. It had the limited mission of forcing the Khyber and linking up with Sale at Jalalabad, since, as Auckland pointed out, "Ten brigades could not, at this season of the year, force the passes to Kabul." After news of the massacre of the Kabul force arrived—Auckland is supposed to have turned white when he heard it—two more brigades were ordered up with the somewhat curious instructions "to curb the violence of excitement which may be expected in that quarter, and to protect the Sikh territory from aggression."

The last item refers to a then-current fear that at any moment a force of Afghan cavalry might come galloping out of the Khyber. Nor was the fear limited to Calcutta: as able a frontier officer as Captain Frederick Mackeson wrote that "a few days more may see a party of the Barukzye troops, and then thousands will be required where hundreds would now do the work."

The immediate task was the relief of Sale, and in early January the single brigade at Peshawar under Brigadier Wild was a poor candidate for the task. It had been sent forward without adequate staff officers, with no artillery, no cavalry, and no commissariat. It was made up of four very green sepoy regiments, and what they heard from the Sikhs about the terrors of the Khyber did not improve their morale. Mackeson tried to buy a passage through the pass, but the fervor of the Afridi tribesmen exceeded their avarice. If Wild was to move north, he would have to fight his way with whatever help he could get from the Sikhs, to whom an appeal had been made under the terms of the old Tri-Partite treaty.

Five miles into the Khyber, high on an isolated rock, stands the fortress of Ali Masjid. It is actually two small forts, and though they are commanded by the higher walls of the pass itself, anyone coming up the floor of the pass would be in for a very bad time if a foe held Ali Masjid. Wild had a tiny force there and on the night of January 15 attempted to reenforce it with two regiments with enough supplies for a month. The men got through against unexpectedly light opposition, but someone blundered; instead of grain for a month, only enough for a week came up. Wild determined to go forward with his other two regiments and some Sikhs to take the rest of the supplies. The Sikhs promptly deserted, and the green regiments bunched up in the mouth of the Khyber, where the Afridis hit them so hard with jezail fire that they refused to go farther. Wounded himself, Wild withdrew the force and a few days later the regiments at Ali Masjid decided that no supplies were coming through and fought their way out. The "key to the Khyber" was in Afridi hands.

Fortunately, the demoralized men were about to receive a new commander. The man selected to command the three brigades which would eventually be assembled at Peshawar was Maj. Gen. George Pollock, and he turned out to be one of Auckland and Jasper Nicolls's happier choices. As a contemporary said, he was "not the first Major-General on the roll, nor the oldest alive in the Army List, nor him who had most grandfathers in England, but for once—this terrible once—the man best suited to the service at hand."

The new man arrived to find nearly half his troops on sick list and the rest close to mutiny. Pollock busied himself providing winter clothing for them and infuriated a number of his officers by making them cut down on the vast amounts of baggage they were accustomed to carrying about. It was the general expectation in India that once the weather improved, the new army would march north to relieve Sale, then, in conjunction with Nott's Kandahar force, press on to Kabul and free Akbar's hostages. In actual fact, Pollock was on a good deal shorter leash. In a letter to Sale in March, he explained his instructions: "Our only object in going to Jalalabad is to relieve you and bring you back with us to this; but it is necessary that this should be kept a profound secret."

Pollock had reference to the last orders he had from Auckland, which ordered him only to bring Sale out and keep an eye on events in Afghanistan, but said nothing about going to Kabul. On March 31 he marched off to carry out the orders. British and Indian troops crowned the heights on either side of the Khyber and his central column got through with only minor casualties. It is only about a hundred miles from Peshawar to Jalalabad, but Pollock's supply train slowed him down and it was April

16 before he was in contact with Sale's outposts. "The illustrious garrison" at Jalalabad had stood a five-month siege, recovered from an earthquake which knocked down most of its fortifications, and now came out to play their relievers in with the Scots air "Oh, but ye've been lang o'coming."

A great many very unkind things have been written about Ellenborough's handling of the last stages of the war, and while it is quite true that some of the things he did were quite odd, he was not mad. On March 15 he set out plans which said about what British India expected: there was to be a victorious movement into Afghanistan ˑˑrd then the troops would be withdrawn. There was, however, one fertile source of misunderstanding in the statement. To British India, a victorious movement into Afghanistan meant going all the way to Kabul. Precisely what it meant to Ellenborough at this time is very hard to say.

As far back as 1838 he had taken the position that the Russians had "as much right as we have" to be in Afghanistan and that any effort to exclude them could only lead to a costly war. These were not the words of a man likely to plunge headlong back into Afghanistan. Moreover, his superiors in London were in no particular hurry. Peel wrote in early April after hearing of Wild's repulse at the Khyber, and while he made the usual bow to "retrieving our military credit," he devoted a good deal more space to the desirability of moving "cautiously and deliberately."

Finally, there was a matter of money. The Afghan campaign had been paid for by the Indian treasury; that treasury was now bare and no one was quite sure where the money for a return to Kabul was to come from. British India thought it knew; as a correspondent wrote the London *Times*, "The pecuniary situation is a grave one. . . . I think England should contribute to the costs of this campaign . . . the policy of moving beyond the Indus was undertaken, whether with or without the consent of the British cabinet, for the purpose of checking Russia and England should therefore assist to recover what has been lost." The proposal was not well received in Britain, where the budget was in such a state of imbalance that Peel had been compelled to impose an income tax.

Out of some combination of all these reasons—his own

dislike for adventuring in Central Asia, the wishes of his masters, the fiscal situation—Ellenborough issued orders on April 19 which were exactly what British India did not expect. Nott was ordered most specifically to evacuate Kandahar, go down the Bolan to Quetta, and thence south. Somewhat looser orders went to Pollock. He too was to retire, but the wording left him more room to stall if he wanted to.

On the frontier, where the feeling was that "the city of Kabul should be laid in ruins by a British force," there was rage. "Monstrous," "sickening thought," and "cowardly counsels" were the words of the day. One of Pollock's aides wrote a friend, "If I were the General, I would move at *once* towards Gandamak, and let them make the most of it at head-quarters. We shall never survive the disgrace of retreating without making an effort to recover our prisoners and, what is more, we shall *deserve* the ruin which will befall us."

Ellenborough's position was that the relief of Sale was sufficient. As he wrote Peel, "At last we have got a victory, and our military character is re-established." He seems, however, to have been quite aware that his generals did not agree. Another order went off to Pollock to get home as quickly as possible, but Pollock stalled and pleaded lack of transport; by June 1 he had extracted permission to stay where he was until October. Ellenborough was thoroughly out of sorts. His generals were recalcitrant. The Indian press was flogging him, and although he liked to pretend that he paid no attention to it, he was finally galled to the point of writing, "If I save this country I shall save it in spite of every man in it who ought to give me support, but I will save it in spite of them all."

Moreover, the withdrawal order was not popular in London, where the press was "getting up a clamour about the women and unburied bones of our soldiers." A representative editorial in the *Times* announced "the impossibility of retreating with honour. . . . If Lord Ellenborough has seriously contemplated such an act, we have no more to say to him." Peel felt the heat and wrote Ellenborough a letter in which a good deal less was said about proceeding cautiously and a good deal more about "political considerations."

Ellenborough did not, however, have this letter in hand when he issued his orders of July 4, 1842, for which he has been roundly roasted ever since. They were not quite so bad as they have sometimes been represented, but even in the most charitable view possible they were unfortunately phrased. Two documents went to Nott. In the first Ellenborough said all over again that he wanted to bring the troops back as soon as possible, but he did tell Nott that he left "to your option the line by which you shall withdraw your troops from that country." In the second, he first expatiated on the relative ease of retiring by the Bolan Pass. He then specifically set out an alternative by saying, "If you determine upon moving upon Ghuzni, Kabul and Jalalabad . . ." and then going into a great deal of quite sensible detail about the problems of retiring by such a route. Pollock got a copy of the instructions to Nott plus orders which reminded him that he was supposed to be back by October but then muddied the water with, "You should make your strength felt by the enemy during the period of your necessary detention in the valley of the Kabul River." Pollock was to make "a forward movement," but it was "not expected that he could go to Kabul."

On July 20 Nott replied, as Ellenborough must have known he would, that he was retiring via Kabul. Significantly, he neglected to inform Pollock of the decision until a week later, and Herbert Edwardes* wrote very dead pan that ". . . the military reader . . . will frown a little, and smile more, as he fancies he detects a professional jealousy between the brother generals as to which of them shall get first to the enemy's capital."

Inevitably, Ellenborough was criticized, as even Peel said, for putting upon Nott responsibility for a decision which "he ought not to bear." On the other hand, Nott was delighted. Pollock, who saw plenty of leeway in his orders to enable him to race Nott to Kabul, chortled at being "unshackled." Wellington defended Ellenborough on the grounds that the decision had to be made by the man on the spot. The case for the defense, however, would be a good deal easier if Ellenborough had not left the decisions to two generals whom only weeks before he had declared to be "without a grain of military talent" and if, once the victory was won, he had been more sparing in his use of the first-person singular.

* Then just a very young officer; later one of the great men of the Punjab.

Nott put Kandahar behind him on August 9 and with two brigades and ten thousand camels moved north against negligible opposition. By September 5 he was at Ghazni, where he expected to have to fight; but the town was abandoned, and he moved on after blowing up the citadel and a considerable portion of the walls, and burning as much as he could of the town itself. A few miles farther along he paused again, this time at the tomb of Mahmud of Ghazni. The doors to the tomb were supposed to have been looted by Mahmud from a temple near Bombay in the year 1025 and it had struck Ellenborough that their return to India would be a particularly felicitous means of impressing the world with the reassertion of British power in Afghanistan. Nott had, in fact, direct orders to bring them back. In the long run, the coup went sour when the gates got back to India and turned out not to be the originals—which could scarcely have been expected to last some eight hundred years—but considerably more recent copies.

Pollock started from Jalalabad on August 20, and if he had only a hundred miles to go as against Nott's three hundred, he was facing tougher country. He had his men traveling light; he lacked baggage camels and he knew if he waited any longer for them Nott would surely beat him to Kabul. Accordingly, he moved off with his officers sleeping four to a tent.

The advance meant that the negotiations that had been going on for the release of the prisoners held by Akbar Khan came to a halt. The captives—"nine ladies, twenty gentlemen and fourteen children"—were in a fort north of Jalalabad, where even Lady Sale conceded that their accommodations were decent and that they were well treated. Akbar had been talking with Pottinger, who found him "very anxious" to trade the prisoners for the Dost. Pottinger explained that he had no power to make terms, but offered to write Jalalabad.* He saw, as he wrote, nothing wrong with releasing the Dost "unless government intends making an example of the city of Kabul."

When word came that Pollock had relieved Sale, the prisoners fully expected to be massacred, and as one of them wrote, "our suspense was great." Instead, they were simply moved to another fort farther north. Here Elphin-

---

* Exchanges, including money and clothing for the prisoners, were regular between the two camps.

stone finally died of his accumulated infirmities and Akbar sent the body to Jalalabad for burial. A month later, the prisoners were moved again, this time to very pleasant quarters outside Kabul.

For all the talk about freeing the prisoners, Pollock was playing dice with their freedom and perhaps their lives. While the negotiations were still going on, he was quite frank about inserting clauses which he was certain Akbar would not accept—since, if he did accept them, the best reason for advancing to Kabul would vanish. Akbar, on the other hand, had no intention of allowing the prisoners to be rescued by a British army. Directly Pollock moved, he planned to send them north of the Hindu Kush, then distribute them in twos and threes to Central Asian tribes.

On September 8 Pollock had to force the pass at Jagdalak, but with Sale's men leading and plentiful artillery support he got through without much trouble. From there it was clear sailing until the thirteenth, when the force found itself in the Tezeen Valley with Akbar's men on the heights all around them. Harry Lumsden, who as Lumsden of the Guides would be a legend on the frontier, left a record of the fight in a letter to his family:

> The enemy's artillery and cavalry came down the valley, and opened a well directed fire on the rear guard from a distance of some 1200 yards. The first round shot they sent at us went within two feet of my horse's legs and sent our doctor, who was leaning on a dooly [litter], spinning, breaking the dooly to pieces, whilst the next shot killed a sowar's [cavalry trooper's] horse.
>
> When the enemy's cavalry had advanced about half towards us I went with an order to the officers commanding the 3d Dragoons to retire before the enemy, and when they should be well out of the hills, to charge.
>
> The moment the Dragoons retired the enemy came out in thousands, horse and foot, thinking our cavalry were repulsed.
>
> The Dragoons retired until joined by the 1st Bengal Cavalry and by Tait's Horse, who, on being formed up, received the order to charge. Every horse shot round and off went the whole line, boot to boot, as hard as four legs would take them.

In a flash our Cavalry was through the broken
enemy line like lightning, back again, and through
them again. We could see nothing of the actual fighting part of the business, only here and there the glim-
mer of a sabre through the dust; but the number of
Afghan horses without riders galloping over the plain
spoke their own tale, and testified to the masterly manner in which our cavalry were being handled. . . .
This lasted about half an hour, when the 1st Bengal
Cavalry returned with crimsoned blades and one of
the enemy's standards.*

The infantry pushed the Afghan jezail men off the
heights, Akbar Khan fled north, and the way to Kabul was
clear. On September 15 Pollock camped outside its walls;
two days later Nott came up furious—it having been his
understanding, or so he said, that the two forces had agreed
to enter the city together.

If the race for Kabul was settled, the fate of the
prisoners was not. Akbar had sent them north as he had
said he would. Pollock ordered Nott after them with a
brigade, possibly with the notion that rescuing the prisoners would make him feel better about losing the Kabul
race. He might have saved himself the trouble. Even on
good days Nott was a man of uncertain temper, and now
he was angrier than usual. He chewed out Pollock's messenger in a most unbecoming manner, then sent a reply in
writing which did not flatly refuse the order but raised so
many objections that Sale, who had a wife and daughter
with the prisoners, was sent instead.

The prisoners had been sent north before the Tezeen
battle under a guard of 250 men commanded by one
Saleh Mohammed. Pollock sent a letter via Mohun Lal
designed to give the commander of the guard something
to think about; it offered him a flat payment of twenty
thousand rupees and an additional thousand rupees a
month for the rest of his life if he turned over his
charges. Saleh Mohammed called in Pottinger and two
other officer-prisoners and told them that he didn't know
Pollock, but that "if you three gentlemen will swear by
your Savior to make good to me," he would turn them
over to their own people.

The agreement was put into writing, the guards were
promised a month's pay apiece to cooperate, and when

* Peter Lumsden, *Lumsden of the Guides.*

word came of the Tezeen victory the entire party marched
south. On September 16 they met a messenger who
told them that British cavalry was on the way. On the
afternoon of the seventeenth, riders were seen in a pass
ahead; Pottinger cautiously put his men into line and
loaded muskets, but the precaution was unnecessary. The
riders were British and when the word got back to London the *Times* headline was "Glorious News."

A great deal was later written about the conduct of the
British troops in Afghanistan, and if it was not quite so
bad as the Indian (as opposed to British-Indian) press
made out, some of it was bad enough. Neville Chamberlain—another young officer who later became a great
frontier figure—wrote his family a sickening account of a
punitive expedition against the village of Istalif. Every
male over fourteen was killed, and a good many of the
women were raped, killed, or both. The soldiers, both
European and Indian, looted under the eyes of their
officers, and when Chamberlain walked through what was
left of the village the next day, he found

> Furniture of all descriptions, wearing apparel, pro-
> visions, books, arms, everything made by the hand
> of man and for his use . . . scattered and destroyed,
> trampled into the mud, soiled and broken. . . . At one
> place my eyes were shocked at the sight of a poor
> woman lying dead and a little infant of three or four
> months by her side still alive, but with both its little
> thighs pierced and mangled by a musket ball. . . .
> Farther on was another woman in torture from a
> wound . . . while scattered through the streets lay the
> bodies of young and old, rich and poor, who had
> fallen in the defence of their town.*

Chamberlain felt himself no better than a "licensed assas-
sin." When the force moved on, there were still ten
houses standing; the engineers promptly burned them. The
next stop was the town of Charekar; the one old man
who hadn't managed to leave was killed and the town
burned.

At Kabul itself, behavior was somewhat better. Henry

---

* G. W. Forrest, *Life of Sir Neville Chamberlain.*

Rawlinson made the wry observation that the sepoys and camp followers, "taking their cue, I fancy, from their officers," did some looting, but considering that there had been talk of burning the entire city to the ground, discipline held fairly well until the very end of the occupation. Then, on October 9, Pollock set about carrying out his orders to leave some mark of British vengeance on the city. He considered blowing up the Bala Hissar, then gave in to the chiefs' entreaties to save it and elected to destroy instead the bazaar where Macnaghten's body had been displayed. Troops were posted at the gates to keep looters out, but once the engineers went to work at demolition the soldiers and camp followers came on with a rush to loot the shops and burn the houses. On October 12 the British marched south again. Shah Shujah had been murdered by the Dost's faction; one of his sons occupied the throne. The boy was obviously not going to last very long after British departure, but for the moment the British wanted nothing further to do with the making or unmaking of Afghan rulers.

Ellenborough did himself no good by succumbing to temptation and issuing a proclamation from Simla dated October 1—four years to the day since Auckland's unfortunate pronouncement. The public might have forgiven the theatrical choice of dates, but Ellenborough could not forbear comment on the failings of his predecessor and spoke of "disasters unparalleled in their extent, unless by the errors in which they originated. . . ." Peel admonished from London; he was attacking not only Auckland but "a course of public policy adopted with the sanction of the Sovereign."

Ellenborough was not that easily dampened. In November he issued another gaudy address to "the Princes and Chiefs, and the People of India," congratulating them on the return of the Gates of Somnauth. Back in London, it occurred to the Board of Control that while despoiling a Mohammedan tomb might delight the Hindu, it was not likely to endear the British to the Mohammedan population of India. The gates, which had been scheduled for a triumphant passage back to Somnauth, were quietly put aside.

In the autumn of 1838 the war had begun with the great military review at Ferozepore, and Ellenborough,

who seems to have had a taste for parallels, determined
that it should be terminated in the same way. The Army
of Reserve under Sir Jasper Nicolls was advanced to meet
the ragged regiments coming down from Afghanistan;
these were thoroughly worn out and grumbled a good
deal about all the *tumasha*, or fuss. An officer who had to
go through it wrote home of the resulting festivities:

> It being feared that the united armies might get
> groggy on Christmas night, the Commander-in-Chief
> resolved on having a parade the next morning to
> prevent seediness. Accordingly, the whole force was
> turned out long before sunrise and marched about
> four miles to an open space beyond the race course
> and a very pleasant walk it was—above all fog and
> below all cotton and turnips. . . . When the fog cleared
> up a little, the ball was opened with a general salute.
> The rest—and by the rest I mean four hours of some-
> thing unpleasant—was inscrutably obscure. The cav-
> alry galloped about—the artillery ran after them and
> the infantry stood at ease on the banks of a wet nullah
> [gulley]—the engineer officers having, by oversight,
> overslept and left the pontoon bridges home . . . a
> very deserving branch of the service was thus ex-
> cluded from this brilliant engagement which is a
> pity, as medals are going to be presented to "all
> those gallant officers with the force beyond the nul-
> lah!"
>
> In the evening, Ellenborough gave a soiree to
> which every officer in or about camp was bidden. A
> ball it could not be called for there were scarcely 50
> ladies and the crush of "great commanders" in the
> tents was such that even these 50 found it difficult
> to dance without treading on each others toes—and
> as for the waltzing, as an Irishman at my elbow ob-
> served, it was for all the world "like jumping in a
> sack, except there were no sacks." The sight was well
> worth seeing however; the tents were all lit up by
> chandeliers of painted glass, reflected from an un-
> limited number of brand new medals in all parts of
> the room, the effect of which was so happy that I
> recommend them on all similar occasions.*

The Dost was duly returned to Kabul and left India

* The *Times* of London.

with an observation: "I have been struck with the magnitude of your resources, your ships, your arsenals; but what I cannot understand is, why the rulers of an empire so vast and flourishing should have gone across the Indus to deprive me of my poor and barren country."

IV

Peccavi—and the Punjab

In all fairness, Ellenborough had more in mind when he paraded his forces at Ferozepore than awarding medals and holding balls. Runjeet Singh was dead. Since his death the Punjab had been an oriental hugger-mugger, with one claimant to the throne after another being struck by rivals and a mutinous Sikh army accepting bribes from the various aspirants and then turning to the next man once the money was in hand. The Governor-General felt the need for a show of force, and a London *Times* correspondent accurately reflected British-Indian opinion when he said that the Sikh army had wanted war for years. Moreover, the Sikhs were a "vain and insolent lot." He then got down to the heart of the matter:

> Politically speaking, the possession of the Punjab is too obviously necessary to admit of doubt and with the Indus our own, we should not only possess the noblest frontier possible for India, but with our steamers upon its water would do more to extend our commerce a hundred fold than has been effected by the advance of our armies into regions they never ought to have seen.

Thus, with the army of the Afghan War not yet disbanded, British India was already looking for a place where the flag might be sent in order that trade might follow it. The maneuver was somewhat more blatant than is fashionable today, but the motives were practical enough. Britain's early lead in the industrial revolution was being cut by continental nations. In some cases British products were excluded, in others the continent was producing for its own needs. In his instructions to Auckland, Palmerston had emphasized the need to open new markets beyond the Indus, and though the *Times* of London might hoot at him, it would also editorialize approvingly that "100,000,000 British subjects in India consume annually 6d per head of British manufactures" and go on in a manner plainly suggesting that many more such subjects would be highly acceptable.

In Britain, manufacturing was depressed and there was serious rioting in the industrial districts. In November, 1842, the *Times* found itself again thinking about the Punjab and observing that the mass of its population was said to be eager for the blessings of British administration. The conquest thereof would remove "every danger of invasion" from the northwest, open up Kashmir, Tibet, and Tartary, and eventually "extend our manufactures throughout the whole of central and Northern Asia."

Ellenborough was not unaware of the expectations. Toasted by officers on his way to Ferozepore, he replied that they would have even greater reason to toast him the next year. For the moment, though, his eye was not on the Punjab but on the territories of the Amirs of Sind. Excellent excuses could be made. The Amirs ran a deplorable government, they had not been faithful to their treaty regarding fixed tolls on the Indus River, and they had not only been audibly delighted when the Afghans thrashed the Kabul force but had threatened "to Kabul" any British who came their way. None of these reasons carried nearly so much weight with Ellenborough, however, as the fact that he had long ago perceived that Karachi, at the mouth of the Indus, was a first-rate seaport. As the general assigned to the task said, "We have no right to sieze Scinde, yet we shall do so, and a very advantageous, useful and humane piece of rascality it will be."

The general in question was Sir Charles Napier, sometimes known as the Devil's brother. The nickname may have been a tribute to his ferocious appearance—long beard, gray hair down to his shoulders, one eye knocked askew by an old wound—or to his equally ferocious manners. A fair sample of Napier's style is his thinking on disorderly troops: "They shall hang on the nearest tree I come to and if no tree is in sight, I shall shoot them on the spot—if need be with my own hand."

The treaty Ellenborough wanted the Amirs to sign included clauses which ceded Karachi to the British and made the Company's rupee the only legal coin in the country. To get the necessary signatures on the treaty, Napier had only 2,800 men—the 22nd (Cheshire) Foot, three sepoy infantry regiments, the 9th Bengal Light Cavalry, and the Poona Horse.*

On February 17, 1843, he came upon his opponents near Hyderabad. There were some twenty-two thousand of them and they held a strong position on the opposite side of a dry branch of the Indus River. To Napier, they looked "thick as standing corn and gorgeous as a field of flowers" with their multicolored robes, large black shields, and gleaming swords. Fortunately for the men who had to advance against them, their firearms consisted only of old matchlocks. Napier's men moved out with the Cheshires leading the way, and as they started up the steep far bank of the Indus, the enemy let fly with their matchlocks. Fortunately, the volley—as it often will when men are firing downhill—went too high, and before the matchlocks were reloaded, Napier's men were in and it was muskets and bayonets against swords. Then the Bengal cavalry charged in the flank and it was all over. One more smaller fight and Napier could message Ellenborough, "This completes the conquest of Scinde." He did not at this or any other time send the famous pun attributed to him: *"Peccavi*—I have Sind."†

It was a grand conquest. Sir Charles's share of the prize money came to seven lakhs of rupees and the Cheshires adopted "Wha Wadna Fetcht For Charlie?" as their regimental march. Ellenborough promptly annexed the territory and proposed to ship the Amirs off to Mecca. London howled. Karachi might be a desirable port to have,

---

* So called because it had originally been raised at the city of Poona, near Bombay.

† The *"Peccavi"* pun was first made by an anonymous author in *Punch* on May 13, 1844, and went thus: "It is a common idea that the most laconic military dispatch was that sent by Caesar to the Horse Guards at Rome containing the three remarkable words 'Veni, Vidi, Vici' and perhaps until our own day, no like instance of brevity has been found. The dispatch of Sir Charles Napier after the capture of Sind to Lord Ellenborough, both for brevity and truth, is however, far beyond it. The dispatch consisted of one emphatic word *'Peccavi'*—I have Sind (sinned)." Note that even in a day when Latin was a great deal more studied than today the author was taking no chances on anyone missing his point. The story was so widely regarded as true that The Cambridge Modern History used it as evidence that Napier had a bad conscience about his conquest.

but the administration of the whole area was bound to cost a great deal of money. Moreover, there was a general feeling that the action had in fact been a piece of rascality and the treatment of the Amirs shabby. Peel wrote Ellenborough, "I wish I could say to you with truth that I felt perfectly at ease about the affairs of Scinde." A Mr. Tucker, who was a director of the East India Company, went a good deal further in a letter to Mr. Cotton, the Chairman: "Throughout my long experience in India," he said, "I have never known or heard of anything so atrocious as our conduct towards these princes and their families." What he proposed was nothing less than the recall of Ellenborough—a power the Court of Directors did have, but had never used. Peel defended, without much heart, what his Governor-General had done, but the Chairs* had been waiting too long to get Ellenborough to let the opportunity pass. In April, 1844, the Company made the proper announcement to the Queen, and since Victoria had no choice, she accepted it—although not without pronouncing that she considered the move both "unwise" and "ungrateful." Peel did what he could to sugarcoat the pill by nominating Ellenborough for an Earldom and sending out his friend and brother-in-law, General Sir Henry Hardinge, as his successor.

The eyes of both Peel and Hardinge were on the northwest. The Sikh court was still all turmoil, and the newspapers were working up public opinion with accounts of "the grossest debauchery" and "atrocious crimes" at Lahore. Beyond the Sikhs were the Russians. They were alarmed by the conquest of Sind and felt, rightly enough, that the conquest of the Punjab was only a matter of time. In June, 1844, Nicholas I visited London and was quite frank with Peel about his distaste for any British movement north of the Sutlej. Later the same year, the Russian foreign minister told Peel that a considerable party in Russia believed, in Peel's words, ". . . that there was no assignable limit to the progressive aggrandisement of our Indian Empire, and that Russia and England must ultimately, and at no remote period, come into hostile contact on that account."

Peel did his best to reassure him and, while he admitted "the cravings of an army for more conquests and more

---

* Chairman and Vice-Chairman of the East India Company.

glory," said he would make no move across the Sutlej unless the Sikhs forced him to it.

Considering recent experience with inept generals in Afghanistan and the fact that a Sikh war was at least a possibility, it might have been supposed that a capable Commander-in-Chief for the Indian army might have been found to replace the retiring Jasper Nicolls. Nevertheless, "the bane of the Indian service," seniority, prevailed. The official attitude deserves to be presented in its own words: ". . . command should be considered in the main degree essentially on the principle of it being a final reward for zealous services, and as a means of enabling old officers, each in his turn, to gather from it wherewithal to pass the remainder of their old age in pecuniary ease and comfort as well as respectability."

The Duke of Wellington fully agreed, and out to India went Sir Hugh Gough. He was a handsome, heavily brogued Irishman who had been, like almost everybody else who got very far in the service in those days, with the Duke during the Peninsula campaign. When he came to India, he was already sixty-four years old, and although his bravery was unquestioned, his chief claim to fame as a commander of armies was a victory over an ill-armed and untrained assortment of Chinese in the first Opium War. Ellenborough had had a brief look at him in action during a scuffle with the little state of Gwalior and wrote home that the man "despite his many excellent qualities, had not the grasp of mind and the prudence essential to conduct great military operations."

Peel had similar doubts and begged to have Gough transferred, but the Duke would not hear of it. Accordingly, Henry Hardinge arrived in India in July, 1844, with the Sikhs "a vagabond army in a state of mutiny on the frontier" and his own troops under an officer about whom he had increasing doubts. Hardinge tripled the number of troops on the Sutlej and then tried to convince the Sikhs that these were mere "precautionary measures and not measures for future conquest." The Sikhs didn't see it that way. In addition to the troops, they knew that the British were building boats for pontoon bridges over the river, and the Indian press was full of war talk. As Hardinge said, "Every military and civil officer . . . is for conquest, honour and promotion; and so is the press, which lives for the two services."

The prospects for peace were not improved by conditions north of the Sutlej. Runjeet's successor, Kharak Singh, had been a thorough incompetent; as a Hungarian who served as court doctor at Lahore observed, "Besides being a blockhead, he was a worse opium eater than his father." His murder set off a spectacular succession of deaths and murders; by 1845 the royal house was pretty well cleaned out and the nominal rule was in the hands of Runjeet's last wife, the Rani Jindan, who sat as regent for her seven-year-old son. Given Runjeet's age at the time he married Jindan, the biological possibilities against the boy actually being Runjeet's son were staggering, but no one seemed to mind. As ruler, the Rani was assisted by her lover Lal Singh and her brother.

The exotic names and titles of the Punjab need not confuse what was fundamentally a fairly simple situation. There was no real ruler. The chiefs—large landholders —were frightened to death of their own army and quite willing to have the British destroy it for them—providing the British assured them that they would retain their own positions. Any hesitation they may have had vanished in September, 1845, when the army murdered the Rani's brother and announced itself ruler of the Punjab. Firmly convinced that they were about to be attacked by the British, the army demanded to be led against the enemy. On December 11 its extremely reluctant chiefs, Lal Singh and Tej Singh, took it south of the Sutlej. They were thirty thousand strong with 150 cannon, and if they had acted quickly they might have demolished a smaller British force in cantonments at Ferozepore. However, while "Singh" means lion, Lal Singh was not feeling anything like one. He sent a message to Ferozepore assuring the British of his friendship and asking instructions. An answer came back telling him to stall for as many days as he could.

The delay lasted a week and gave Gough time to get his troops together and Lal to send another message urging the British "to consider him and the Rani as their friends and to cut up the ruffians [his army] for them." On the eighteenth, however, there was a brisk little action which cost the British 215 dead, including Sir Robert Sale, and the suspicion began to grow that the Sikh was going to be a difficult nut to crack. Whatever their natural bravery, it is more to the point that they had an excellent artillery and, under Runjeet, had been properly trained by an assortment of European officers.

One, an Italian named Ventura, who claimed to have been a colonel in Napoleon's armies, changed a large part of the Sikh irregular horse into a disciplined infantry. By the time the war began, he had retired to Paris. His friend and counterpart for cavalry was Jean François Allard, a Frenchman from Saint-Tropez, who had also served with Napoleon and after Waterloo had come east at Ventura's suggestion to serve with the Shah of Persia. Neither man was happy with Persian pay and came south to Runjeet. The cavalry Allard trained up was good enough to elicit from a British officer the comment that they were "well mounted and form a fine body of men and horses." Like Ventura, Allard departed before the war.

The third of Runjeet's European generals and the best known to the British was Paolo Avitabile, a Neopolitan of notable cruelty, rapacity, and ability, who arrived in the Punjab in the course of an unsuccessful effort to get to Philadelphia. Dissatisfied with his progress in Napoleon's artillery, he was sailing for the United States when a shipwreck put him on the beach at Marseilles. From there, he went to Persia, where according to his own account, he achieved the rank of colonel and numerous decorations. The facts are disputed by an Englishman who claimed that he made his living in that country as a peddlar. Whatever the truth, he and a French officer, Claude Court, headed for the Punjab, where Runjeet made Avitabile governor of the province of Wazirabad. The area, previously quite turbulent, became quite calm, as Avitabile hung anyone who caused trouble or, indeed, seemed likely to cause trouble. Runjeet sent him along to Peshawar, reputed an even tougher town to run, and Avitabile did equally well there, although a gibbet shortage frequently forced him to hang two or three malefactors at the same time from each gallows. He was an imposing figure—a big man whose customary uniform was a tight blue jacket, baggy crimson trousers cut on the Zouave model, and a heavy sword. In spite of his brutality, the British found him useful in operations around Peshawar at the end of the Afghan war. Accordingly, when he decided that the troubles following Runjeet's death made it desirable for him to depart, he had no

Chiefs of the Indian States assemble with their entourages for the great Durbar of 1877, at which Lord Lytton proclaimed Victoria Empress of India

Lord Lytton's hexagonal throne pavilion and the pavilion for Indian princes and British officials at the Durbar of 1877

Rajputs

Mountaineers of Afghanistan

Runjeet Sing

Sikh soldier

Dost Mohammed Khan

The Hindu Kush Mountains

Akbar Khan

Sir Robert Sale

The assassination of Sir Alexander Burnes

View of Kabul

Lady Sale

Lord Ellenborough

The Battle of Ferozeshah

Sir Herbert Edwardes

The surrender of Moolraj

Noncommissioned officers of the native Bengal infantry

Flight of Europeans from the mutineers, 1858

Captain Hodson arresting the king of Delhi

Mountaineers of the Northwest firing on the British

The Maharajah of Oodeypore and the British resident

Lord Lytton

Sir Frederick Roberts

Lord Dufferin

King George V at the final Royal Durbar, 1911

trouble finding refuge in British India before retiring to Naples.

Avitabile's friend Court was a good deal less colorful, but of the European generals in the Sikh service he was perhaps the most important because it was he who brought the Sikh artillery to an excellence which took the British by surprise. Like the others, he was gone before the war started. Indeed, of all the Sikh's European and American* officers only a Spaniard, Colonel Hurbon, was actually present during the fighting with the British, and although he is credited with some of the engineering of the Sikh defense, it appears more likely that he was simply a regimental commander.

Herbert Edwardes, now risen to be an aide-de-camp to Gough, left a brilliant picture of the troops marching to assemble on the Sutlej:

> Here, Jack Sepoy, bitterly cold, has tied up his head like a stagecoach traveler and then stuck his full dress shako on the top of it, much askew. Behind him, rejoicing in the privilege of his rank, jogs along on a miserable bare-ribbed tattu [pony] a grey-haired subadar [sergeant]; his very oldest clothes are put on economically for the occasion, but round his throat glitters through the dust his gold-headed necklace, and on his left breast, perhaps, dangles on a ribbon twice too long, a medal or a star. Next, covering the entire column with dust, canters by, a devil-may-care subaltern, his forage cap cocked knowingly over one ear, and under him the best Bombay Arab that could be got for money, though it would not carry his bills. "Bless my soul, sir," croaks a wheezy voice on the other side of the road, "how often *must* I tell you to keep that beast in the rear?" It is the fat major, who has pulled up in his buggy, to spit the ensign's dust out of his mouth and knuckle it out of his eyes.

> On one side of the road a hackory [cart] has fallen in the dark into a ditch and on the other, a gun. The former will be there half the day; for the driver is

---

* The American Harlan had long since departed the Punjab for service with Dost Mohammed, but the remarkable Colonel Alexander Gardner was still there. By his own account, he was not involved in the fighting, but devoted himself to protecting the Rani. The Colonel's book about his Asian adventures is fascinating reading, but too much of it sounds like the work of a lively imagination to be taken seriously as history.

smoking his hookah and waiting till Providence sends someone to help him. The other will be all right in ten minutes; for a dozen strapping Horse Artillerymen have "put their shoulders to the wheel" and are hauling away to a jolly chorus. Chaque pays, chaque mode.

Look at that half clad, knock-kneed wretch shuffling along at one untiring pace, with a bamboo over his shoulders and at either end of it a heavy green box, slung by ropes. He is a "banghy-Bearer" and you take an inventory of his load without opening the pitarahs; one of them is always devoted to a guthri (bundle of clothes and "something of everything master possesses") and the other to plates, dishes and a teapot; for woe betide the khitmutgar [body servant] who has not breakfast ready the moment the regiment comes upon its ground.

But mind your head or it will be knocked off by that half-mad camel who is overladened with tents and tots [tin pots from which the European soldiers drank] and is dancing about the road, furious at the clattering on his back.

That red-haired grenadier with the yellow facings is one of the gallant 9th Foot and if what he is now swearing at the camel was not pure Irish, there could not be a doubt about his country; for at the end of his bayonet he has slung his boots, and is walking barefoot "to warm himself."*

The Afghan campaign had still not taught the British to travel light; a young officer still went to the front with a tent twelve feet square, a bed, a table, a chair, two trunks, and a brass basin for washing.

On December 21 Gough, with much spurring from Hardinge, had his force of some fifteen thousand drawn up in front of about the same number of Sikhs near the village of Ferozeshah. About a third of his men were Europeans; his artillery was on the light side and artillery ammunition none too plentiful. In terms of past experience, however, it was more than adequate for meeting Indian troops in the open field. Hardinge himself had come up to take service as second-in-command under Gough (and to keep an eye on him) and, as was not

---

* Edwardes's *Memorials.*

uncommon in nineteenth-century fighting, distinguished visitors were present to witness the action—in this case, Prince Waldemar of Prussia and two of his counts.

Gough was to be much criticized for his tactics in this and later battles, but in truth he simply did what had always been done. As John Lawrence, later a Governor-General of India, said, "We began the campaign as we have begun every campaign in India before and since, by despising our foes; but we had hardly begun it before we learned to respect them, and to find that they were the bravest, most determined and most formidable whom we had met in India. Hitherto, we had found in all our wars that we had only to close with our enemies, when, however overwhelming might be the odds against us, victory was certain. But in this campaign we found that the Sikhs not only stood and died at their guns, but that their infantry, even after the guns had been lost, were undismayed and were still willing to contest the victory with us."*

In this case, the Sikhs not only had more artillery, they had the heavier pieces. From four in the afternoon until dark, Gough threw his infantry at it with a single-mindedness worthy of a Haig on the Somme. The sepoys gave way under the cannonading with a resulting heavy loss among their British officers, who exposed themselves more and more recklessly to get their men to advance. The European regiments in the assault advanced with artillery tearing "considerable gaps" in their ranks. At the Sikh lines, the smoke and dust made it "dark as night." The Sikh infantry fired a volley and then came on with *tulwars,* or swords, while the Europeans tried to spike the enemy guns—in some regiments every fifth man having been equipped with spikes and a small hammer for the purpose. The men were so tortured by thirst that many of them kept pressing toward a well inside the Sikh line in spite of the fact that the enemy kept it under musket fire so steady as to make it a death trap.

At dark, the Assembly sounded and the plain echoed with regimental bugle calls as officers tried to get their scattered troops together. It was a miserable night to be caught in the open; "dying and dead all around us, balls whistling around us in every direction, no food and above all, no water, and the cold intense." It had been a bad

* Bosworth Smith, *Life of Lord Lawrence.*

day. A Victorian writer, trying to convey how desperate the situation had been, found it necessary to record of the 80th Foot that at one point it had even required the "stirring call" of "80th, do your duty!" to get it to advance.* Prince Waldemar of Prussia's personal physician was felled by a cannon ball, and though the prince dismounted instantly to see what might be done, "the unfortunate gentleman had already ceased to exist." As one young officer said, "It was all confusion from beginning to end," and Gough had run up a formidable butcher's bill of 2,400 men—or about one out of every seven in his command. News filtering back to the rear areas made the day seem even worse. An officer at Ludhiana made a diary entry which called the attack a failure, said that the officers were desperate, that all state papers were to be destroyed, and that if the next day's attack failed, an unconditional surrender was to be arranged to save the wounded.

It was true that Lal Singh's men had also been through a severe day's work, but the Sikh reserve under Tej Singh could be expected in the morning and there was virtually no artillery ammunition left with which to meet them. Fortunately for the British, Tej Singh appeared, but only to skirmish a bit and then retire behind the Sutlej to wait for a day when the British would be strong enough to whip his army for him.

Hardinge wrote Peel of "the bravery of the British troops" and the "great victory" and then got down to business. "We have been in the greatest peril," he said, "and are likely hereafter to be in great peril, if these very extensive operations are to be conducted by the Commander-in-Chief. . . . Gough is a brave and fearless officer, an honourable and amiable man, and, in spite of differences, a fine-tempered gentleman and an excellent leader of a brigade or a division. . . . He is not the officer who ought to be entrusted with the conduct of the war in the Punjab. . . . Sir Hugh Gough has no capacity for order or administration. He is at the outposts wonderfully active, but the more important points, which he dislikes, of drafting proper orders and looking to their execution, are very much neglected."

* This is a libel on the 80th. An officer of the next regiment in line recorded that the actual order, delivered by Hardinge himself, was "80th! that gun must be silenced!" and that the regiment promptly lost forty-seven men getting the job done.

Hardinge wanted the command turned over to Napier and the sooner the better. Nor was he alone in the opinion. An Indian correspondent for the London *Times* wrote of Gough's "most egregious want of skill and management," and the Bombay *Times* recalled that even in China Gough had been a weak commander and "the troops were in great measure left to act as they liked best." Everyone agreed that the troops themselves had been brave as brave could be, but as one critic pointed out, "Surely we do not require to constantly show the world how doggedly brave we are." Napier, he said, was the man "to whom public opinion in this country unhesitatingly turns."

In plain fact, British public opinion or a good piece of it was still too indignant over Sind to give Napier the top spot. Instead, Peel sent back a letter giving Hardinge himself the title of Commander-in-Chief as well as Governor-General. Communications, however, being what they were between London and the frontier, the letter didn't arrive until the war was over, and Hardinge, chivalrous soul, neither put the instructions into effect nor told anyone about them. As he wrote home, "I shall be rejoiced to find him retained as Commander-in-Chief . . . in time of peace." Thus was Sir Hugh Gough, who didn't do particularly well with the first Sikh War, left to do equally badly with the second.

That the Sikh army was betrayed by its leaders is quite clear; the exact time and place of the arrangement is still and perhaps always will be unclear. Tej Singh visited Hardinge in camp shortly after the Ferozeshah battle, and while there is no record of what was said, Hardinge was able to write Peel on January 18, 1846, "They say they are ready to submit to any terms. But they can offer no guarantee for the performance of any pledge, in the ungovernable state in which their army remains. . . . The Chiefs urge the army to make another attack in order that it may suffer another defeat. Its destruction and disgrace by the British army is the object which they still have in view."

The desired defeat could not be immediately forthcoming. First, Hardinge waited a month while men and supplies came up. Then on January 28, a wing of the British— about 11,000 horse and foot—faced some 15,000 Sikhs who had recrossed the Sutlej with hopes of raiding the supply base at Ludhiana. The Sikhs, some fighting in full

coats of mail, did not handle their cannon quite so skill-
fully as before, but they held quite firmly until a charge
of lancers led by the 16th—the Scarlet Lancers—came
down on their right flank. The first time the lancers rode
through, the round Sikh shields proved too tough for
them and a number of the ash lance-shafts were broken.
Wheeling, however, they shifted their lances to the bridle
hand and galloped in again, this time to take the Sikh
infantry on the side undefended by the shields. On the
third pass, the Sikhs cracked and moved back north of
the Sutlej, fighting a very decent delaying action to cover
their river crossing but leaving fifty-six pieces of artillery
behind them. Until the Scarlet Lancers were motorized
and had to give up their lances, the pennons thereon were
always crimped in memory of the bloody crumpling they
received on the day of the battle of Aliwal.

The threat to Ludhiana removed, the Aliwal force
rejoined the main British body near the village of Sobraon. Here the Sikhs had thrown a bridge over the river;
Hardinge had let them do it because he frankly feared
that any interference might bring on a general action
before he was ready for one. Around the bridgehead the
Sikhs had thrown up a considerable semicircle of breast-
works. To the British facing them it looked like another
very bad day's work for the infantry, and on the night
before the assault the colonel of one regiment got his
officers together and urged them all to shake hands with
one another "so that, should there have been ill-feeling on
the part of any, it might end forever," since by the next
evening many of them were likely to be dead.

The task facing them was not quite so severe as it
appeared. Before the battle, Hardinge had completed his
arrangements with the Rani and the Sikh chiefs. He felt
quite certain that he had the force to win at Sobraon, but
he was anxious to avoid a long campaign with hot
weather ahead; it comes in March in the Punjab and was
bound to mean a great deal of sickness for European
troops. On her side, the Rani wanted assurances that she
would be retained in power after the British victory. The
deal was made; the British would defeat the army, Tej
Singh would promptly desert as soon as the attack began,
and after the battle he would not resist the disarming and
disbanding of the Rani's troops. Hardinge even had the
plans for the Sikh fortifications.

Through the day of February 9 elephants dragged the

heavy artillery just arrived from Delhi into firing position. The infantry was held back until after dark to keep from the Sikhs the fact that Gough intended to put the heaviest concentration of them on his own left. At 2 A.M. on the tenth, the men were paraded and stumbled forward into their jump-off positions without lights; the job was made worse by a dense fog which came along before dawn. The sun rose, the fog burned off, and the British artillery opened. The surprise was successful; only then did the drums and trumpets in the Sikh camp sound the alarm.

For two hours, the artilleries dueled, neither side doing the other any particular damage, and then Gough ordered his left to charge. The Bengal Horse Artillery galloped forward, unlimbered within three hundred yards of the Sikh earthworks, and went to work as the infantry moved up behind them. The infantry got into the fortifications and were promptly thrown back out as the Sikhs rushed reserves to the point. Next the British right and center, which had been feinting, went forward in earnest; there is some doubt as to whether Gough ordered the charge or whether they went ahead on their own. One reasonably good authority reports that Gough saw them go off and remarked, "Good god! They will be annihilated."

Annihilated they were not, but one soldier remembered bursting into tears at the sight of so many dead and wounded comrades around him. Tej Singh fled the field on schedule, but his troops did him more credit than he deserved. It was eleven in the morning before the British were inside the fortifications all along the line and the Sikhs were struggling to get back across the bridge. In the crush, the bridge began to break up (there are those who accuse Tej Singh of having had the key pontoon removed) and the men tried to struggle across the river itself, swollen by recent rains to over seven feet deep. The British horse artillery moved up to the bank and flogged them with grapeshot. Gough had another 2,400 casualties for the day and the Sikhs somewhere between 5,000 and 8,000, but before sunset Hardinge had regiments over the river and was preparing to march for Lahore.

By February 14 the army was outside the city and Hardinge was faced with the question of what to do with the Punjab. He knew that Indian opinion was all for annexation; as he wrote of the civil servants, "the extension of territory opens a wider field for the display of their administrative talents—affords to them and to the officer in the army quicker advancement; and scarcely one of these gentlemen reflects upon the consequences, being dazzled by the brilliant prospects of British conquests to make the Indus and the Khyber mountains the boundaries of our Empire." Hardinge himself was far more inclined to agree with the London *Times,* which editorialized, "Expences of such a dependency would be ruinous."

His arrangements with the Rani aside, Hardinge's army was down to 3,000 Europeans—not nearly enough for the long campaign that annexation would involve. Accordingly the affair was settled by a rather involved bit of treaty writing. Young Dalip Singh was put on the throne with the Rani and Lal Singh as his advisers. The Sikh army was cut down to 30,000 men, and 250 pieces of its best artillery were sent down to Delhi. The British took over Kashmir, a considerable amount of land north of the Sutlej, and levied an indemnity of seven and a half million dollars. Since the Sikhs didn't have that much money on hand and there were the expenses of the campaign to be met, Hardinge promptly sold Kashmir to a local chief for three and a half million. To keep an eye on the Rani, a resident was to be left at Lahore and, until December, a garrison of 12,000 men would remain with him. Nominally, the Punjab was still independent, but as Hardinge wrote later, ". . . by the Treaty of Lahore, March, 1846, the Punjab never was intended to be an independent state. . . . The native Prince is in fetters, and under our protection, and must do our bidding."

The fetters were bound a little tighter in December when Hardinge revisited Lahore, presented each of the chiefs with a watch, and prevailed upon them to request that the British leave their troops there and run the state until young Dalip came of age eight years hence. The chiefs needed a little coaxing, but as Hardinge said, "The coyness of the Durbar and the sirdars is natural, but it is very important that the proposal originate with them . . . and our reluctance to undertake a heavy responsibility must be set forth." The thing was done and Hardinge wrote London, "It is really annexation without the expense."

So ended the first Sikh War and one officer wrote home, "The order is out giving the army 12 months batta [combat pay]; this is 2,200 rupees for me and it is said we are to have medals for the campaigns. Lahore looks well in the distance, but when you get into the city it is the most filthy place you can imagine—the stench quite frightful and the streets so very narrow that only one elephant can pass through at a time."

For once, youth instead of Peninsula veteran was going to get a chance to do a job. The man Hardinge left as resident to make his "great experiment at Lahore" was Henry Lawrence, then just turned forty, and the handful of bright young men Lawrence took with him was headed by a twenty-seven-year-old who had been Gough's aide— Lt. Herbert Edwardes. Lawrence (one day he and his brother John would be known as "the titans of the Punjab") was the son of an Irishman who rose to be a colonel in the British army; the boy was born during his father's tour of duty in Ceylon. At the proper age, fourteen, he followed his older brothers Alexander and George to Addiscombe, a military school near London maintained by the Honorable Company for the instruction of its young hopefuls. The Directors of the Company enjoyed the patronage of appointing to the school, and students were passed out in very much the same way they are today by military academies—the brightest went to the engineers, the middle crop to the artillery, and the culls to the infantry. For those who failed to complete the course or who lacked the desire to take it, there was always the cavalry, to which commissions could be given directly by the Directors on the assumption that all a cavalryman needed was the ability to stay on a horse and whack at the other fellow with his sword. Lawrence's two older brothers seem to have done poorly; both were put over to the cavalry shortly after entering school. Henry himself stuck it out "lest it should be supposed that no Lawrence could pass for the Artillery," and in 1823 he arrived at Dum-Dum, near Calcutta, the headquarters of the Bengal artillery.

By the time Hardinge sent him to Lahore, he had seen service in a war with Burma, where he picked up a fever which never fully left him, and made himself a first-rate reputation in the Afghan War when he was sent to the northwest to help keep the Sikhs in line after the death of Runjeet Singh and, later, to organize supplies for Pollock's force moving on Kabul. At forty, he was a tall, well-set up man, but with a gaunt face made gaunter by a long straggly beard and his fever. Even one of their most affectionate chroniclers concedes that both John and Henry Lawrence were probably "a little mad"; certainly both had eyes which are haunting reminders of the American abolitionist John Brown. Henry had a ferocious temper, an appetite for praise which must have driven his superiors to distraction, and, withal, a warmth which made him quite literally loved not only by the officers who served him but by the enlisted men as well. As a manpower expert, he was superb—virtually every one of the youngsters he took to the Punjab with him turned out a brilliant choice. It is fortunate that they did. The Punjab was nearly half the size of Texas, wilder and woolier than that state at its worst, and its nominal rulers—the child Maharajah, his mother, and Lal Singh—had next to no control over it. Lawrence sent his lieutenants into the countryside with no further instruction—if one can believe Edwardes's fondly exaggerated version—than "Settle the country; make the people happy; and take care there are no rows."

Lawrence had to send them out alone, or virtually so, because he was under the strictest instruction from Hardinge to keep the twelve thousand troops assigned the Punjab tightly in Lahore. Hardinge had the Kabul fiasco firmly in mind; the troops were to be kept together—not sent about the country in penny packets—and they were to occupy the citadel at Lahore from which they could easily stand off any Sikhs, particularly since the Sikhs were now short on artillery.

To give himself some sort of field force other than the dubious Sikh army, Lawrence reverted to a notion which he had first put forward eight years earlier when the Army of the Indus was being assembled for the invasion of Afghanistan. At that time he had proposed to Sir Henry Fane that a "corps of guides" should be raised to operate outside the framework of the regular army for "ascertaining the position of the enemy, the resources of the country, the state of the roads, passes and fords, and the numerous et cetera necessary to the success of an army." The force was to consist of a minimum number of European officers and a maximum number of Indians familiar with the frontier and its languages. The budget was also to include a sum for the "liberal remuneration" of spies. For the latter purpose, it was Lawrence's intent to employ horse merchants, camel drivers, and similar sorts who traveled freely through the Punjab and Afghanistan. Fane was interested in the project but resigned before doing anything about it.*

In early 1847, Lawrence revived the idea and nominated an ebullient twenty-six-year-old lieutenant, Harry Lumsden, to raise the Guides. Though the force was to be small at first—only 109 cavalry and 190 infantry—Lumsden was nevertheless jubilant: "It will be the finest appointment in the country," he wrote his parents, "being on the right hand of the army and the left of the political." For a second-in-command, Lawrence gave him Lt. William Hodson, a turbulent soul about whom there would eventually be a good deal of scandal. As Hodson saw it, it was their job "to give *accurate* information, not running open-mouthed to say that 10,000 horsemen and a thousand guns are coming, (in true native style), but to stop to see whether it not be really only a common cart and a few wild horsemen who are kicking up all the dust; to call twenty-five by its right name, and not say *fifty* for short, as most natives do."

Lumsden's guides were going to be different. Instead of the scarlet coats and choking stocks of the regulars, British and sepoy, the Guides wore loose-fitting khaki, which suited the climate, blended into the land, and won them the nickname Mudlarks. They were to be trained to fight, not drill. A set of rifle-practice instructions which he put on paper in later years is not only an insight into the training the Guides got, but an insight into the training the regular regiments did not get. "The most important of the education of the soldier is his ball practice," says Lumsden, and adds sensibly,

> for after all, what is the object of maneuvering but to get your men into the most advantageous positions for shooting down their enemies? And the effect of the most skilfull dispositions must be marred if men cannot use their arms when they have gained the vantage ground. Of course, the first thing in the training of your men is to make them individually

---

* The notion of "guides" was not original with Lawrence. A similar force—on a very small scale—had been raised during Wellington's Peninsular Campaign with Portuguese filling the role of border tribesmen. Given the number of "Peninsula Generals" in India at the time, it seems safe to assume that Lawrence might have heard of the project. (See Sir Charles Oman, *Wellington's Army*.)

good shots at single targets, at known distances, but this I hold to be only the ABC of the shooting art, so far as the soldier is concerned, the finishing of his education in this department requiring much patience and careful supervision, and I have reason to know that this part of his training is entirely neglected in many native regiments. A regiment should be frequently practiced in maneuvers with loaded arms, and thus positively taught how little danger there is with ordinary care in carrying loaded arms. Companies might next be practiced in extended order, firing at marks scattered about at all sorts of distances, elevations and angles. . . . Too large marks are not required, as skirmishers in the field against men who know their work will seldom get a shot at more than the head and shoulders of a man. Common ghurrahs [clay pots] are about the right size and can be easily placed.*

The Indian army was apparently somewhat shaky about other men with guns. Lumsden has some remarks about firing in regimental formation and notes that "in many regiments the front rank men will be so nervous of the loaded arms of the men behind them as quite to lose all their senses."

He saw to the training himself, directing much of it with a short, weighted stick which became known in the Guides as "Cease Firing" because it was their commander's habit to apply it sharply between the shoulder blades of anyone failing to heed the order.

By March, 1848, the Guides had been raised and trained and had seen a little field duty visiting villages reluctant to pay their taxes. Henry Lawrence had gone home to England on sick leave and in his place as Resident at Lahore sat a civilian from the Bengal establishment, Sir Frederick Currie. Currie had arrived to find that he had a very troubled and troublesome Rani on his hands. To turn back a bit, at the end of 1846, the Rani's lover, Lal Singh, had been tried and found very guilty of trying to stir up a revolt against the British-sponsored ruler of Kashmir. Lal Singh was clapped into the state prison at Agra. The Rani sulked, stirred up what sentiment she could against the British, and finally worried Henry

* Lumsden, op. cit.

Lawrence into issuing a proclamation "for the Information of the Chiefs of the Lahore Durbar, the Priests, Elders and the People of the Countries belonging to the Maharajah Dalip Singh." It said that the Governor-General of India felt "the interest of a father" in the young prince. This fatherly interest had just been extended to having the boy's mother removed from Lahore and put under what amounted to house arrest at Sheikhopoorah, twenty miles away. This was necessary because the Rani had been "intriguing to disturb the government." Moreover, it was "only too probable" that if the Rani were left near the boy she would "instill into him her own bitter feelings of hostility."

Bitter she was. Her exit lines from Lahore suggest a woman of a good deal more character than the drunken "Messalina of the North" usually portrayed in the British press. To quote her exactly: "Instead of being secretly king of the country, why don't you declare yourself so. You talk about friendship and put us in prison. . . . You have not only destroyed my character, but have also imprisoned me and separated me from my child. . . . I am the owner of a kingdom; I will have redress from your queen. You have acted towards me unjustly."*

In January, 1848, Lawrence left India for England, accompanying his friend Hardinge; Hardinge was retiring as Governor-General, having assured his successor that "so far as human foresight could predict, it would not be necessary to fire a gun in India for seven years to come." For a man of Hardinge's intelligence, his margin of error was considerable—he was wrong by six years and eight months.

Hardinge's successor, James Ramsay, Lord Dalhousie, was a tough, imperious bantam on the Wellesley model, and he had been scarcely two months in office when it became plain that the Punjab was on the verge of an outbreak. The Guides were ordered down from Peshawar to see what their spy system could do about the Sikh efforts to win over the sepoy garrison at Lahore. Before they got there, however, much more serious news came from Multan, a good-sized city some 250 miles southwest of Lahore.

A civilian, Vans Agnew, and a Lt. W. C. Anderson had been dispatched thence to speak with its governor—one

* Khrushwant Singh, *History of the Sikhs.*

Mulraj—who had resigned in a revenue dispute with Lahore. Although Mulraj himself was regarded as a docile sort, his army was not, and Agnew and Anderson traveled with a remarkably large escort—1,400 Sikh infantry, 600 Gurkhas, 700 cavalry, and 100 artillerymen with six guns. The first thing the two Englishmen did on arriving was to have Mulraj's troops paraded and assure them that they were not to be mustered out of service. They then turned and were riding out of the fort with Mulraj when a soldier standing near the gate ran a spear into Agnew's side and Mulraj's escort sabered Anderson. The two men, with their own escort, made it back to a building outside the walls and got out a note asking for help. Agnew reported their condition as: "I am cut up a little on my back. Lt. Anderson much worse. He has five sword wounds; I have two in my left arm from warding sabre cuts, and a poke in the ribs with a spear. I don't think Mulraj has anything to do with it."

The next day their entire escort, Sikh and Gurkha, went over to Mulraj, and toward evening, a mob—half soldiers, half civilians—broke into the building and killed both men. Almost two years to the day after the first Sikh War had ended, the second had begun.

Agnew's note went to Herbert Edwardes, who was at a village about ninety miles north of Multan. He was, as an officer on the frontier was likely to be in those days, seated among a group of locals who were "either robbers, robbed or witnesses to the robberies" and trying to administer justice. There was a sound of running feet and the *kossid,* or messenger, came in stripped to the waist and streaming sweat. Edwardes read the letter, dismissed the kossid, and—marvel of composure—sat down to complete the trial. He does admit that his mind was not entirely on the subject. Since Edwardes's few hundred Sikhs were at best of doubtful loyalty against their coreligionists, he set about raising a new force from the Muslim Pathans along the Afghan border and prepared to threaten Multan as "the only move which can save this frontier."

Neither Dalhousie nor Gough was going to be much help. Although Dalhousie declared that he was "painfully" alive to the effects of delay, both men agreed that European troops could not stand the heat of a summer campaign in the Punjab, and, into the bargain, both were hopeful that the Multan affair would remain localized. To that end, Currie at Lahore ordered the Guides to remove the Rani from Sheikhopoorah before she could become a rallying point. Lumsden and his men rode all night, arrived at the Rani's just before dawn, and told her she was badly wanted at Lahore. The lady got into a carriage, Lumsden climbed in beside her, and off the party clattered—not to Lahore, but down to Ferozepore in British India from where the Rani could be sent even farther south. Currie's official report to Dalhousie says, "Happily there was not the slightest opposition; all was acquiescence and civility." Lumsden's version is that once the lady found where she was headed, she turned the air blue.

On June 18 Edwardes commended his cause to the Almighty, reflected that no Englishman was likely to do badly on the anniversary of Waterloo, and led his three thousand Pathan recruits plus some troops provided by the Nawab of Bhawulpore against Mulraj. They were mostly infantry and all badly disciplined, all Edwardes could do was hold them for one mad rush, since there was no hope of rallying them if it went wrong. It went right. Mulraj fell back on Multan and Edwardes took most of the guns his opponent had brought into the field. In early July he pushed Mulraj all the way into Multan and then set to pleading with Lahore for heavy guns to use against its walls. Currie did what he could—sent a light siege train, some British infantry, and a Sikh force under its own general. An older Punjab hand, John Lawrence, had warned him against sending Sikhs "for they will assuredly fraternize with the rebels." The Sikhs not only fraternized, they marched off in September to join the rest of the Sikh army gathering to chase "the cruel Feringhees" out of the Punjab. Edwardes sat outside Multan too weak to break in and Mulraj sat inside too weak to break out.

The Punjab was up, and as John Lawrence said, "These men will fight desperately and die hard." There was a general assumption that the rising was a carefully planned affair, organized by the Rani, in which the whole north—Sikhs, Afghans, Beluchis—would join together to drive the British all the way back to Delhi and if possible beyond. Dalhousie repeatedly asked Currie for evidence to support the general conspiracy theory, but Currie was never able to supply it. Rather, it would appear that in an occupied country with a large number of disbanded soldiers, gener-

als as well as privates, there was bound to be trouble
sooner or later and no vast amount of plotting was
necessary to bring it about. Once the thirty-two-thousand-
man army the Sikhs had been allowed to keep after the
first war went over, the fat was in the fire.

In the cooler October weather, Dalhousie ordered the
Army of the Punjab assembled and made a real rouser of
a speech to the effect that "I had hoped to see prosperity
and peace realized over this vast empire. I have striven
for peace, I have longed for it. But since the Sikh nation
desires war, on my word they shall have it and with a
vengeance!"

His eloquence was such that one colonel burst into
tears and a younger officer declared himself "so inspirited
as to be able to fight a regiment."

Once again, the British were marching off to war with
Lord Gough—the increase in title was in recognition of his
services in the first Sikh War—leading the parade.
Gough, as even the Duke of Wellington admitted, was
inclined to use bayonets where guns would have done
better, and his second Sikh War was going to be remarkably like his first. Moreover, he was seventy and probably
senile. Dalhousie was sure that he had "utterly lost any
power of memory which he may have ever possessed."
Nor had the seniority system produced much in the way
of helpful subordinates. General Pope—of whose unfortunate cavalry brigade more shortly—was unable even to
mount a horse without the assistance of two men, and
Hodson reports in all seriousness that there was an infantry brigadier so nearsighted as to be unable to tell in
which direction his command was facing.

On January 13, 1849, Gough came up to the Sikhs near
the village of Chillianwalla with thick brushwood and
ravines in front of their position. Two badly handled
skirmishes and a row with Dalhousie had not improved
Gough's disposition; there is a myth, in fact, that he
fought at Chillianwalla simply because the Sikhs dropped
a couple of cannon balls near him and "roused that spirit
of defiance and antagonism which were so natural to
him." In actual fact, he was out of range of the enemy
fire but the firing does seem to have inspired him to
attack that afternoon and to do so straight ahead rather
than wait to take his foe in flank the next morning.
Gough order his artillery to commence, the Sikh artillery
returned the compliment, and the battle was on.

To get at the main Sikh positions, the infantry had to advance nearly a mile through heavy brushwood, a good part of it growing in swamp. Their artillery preparation did them very little good because they had to fire blind. Nevertheless, at the first slackening of the Sikh artillery, the order was given to advance and there were stern admonitions about not firing: "The bayonet must do the work." In later years, indeed, there grew a legend that one brigade had actually been sent forward with its muskets unloaded. In any event there was very little to fire at; as one officer said, "We could see no distance on our front."

The infantry suffered fearfully getting through the wood and worse as they struggled for the Sikh guns. "The Sikhs fought like devils . . . fierce and untamed in their dying struggles . . . they ran right on the bayonets and struck at their assailants where they were transfixed"— thus a lieutenant on the day's work. The woods broke up the British line, the Sikhs kept slipping in behind them, and one British regiment lost nearly half its men before it even reached the enemy gunline. There was worse to come.

On the British right, General Pope had his cavalry brigade—two squadrons from the 9th Lancers, three of sepoy cavalry, four from the 14th Lancers—ready to advance. In addition to his problems as a horseman, Pope had never before commanded cavalry, even in peacetime. Finally, there is the question of what horsemen were expected to accomplish in woods so thick that the troopers would scarcely be able to see one another. The brigade was ordered to mount, swords were ordered drawn, and in one long, thin line they went forward at a trot. A number of things went wrong almost immediately.

First off, Pope had gotten his men lined up at a slight angle to the main British line, so as they trotted out, they began to move across their own front and through their own artillery fire. There was nothing for the artillery to do but stop firing. Next, the line of horsemen started to come apart badly in the trees, the trot slowed down to a walk, and the troopers felt a great deal less like a wave sweeping forward and a great deal more like being lost in the woods. The men were halted in an effort to get them back into some sort of order and at this moment the Sikh cavalry came plunging at them out of the forest. Someone —very likely several someones—shouted "Threes about!"

and suddenly everybody was turned around and heading pell-mell back for the start line. The Sikhs came hard after them, the 14th Dragoons ran right through a British horse artillery position, Sikhs and Dragoons were so mixed the gunners couldn't fire, and before it was over the artillery and cavalry retired, leaving the Sikhs with six British cannon.

According to Dalhousie's own report to the Duke of Wellington the 14th didn't even stop at the British gun line but kept right on going until they came to a field hospital and were only stopped there by a chaplain, the Rev. W. Whiting, who, pistol in hand, threatened to shoot the first man who retreated a step farther. Even Dalhousie's biographer concedes that the story may have gained a bit in the telling.

General Pope was probably fortunate to have been killed in the melee. The colonel of one of his regiments felt himself so thoroughly disgraced that he blew his brains out a few weeks later.

Both sides drew off for the night, and if either of them had any heart for immediately renewing the contest, the rain that started that night and lasted for three days took it out of them. Gough—he was remarkably consistent about casualties—had another 2,400 of them, but this time the figure represented one out of every five men he had. The Sikhs felt strong enough to send a messenger offering peace in exchange for the British getting out of the Punjab. Dalhousie turned them down, but his letters to London sound very like Hardinge's during the first Sikh War: "In public I make, of course, the best of things. I treat it as a great victory. But ... I do not hesitate to say that I consider my position grave." On Gough he was emphatic: ". . . if he again fights an incomplete action with terrible carnage as before, you must expect to hear of my taking a strong step; he shall not remain in command of that army in the field."

Whatever Dalhousie may have been making of it in public, the public, not only in India but also in London, was quite aware that it had been a very bad day's work. "Lord Gough's generalship," announced the *Times,* "in attacking the Sikhs so late in the day, with such precipitation and in a manner so disorderly, has been severely censured by the press." Their Indian correspondent said, "I have received three letters from camp and they all

contain the same account of the 'Tipperary tactics.' "*
"Several people advised him not to fight that day," he
went on, "but he would listen to no one and even said he
would put any officer under arrest who presumed to
suggest anything to him. So at it they went—every General and Brigadier his own way, receiving no orders."

Indeed, Gough does seem to have been guilty of the old
charge Hardinge had made against him—that he spent his
time way up front, where a lieutenant should be, but a
general should not. "His Lordship fancied himself at Don-
neybrook Fair," wrote an officer who was present, "and
was in the thick of it . . . lost to sight." Two days after the
news of Chillianwalla reached London, Napier was ordered out to India to take over as Commander-in-Chief.

For the moment, however, Gough was still in command and events were not going to wait for Napier.
Edwardes's little force before Multan had been reinforced
up to 10,000 men under a General Whish. Dalhousie
thought Whish was taking altogether too long with the
seige—"Tomorrow and tomorrow and tomorrow should
be the motto on General Whish's new coat of arms," he
wrote a friend—but on January 22 the place finally surrendered. The Multan-wallahs, as they called themselves,
marched off to join Gough. When they came up, Gough
would have about 25,000 men and there was a good deal
of worry that he might well need every last one of them.
From the beginning, the Sikhs had been urging Dost
Mohammed to throw in with them. They even offered
him Peshawar, and the British felt that the offer of the
city he'd wanted so long plus a chance to settle an old
grudge would be more than enough to bring the Dost and
his Afghan horsemen into the Sikh camp. "If the Dost
does come in to stir the storm," Dalhousie conceded, "the
steering will become ticklish."

The Dost, however, proceeded more carefully. He
came down through the Khyber and, since there wasn't
much the Sikhs could do about it, simply took Peshawar.
Then he offered to mediate between the two warring
parties. The British rejected the suggestion as impudent.

At Chillianwalla, the two armies sat facing each other—
Gough waiting for the Multan men to come, the Sikhs
trying to bait Gough into another headlong frontal at-

* The press never let Gough forget he was Irish. If he did well, it
was attributed to native Irish ferocity; if badly, it was "Tipperary
tactics."

tack. On February 13 the Sikhs gave up the game and marched around Gough's right and down to the town of Gujerat on the north bank of the Chenab River. From there, they could either threaten Lahore or intercept Whish. Neither plan worked out. The Indian army was learning to march a great deal lighter than had been the rule in the past. Gough had cut himself down to one tent and his officers were sleeping doubled up. Accordingly, they were able to move with "the requisite celerity." Gough swung around, moved south on a parallel track, and on February 18 was joined by Whish just west of Gujerat. The Battle of Gujerat is worth describing in some detail because it went off by the book; it was the way a battle was supposed to be fought in India in 1849. In fact, it went so well that a story was passed around that Gough wasn't even there, having been imprisoned by his staff in a nearby windmill. The story is not true, but he was getting better advice from his staff and listening to it. Moreover, he was in the pleasant position of "the balance of metal being happily on our side." He had more guns than the Sikhs and bigger ones. His biggest were 18-pounders—that is, they threw an 18-pound projectile—and it makes a helpful comparison to recall that the standard British gun in the African desert campaigns of World War II was a 25-pounder. The small guns of the horse artillery were 6-pounders. The Sikhs had a man-power edge—35,000 to about 25,000—and had been supplemented by a modest contingent of about 2,000 Afghan horse.

On February 21 the troops rose at dawn, packed all their extras on baggage camels, and about 7:30 formed up four miles west of Gujerat. It was a beautiful morning: the sky was clear blue, the day was cool enough to remind some present of a spring dawn in England, and to the northeast the snow sparkled on the mountains which would shortly mark the new northern boundaries of British India. The ground across which the men were to move forward was level farmland and the young crop a gentle green still wet with the morning dew—the dew also, as a practical soul pointed out, serving to keep the dust down. The advance began with each regiment moving forward in column and staying far enough from the regiment next to it to be able to shake out into line when the time came. Between the columns of infantry in their scarlet jackets rode the horse artillery in their blue, and at the

center of the whole force came the big 18-pounders—
each pulled by an elephant. From one side to the other
they covered a front of some three miles of scarlet cut
with dark blue, and on each flank rode the multicolored
cavalry. Sepoy cavalry wore French gray throughout, the
9th Lancers on the left wore scarlet, the Sind Horse had
their troopers in olive-green coats and red turbans while
their officers courted sunstroke in silver helmets. The
regiments of irregular horse were similarly gay—bright
yellows, blues, and greens.

In one hour this magnificent array slowly advanced two
miles and then the Sikh guns in Gujerat opened fire. The
infantry was ordered to open out into line and lie down.
The horse artillery galloped three hundred yards ahead,
unlimbered, and commenced fire. The elephant-drawn
heavies went a hundred yards ahead and did the same.
Gough had promised his infantry a good, thorough artillery preparation this time, and they got it. For three
hours their guns pummeled the Sikhs while the men lying
behind the guns were "chatting, laughing, joking." The
artillerymen took severe casualties from the Sikh guns,
which were well served as usual, but after three hours the
weight of metal began to tell and the Sikh fire slackened.
The infantry knew that its time to go to work was at
hand. Staff officers who had been galloping about with
orders checked their pistols, for the galloping was likely
to shake the shot loose. One officer remembered lighting
a cheroot and that in going forward the men hardly fired
a shot—"it being the custom in our brigade to take the
guns at the point of bayonet."

The Sikhs gave way, made one gallant counterattack
when a gap opened in the British line, and then collapsed.
On the flanks, the cavalry held off the Sikh cavalry and
finally drove them off altogether with the Sind Horse and
the 9th Lancers winning particularly golden opinions for
their efforts. It was over; it had been a textbook effort,
there was a flying column in pursuit of what was left of
the Sikh force, and there had been only six hundred
casualties. As the *Times* gratefully observed, "Our loss,
though sufficient to keep up with that honorable prescrip-
tion of danger which the Duke* tells us necessary to the
enjoyment of an occasional triumph, is trifling compared
with the late massacres."

Out of fifty-nine Sikh guns engaged, fifty-three were

* There is only one "the Duke"—Wellington.

captured. What was left of the Sikh army turned in its arms and the British cavalry chased the Dost out of Peshawar and back through the Khyber. Dalhousie offered the Khyberees two lakhs of rupees to close the pass and trap the Dost on the Indian side, but they either couldn't or wouldn't do the job. All that remained was to decide what to do about the Punjab. Dalhousie and London had been debating the point since the previous summer, and when, by late March, London had not been able to make up its mind, Dalhousie acted with characteristic decision and annexed it on his own authority. The treaty which the Sikh durbar signed on behalf of the young Maharajah took scarcely one printed page; by it Dalip Singh resigned all his claims to the Punjab, and all the property of the state was confiscated by the Honorable Company to cover the expenses of the war—except for the Kohinoor diamond, which Dalhousie sent along to Victoria. Young Dalip got a pension.*

British India now ran to the foothills of the Himalayas and the borders of Afghanistan; what Runjeet Singh is supposed to have predicted while looking at a map of India—"One day it will all be red"—had come true.

---

* The boy went to England, lived as a country gentleman, and became quite a favorite of the Queen's.

CHAPTER

V

Border Wars and the Mutiny

In reviewing the war, the *Times* thought it detected a trend in Indian Army affairs. "There is one class of our Indian heroes of whom we have purposely avoided speaking in connection with the veteran warriors whose merits we have just been passing in review. This Sikh warfare appears to have called into existence a younger race of men on whom in days to come the task of defending their country's honour will devolve."

The *Times* was on the optimistic side. The Duke had three more years to live; so long as he lived, youth was not going to prevail against Peninsula veterans. Nevertheless, some changes were on the way. Sir Charles Napier arrived in May to take over from Gough; he was more intelligent than Gough and tougher than Hardinge. Within six months he court-martialed no less than forty-six officers and administered a series of tongue-lashings of which the following is a fair sample:

At a late review of the troops . . . the following evident deficiencies were evident to all: 1st. That some commanders of regiments were unable to bring their regiments into line. 2nd. One commanding officer attempted to wheel his whole regiment as he would a company. 3d. Several officers commanding companies were seen disordering their companies by attempting to dress them from the wrong flanks. 4th. When the line was ordered to be formed, some commanders deployed too soon and ordered their lines thus improperly formed to "double quick" in order to regain their position. This was all bad, but it was worse to see the regiments on receiving the word to "double quick" at once charge, with loud shouts, no such order having been given by anyone. . . . 5th. Bad as this was, it was not the worst. When these regiments chose to charge,

the Commander-in-Chief, to his astonishment, saw
some of the rear ranks firing straight up into the air;
he saw some of the men of the rear rank actually
firing off their muskets to the rear, over their shoulders, as the bearers—he will not call them soldiers—
were running to the front. If ever such again happen,
it will expose the commanding officer of any regiment that so disgraces itself to reprimand in public
orders to the whole Indian army. In the course of his
service, he never witnessed such a scene. . . . The Commander-in-Chief will, therefore, hold commanding
officers responsible—for they alone are to blame that
any soldier who shouts or charges or fires without
orders be instantly seized, tried at once by a drum-
head court martial, and the sentence executed on the
spot.

On the new frontier, only Peshawar was to have a
garrison of regular troops. The rest of the 997 miles of
Punjab border country was the domain of the Guides—
now raised to 840 men—and ten regiments of the newly
formed Punjab Irregular Force. The Force, eventually
retitled the Punjab Frontier Force but generally known by
its original nickname, the Piffers, consisted of five cavalry
and five infantry regiments. The cavalry regiments were to
have 588 troopers each, the infantry 800 privates; in the
beginning the number of Sikhs permitted to enlist was
severely limited. The remainder of the men were drawn
from the same sources the Guides had found so fruitful—
the border tribes who knew the ground and the languages.
All but one of the new outfits adopted the Guides' khaki
uniforms, each working out its own formula for dyeing
the white drill uniform material brown. Some units used
tea, others coffee, mud, or curry powder, and the stink
around a camp when dyeing operations were in progress is
said to have been considerable.
Enlisting Pathan tribesmen never seems to have been
any trouble. Lumsden always had a number of them
trailing after the Guides and waiting for an opening,
which was filled by competition on the rifle range. Recruiting Sikhs—particularly since policy permitted recruiting
only men too young to have been in either Sikh war—
seems to have been more difficult. A Frontier Force
officer of a slightly later period, when more Sikhs were
sought, set down very precisely the techniques involved.
The men detailed to recruiting should be "plausible men,
who are good at talking and sociably inclined." They

should be well dressed and provided with small sums of
money to spend on rum and sweetmeats. "It cannot be
denied," he says, "that the majority of recruits are hum-
bugged into enlisting." Accordingly, "wonderful stories of
the delights of service, charming stations, no work, fed on
fruit and other luxuries and plenty of pocket money" are
to be told them. If a British officer goes along, he is urged
to set up a small fair, enlisting any "local acrobats and
mountebanks available" for a few rupees and arranging a
program of "wrestling, flat racing, long jump, race for
children, three legged race, etc. etc." with prizes for first
and second places.*

The new frontier regiments had only four British
officers apiece, and the sort of thing a young man could
expect can be quite nicely judged from some notes a
colonel drew up for a nephew headed that way. In *Hints
To Cadets*, the colonel† said in 1850:

1. Take care before the ship leaves the dock to
have all your baggage on board and that part of it
which you will not require during the voyage (your
box of saddlery, for instance) marked accordingly
and at once stowed away in the hold.... Avoid sending anything into the hold that may be injured by the
heat (such as epaulettes, sword knots or anything
gilt).

2. Have your cot screws put in all right and to be
sure that they are so, hang up the cot, get into it and
jerk it well. . . . Cot screws are sometimes tempered
so high as to break with a jerk.

3. It is perfectly useless to take any *English* seal-
ing wax with you.

4. Keep all hammers, nails etc. very close or they
will be borrowed, even by the ship's carpenters; and
if lent, you will most probably never see them again.

5. Be provided with two pairs of *stout* walking
shoes, for use during the passage; it is curious how
quickly shoes wear out on board ship.

6. Secure the attendance of a servant for the voyage
as soon as possible. If there are troops on board, you
will find little difficulty in obtaining permission of the
officer to employ one of the men.

7. The pilot will leave your ship about the Land's

---

* Robert Falcon, *Handbook on Sikhs for Regimental Officers.*
† Colonel Sir Charles Hopkinson, CB.

End. Have a few lines in a letter ready for wafering to send ashore by him, however sick or ill you may be . . .

9. Avoid *all* card playing.

10. Take not more than four or five rupees with you on shore in your pockets. None but "Griffs" carry money with them. Your cousin Harry, with all his sharpness, lost every rupee he took ashore—about 100.

11. After joining your corps and performing your duty as an officer you will occasionally receive orders from your superiors, which to you, may appear incomprehensible, nay even useless or ridiculous. To form any opinion of them whatsoever, is, *remember,* no business of yours.

12. Above all things, determine to act with the utmost good temper, mildness and patience in all your intercourse with the native, particularly those under your command. This is even more especially called for with your own servants—whom you cannot expect to understand your language as well as yourself.

> I conclude by earnestly enjoining you
> Never to do anything in a hurry.
> Never condescend to be put out of temper.
> Never, *never* get into debt!

This counsel of perfection was considerably honored in the breach. Young officers were wont to refer to their servants in particular and Indians in general as "niggers." Far from not being put out of temper, they quite often were put so far out as to come to duels. Officially, invitations for "two for pistols and one for coffee" were against regulations by 1850, but as an officer of the period said, "It was for some injuries the only mode of obtaining satisfaction, and it is a pity that it was altogether abolished."

Life for a European officer was pleasant. Although the son of an Indian army officer coming out himself for the first time might reflect that things were not so good as in Father's day, when they had had numerous servants, "a couple of elephants," dozens of horses, ponies, and dogs and some hunting cheetas, he could still describe his station as a "jolly place." Each regiment had its own billiard room; there were cricket teams in the Indian as well as in the British units. In addition to horse racing, there was an extraordinary amount of *shikar,* or hunting. At the death of one notable shikarhi, an officer named Nightingale, it was estimated that in his lifetime he had killed scores of tigers and speared thousands of hogs and hundreds of bears.

Dalhousie had forbidden wives and families on the frontier, and even in India proper there was a considerable shortage of white women. There is an old British-Indian saw to the effect that necessity is the mother of invention and the father of the Eurasian. Indian women were taken in under the euphemism "housekeepers" or the more elaborate rationale "sleeping dictionaries." The argument in the latter case was that an Indian mistress helped a young man learn the language faster. The available white women were either British or half-British, half-Dutch girls from South Africa, where many Indian army officers took their leaves. These last were widely admired on the grounds that they rode well, could dance and flirt, and were not so straitlaced but quite as virtuous as the girls from England.

For the British enlisted man, the prospects were somewhat less attractive. Not that they expected much; the vast majority were, on the word of one of their own number, "the idle, the depraved and the destitute" of British society. Occasionally a young man of the better sort turned up—Durand's sergeant at the storming of Ghazni, a sergeant for whom Lady Sale has many kind words during the worst of it at Kabul, a young Irishman who joined up in the 1840's because ". . . of a mercantile friend, whose affairs were inextricably interwoven with mine, sustaining several heavy and unforeseen losses in trade."

The latter young man joined simply by meeting on the streets of Dublin a noncommissioned officer with the recruiting ribbons on his shako and accompanying him to the recruiting office. He was given a selection of regiments and picked the 13th Light Foot partly because it had become quite famous as a result of Jalalabad and partly because he seems to have felt it wise to get out of the British Isles and the 13th was still in India. The traditional shilling was pressed into his hand and he probably began regretting his decision almost immediately. Shipped to a receiving station in England, he found his fellows "in no way distinguished for orderly conduct" and inclined to devote what spare time they had to fleecing their less sophisticated mates at cards. His first breakfast consisted of weak coffee and a brown bread so miserable that it would stick to the wall like paste. A few days later, he saw his first flogging—150 lashes delivered in slow time. He cannot have been sorry to have promptly been shipped out to India.

The passage in those days took about four months. Recruits, old soldiers returning, and any old soldiers' wives all lived in one compartment. The men slept in hammocks, which sea-going wits then as now thought it comic to cut down at night, and the women slept on the deck. The voyage was reasonably pleasant if the weather was good. The soldiers were required to assist with ship's work—probably a welcome antidote to boredom—but could not be required to go aloft.

Once settled with his regiment, the private soldier found that due to the cheapness of Indian labor he had an enormous number of services available to him which would not have been available in Britain. For two rupees—about a dollar—a month out of his five dollars a month pay, he was served by a bobagee who fixed his breakfast, a dhobie who did his washing, a nappie to trim his hair. His government allowed him a pound of bread, a pound of meat, 5/7 of an ounce of tea or coffee a day, plus sugar, rice, and salt. As one of the men who had to eat it said, it would have been an adequate diet if it had been of decent quality—but it wasn't.

The arrangements for the soldier's leisure were astonishingly meager. There were divine services and in cantonments there was usually a library for those who could read. For the rest there was a canteen at which the soldier was allowed to purchase two drams of spirits a day—except on special occasions when he was permitted to get roaring drunk. For those who wished to get drunk more often there was a native moonshine—going by the name of Dharroo—more notable for cheapness than quality.

An enlisted man's social life was exceedingly circumscribed. For those who wished, there were the lall bazaar women—prostitutes—and on the frontier Peshawar had a notable reputation for the quantity and variety of vice. The soldier who wished to marry could, by permission, and one famous source of wives was a Bombay orphanage for half-caste girls which would provide any enlisted man certified to have a good character with one of their young ladies.

If the station was temporary, the men lived in tents 16 by 18 feet, sixteen men to a tent, eight down each side. In cantonments, they lived in barracks made of sun-dried brick and whitewashed. On very hot stations where temperatures might reach 125 degrees in May, the men were ordered to remain indoors from 9 A.M. to 5 P.M. and derive what cool they might from straw mats put in the way of whatever wind might be blowing and kept wetted by Indians known as *pani wallahs*.

Between the monotony, the drinking, and the heat there was a good deal of violence on an Indian post. As noted, dueling still went on between officers. Among enlisted men, it was simply a fight with a violent ending, and for the culprit there was hanging. For the occasion, the troops on the station were drawn up to make three sides of a square; the gallows stood on the fourth side. The prisoner was led out, dressed in a white gown, and put onto a small cart which became part of a little procession that marched around inside the square. First came the band playing the Dead March, then part of the guard, then four men carrying a coffin, then the criminal himself with a chaplain if one was available and a friend if one was not. The rest of the guard brought up the rear.

The procession halted at the foot of the gallows; the condemned man, his guards, and his executioner climbed the steps to the platform. If the executioner was an Indian, it was not unusual for the condemned to ask that the sergeant of the guard adjust the noose rather than permit himself to be touched by an Indian. The noose adjusted, the trap was sprung, the body fell, and the troops were marched away, taking a smart "eyes left!" as they passed the gallows.

In May, 1850, the men got a new commander. Napier had one run-in too many with Dalhousie and resigned. Out to relieve him came Sir William Gomm. Predictably, Sir William was a friend of the Duke's, a Peninsula veteran, and an antique. As a contemporary said, "He ought not to have been selected for such a command at the age of seventy and with no recent military experience." Dalhousie simply philosophized that all military men sent out to command were antiques, and at least, unlike Napier, Gomm was "quite content to sit inside the coach and let another drive it."

Along the northwest frontier, the Piffers settled down to the not inconsiderable task of keeping the peace. Central Afghanistan has its fertile valleys, but the border tribesmen lived among very bare rocks indeed, and their principle export was armed men who descended onto the Indus plain bent on robbery, cow theft, the kidnapping of rich Hindu merchants for ransom, or the murder of the unbelieving British in the name of the Prophet. A frontier officer described them as

> . . . savages . . . noble savages perhaps—and not without some tincture of virtue and generosity, but still absolutely barbarians. They have nothing approaching to government or civil institutions. In their eye, the one great commandment is blood for blood and fire and sword for all people not Mohammedans. They are superstitious and priest ridden. But the priests are as ignorant as they are bigoted, and use their influence simply for preaching crusade against unbelievers and inculcate the doctrine of rapine and bloodshed against the defenceless people of the plains. The hillsmen are very avaricious; for gold they will do almost anything except betray a guest. They are thievish and predatory to the last degree. They are utterly faithless to public engagements. They are fierce and bloodthirsty.*

Thus one of the more intelligent Englishmen of his day in India.

Kabul made no pretense of claiming the border men as subjects; each tribe ruled itself, conducted blood feuds with its neighbors, and organized raids on the plains. When a raid was decided on, a few veteran raiders consulted together and listened to reports of spies just up from the plains. Word then went out to the young men of the tribe that a raid was on and that anyone interested in joining should appear at a given date at the rendezvous point with supplies for so many days. The raiders having assembled, they marched at top speed to their objective, usually thirty or forty miles away, and arrived a few hours before dawn. At first light, the unfortunate village was attacked, the cattle driven off as rapidly as possible, and the raiders usually back in the hills before resistance could be organized or help summoned.

There were three methods of enforcing good frontier behavior. First, if a tribe had any considerable commerce with the plains—salt, wood, and some iron were the major

---

* Sir Richard Temple quoted in Sir William Lee-Warner's *Dalhousie.*

items—it could be blockaded until it showed better manners. If a section of a tribe was felt to be planning trouble, a small force could suddenly be sent against it before its plans had matured. Finally, if an entire tribe had been raiding with such regularity that there was no alternative, a major expedition—two or three thousand men—would be sent against it to destroy its villages, burn its crops, and carry off some of its *maliks*, or headmen, as hostages until it paid the fine levied against it. No less than nineteen of these punitive expeditions were necessary between the end of the second Sikh War and the outbreak of the Bengal Mutiny in 1857, and they were not always popular back in London. In 1852, the *Times* charged Dalhousie with always being "at blows with the swarming tribes about the Khyber Pass" and pronounced that "it seems impossible that anything can be gained by such measures. If we pushed our posts to the very center of Tartary, our neighbors would be robbers still and why should we not make the best of matters on our boundaries, instead of going to fight the same game 500 miles off?"

Dalhousie always claimed to ignore newspapers, but the attacks nettled him sufficiently to produce a letter to the Board of Control: "I told the Government from the first that for many years to come they must expect perpetual forays and skirmishes on that frontier. These hills have been held by plunderers for centuries upon centuries. They regard the plains as their food and prey. This state of affairs cannot be remedied at once, and it ought not to be expected."

Of all the tribes along the border, the Afridis and the Waziris were generally conceded to be the most difficult to keep in control and the Mahsud Waziris the worst of all. There were 12,000 men in the clan—long, lean types with dark blue or red turbans, an outer garment of rough lamb's wool, white cotton trousers, and sandals. They lived in the ruggedest sort of hill country in Bannu and boasted that none of the armies that had passed through Afghanistan had ever penetrated their strongholds. A major source of their revenue came from raiding the caravans which came down each fall—and still do—from Ghazni to bring goods from Central Asia into the Indian market. Although the caravans were large—5,000 to 15,000 men, women, and children—the Waziris caused them enough trouble to make the caravans attempt to bribe their way through. The tribesmen annually refused the bribe and went on raiding. As early as 1855 John Lawrence had recommended an expedition against them, and in 1859 Brigadier Neville Chamberlain, commanding the Frontier Force, reported that the border was generally quiet until he came upon people within reach of the Mahsud Waziris. In the five-year period 1855–1860, the clan ran up a police record of 184 major offenses. The government was never anxious to sanction an expedition because expeditions were expensive, but in March, 1860, the Mahsuds forced the government's hand.

Some three thousand of them descended onto the plains with the intention of sacking the town of Tank. Tank was garrisoned by a fragment of the 5th Punjab Cavalry—158 sabers under Ressaldar* Saadat Khan—but the Ressaldar was a resourceful man. First he pretended to retreat in order to pull the Mahsud footmen well out of the hills and into the open, then wheeled around, galloped between them and the hills, charged, and managed to kill three hundred of them before the rest escaped.

Saadat Khan received a sword of honor and Brigadier Chamberlain received orders to take a force into the mountains and exact retribution. The resulting expedition was a little bigger than average, but otherwise can be taken as typical of what frontier work was like.

First, as protocol called for on the frontier, Chamberlain's political officer, Lt. Col. Reynell Taylor, issued a proclamation urging the Mahsuds to mend their ways. He pointed out that the Mahsuds had committed "injuries upon the persons and property of British subjects, and likewise upon merchants and travelers," he noted that they had attempted to plunder Tank, and he stated that the government was now convinced that its previous policy of "leniency and forbearance" was misunderstood and hence was coming into the hills to seek "redress for the past and security for the future." If, however, the Mahsuds would care to make restitution for the past and give security for the future . . .

The Mahsuds had no intention of doing any such thing, and on April 17 Chamberlain marched off with five thousand men. For the first day, the force marched north through a huge ravine, its floor covered with stones and boulders with a little stream down the middle. No Mah-

---

* Indian commander of a troop of cavalry. A warrant officer is probably the closest modern equivalent.

suds were sighted, although a barricade where defense might have been made was found and destroyed. On the second day, they came to a small village and burned it; Mahsuds began to appear on the heights to taunt Pathans serving with the Frontier Force and urge them to throw down their rifles and fight with swords as men should. On the third day another village was burnt, and on the fourth, Colonel Taylor, riding ahead with an escort of only four cavalry troopers, was jumped by three Mahsuds; though he and the escort managed to kill all three, the result could easily have gone the other way. Again in accordance with frontier protocol, Chamberlain inquired whether the tribesmen would like to claim the bodies for proper Muslim burial. The Mahsuds declined, but thanked him for the offer.

On the twenty-first and twenty-second, the force continued into the hills, destroying villages as it went, but when the camp turned in on the night of the twenty-second there was still no sign that the Mahsuds intended to make a fight. The issue was settled just as reveille sounded the next morning when three thousand tribesmen hit the rear picket. Some five hundred of them, swords in hand, came bounding down the ridge into the camp proper while their comrades on the ridge kept up a fire with their jezails and beat drums for encouragement. The Guides infantry stopped the front of the assault while a Gurkha battalion with some of the 4th Sikhs got nimbly up the flank of the ridge and put the force there to flight. It had been a neatly executed raid; Chamberlain had 63 dead and 166 wounded.

The force moved on into the hills until April 27, then paused until May 1 while supplies came up, especially a fresh issue of shoes all around to replace those ruined by two weeks' marching over rocky ground. On the afternoon of May 1, Mahsud headmen came into camp, announcing that they had been sent to make terms. Chamberlain, Taylor, and Lumsden sat down with them and Taylor went over his whole proclamation again; he explained that the British government had no desire to be in the country and even less to annex it, but that the Mahsuds would have to pay up 43,000 rupees for damages done over the past eight years and give hostages for future good behavior. The headmen protested, but promised to think it over and send an answer. When no answer came, the force moved forward and the Mahsuds fell back ahead of it. Chamberlain sent a messenger to inquire about the answer and the tribesmen replied by killing the messenger's horse.

On May 4 the force found itself facing the Barari Gorge. Trees screened the narrow mouth, and the hills on either side of it were full of Mahsuds protected by sangars.* On the Mahsud right, there was also a fortress tower and a plentitude of sharpshooters farther back on the ridge waiting for any force that tried to move along the ledge toward the tower. Chamberlain decided to make a fake at the tower and take the sangars on his right first. To this end, the 1st, 2nd, and 3d Punjab Infantry—thirteen hundred men in all—and a four-gun mountain battery struggled up the heights and formed up to attack. The 1st Punjabis were delegated to assault the chief sangar, but as they went forward the broken ground detroyed the line and men began to drop not only from jezail fire but from boulders rolled down the hills on them. They wavered; the Mahsuds sensed it and came bolting out with much shouting and waving of the long Afghan swords. The 1st Punjabis broke back on the 2nd, the 2nd broke too, and the Mahsuds went all the way to the 3d Punjabis and the four mountain guns in the reserve. The mountain guns were altogether too much for them; it was the Mahsud turn to break, and when they did the 1st Punjabis went back and took the sangar.

The mountain guns were now free to fire across the valley into the Mahsud right positions. With the artillery support, the force there under Lumsden stopped faking and cleared its front; by evening everyone was in camp three miles on the other side of the pass. The price had been 30 dead and 86 wounded. In addition to his casualties, Chamberlain now had a fairly heavy sick list and his supplies were running out. Accordingly, on May 9, he started to retrace his steps, destroying any property he might have missed on the way up. As always on the frontier, the withdrawal was difficult, with the Mahsuds nipping at the rear guard. The return march led through the town of Makin, and in a last effort to get terms, Chamberlain offered to spare it. The Mahsuds turned him down and the expedition spent May 11 burning what they could and blowing up the rest while the tribesmen howled from the heights around and took long-range shots with their jezails.

On May 20 the force was back on the plains at Bannu;

---

* A sangar is a stone breastwork thrown up by the defense in country where it is too rocky to entrench.

they had been out a month, they had taken 361 casualties—
high for a punitive expedition, where 50 was usually more
like it—and the Mahsud behavior remained as unsatisfactory as ever. Chamberlain's biography barely mentions the
entire affair.

The technique of the punitive expedition scarcely varied
from first to last. Whether it is Lumsden or Chamberlain
describing some of the first, Kipling writing toward the
end of the century, Field Marshal the Viscount William
Slim telling about a difficult withdrawal just after World
War I, or John Masters going out with his Gurkhas just
before World War II the stories remain the same and
some of them probably shouldn't be subjected to the most
stringent scholarly scrutiny. Slim has one yarn about the
colonel of a regiment and the chief of a recalcitrant tribe
comparing notes after the event. The chief complimented
the colonel on the improvement his men showed over their
previous outing and deplored the performance of his own
crowd, at the same time offering the excuse that their
rifles hadn't been properly sighted for the new ammunition. Slim has another about a chief who wanted to know
why he and his men couldn't have the same campaign
ribbons for the border wars that the British and the sepoys
got.

The expeditions were marked by a good deal of friction
between the military and the political officers—the politicals feeling that they understood the Pathan better than
the soldiers did. One of the most famous of all frontier
stories concerns a political who dropped out of sight
during a day of brisk skirmishing with the Afridis (or the
Waziris or the Mohmands or the Utman Khels—it varies
with the teller), returned at evening, sat down among a
group of infantry officers, and observed, "How were your
casualties today? Our chaps lost two."

Lumsden, who probably knew as much about the subject as anyone, set down the rules for hill fighting in
considerable detail. On entering hill country, advance
guard, flanking parties, and rear guards were to be put
out. The advance, in his opinion, had little to do but keep
alert. The flankers were to see that the ground on either
side of the track was clear. The heavy duty fell on the
rear guard, which was likely to be attacked almost daily.
In the morning, it was the duty of the rear guard to hold
the old campsite until the main force had moved on for
half a mile. In keeping the enemy at a distance during this
interval, Lumsden conceded that artillery could be useful,

but personally preferred long-range rifles. When the time came for the rear guard to move out, he advised burying a few pounds of powder or a live shell with a slow fuse attached before departing. If even one of the enemy is blown up in this way, it has "a great moral effect."

He also had a number of warnings for the novice about the Pathan as a night fighter. An imitation of the jackal's cry was the favorite form of signaling after dark, and when the calls came from all around the camp, the sentries would do well to keep doubly alert. He also describes a trick designed to deprive the camp of its proper rest and undo a young soldier's nerves. The Pathan firearm of the day was the jezail and it was quite literally a matchlock—that is, it was fired by applying a lighted match to the powder. Accordingly, two tribesmen would take a long piece of string, put slow matches between the strands about every two feet, light them, and then advance toward camp with the string pulled taut between them. In the black of a moonless night it required very little imagination on the part of the sentries to believe that a line of matchlock men was bearing down on them. The sentries would start banging away, wasting ammunition and waking the camp. When the matches went out, the Pathans simply rolled up their string and went back to repeat the trick from another direction. In Lumsden's experience, buckshot fired just past the last match on either side proved an excellent deterrent.

In moving what Dalhousie called "the outpost of the Indian Empire" from the Sutlej up to Peshawar, the British had come 500 miles closer to the Russians, but the old Russian base at Orenburg was still something over 2,000 miles away. It was not going to remain that way for very long. If the British moved, the Russians felt they had to respond, and Perovski was still governor at Orenburg; moreover, he had learned something from his earlier fiasco. Instead of trying to go the whole way to the khanates in one step, he started cautiously in 1845 to push forward a string of bases; by 1847 he had one on the Aral Sea and by 1853 he had pushed 450 miles up the Syr-Darya to erect a fort which he modestly titled Fort Perovski.

Here, for the moment, he had to stop. In the west, Russia had been pushing through Rumania toward Turkey, and Turkey declared war. Early in 1854, Britain and France—neither of whom fancied a Russian domination of the Black Sea—came in on the Turkish side and the Crimean War was on. London looked nervously at Fort Perovski and wondered whether the Russians might take them in flank by attacking India. Dalhousie was most reassuring on the subject. "If Russia should invade India with all the power she can command at present, her army would be exterminated even if it ever reached the borders of India," he wrote home. Indeed, he found the prospect quite exhilarating: "I should wish for no better lot than that such an invasion should be led by the Emperor in person and that I should be the Governor-General when it came."

There were, however, steps to be taken. Even before war was actually declared, Herbert Edwardes, now Commissioner at Peshawar, had been told to put out feelers for a treaty with Dost Mohammed—but not to appear too anxious. John Lawrence, now Commissioner of the entire Punjab, didn't really want the treaty and was even more cautious. He felt Edwardes's feelers would only encourage the Dost to "extravagant demands" and suggested that "the best attitude, perhaps the only one with Orientals, is that of complete superiority."

Dalhousie was more optimistic. As he wrote Edwardes:

I do not agree with him. I think his view founded on a fallacy. It proceeds from the assumption that the Afghans are fools, whereas I think, they are in general quite as clever as we are. The Afghans, it seems to me, must perceive that Russia, designing to swallow India, must make the first solid mouthful of Afghanistan. . . . The Afghans no doubt hate us, but they hate the Persians at least as much and the Russian certainly more.

As early as 1850 Dalhousie had been anxious to forget about the Dost's behavior in the second Sikh War and reopen some sort of relations. For one thing, he thought an agreement would help to stabilize the frontier. For another, the Persians were reaching out toward Herat again, and behind any Persian move, any Governor-General of India was apt to detect a Russian hand. The Dost could, if he would, be extremely helpful in keeping the Persians out of Herat. On the other side of the fence, the Dost was equally unenthusiastic about Persians in Herat. Moreover, he was contemplating an expedition against some troublesome brothers at Kandahar and he had no desire to have them in a position to appeal to the British. He too had been after the treaty for some time; as he wrote Dalhousie, "After all, if I have offended you, you are a great nation and can afford to forgive."

Until Crimea, London had been unenthusiastic about any arrangement with Kabul, but once the war started and the possibility of a Russian attack on India opened up, Dalhousie got instructions to go ahead. While Edwardes negotiated with the Dost, Major John Jacob set about securing the other end of the frontier by negotiating for the free use of the Bolan Pass with the Khan of Khelat. The process was a simpler one, since there was less past to forget on both sides and Jacob was authorized to sweeten the package by offering the Khan a subsidy of fifty thousand rupees a year.

At the same time, Dalhousie was busy toning down swashbucklers in India who had a number of ambitious, not to say romantic, schemes for getting at the Russians. Some wanted to send British officers north to lead the khanates of Bokhara, Khiva, and Khokand against the foe. Others wanted to attack with a mixed British-Persian force through the Caucasus. The Governor-General had no intention of letting any regiments out of India if he could possibly avoid it. The Russians might not frighten him, but the Indians did. "There is among the native population a most exaggerated idea of the power of Russia," he wrote London. A rumor that there was a Russian fleet on the way to plunder Calcutta was enough to close down the shops and send the rich scurrying to bury their money and jewels. Dalhousie was emphatic that "with such a people as this to deal with, we must on no account appear to weaken ourselves at such a time." He was only three years away from being altogether right.

By the end of 1854, Edwardes had his treaty and it was just as simple as Dalhousie had wanted it. It said only that there would be peace and friendship between the Honorable Company and the Dost, that the Honorable Company would not meddle in the Dost's territories, and that the Dost agreed to be the friend of the Company's friends and the enemy of its enemies. Note that nothing was said about the Dost's friends and enemies. Ironically, someone with a little dressier title than Edwardes had was needed for the signing, since the Dost was sending one of his sons to sign for Afghanistan. John Lawrence, who had opposed the project all along, got the job and poor Edwardes had to wait a bit longer for his knighthood.

With the Afghan treaty, Dalhousie passes from this narrative.* He left his successor with the comforting thought that while all was serene for the moment, "No prudent man, who has knowledge of eastern affairs, would ever venture to predict the maintainance of continued peace in our eastern possessions."

His successor was Charles Canning—a man with a first-rate mind and the reputation for being a very cold fish. His knowledge of India was not extensive; in Britain he had made his reputation as Post-Master General. Within days after he had arrived to study his new subject, the Persians marched on Herat.

The Crimean War was coming to an end with the Russians on the short end of the stick and the inevitable British suspicion was that they were pushing the Persians forward in Asia to make up for what they had lost in Europe. One school of thought—"the forward school"— pressed on Canning the desirability of moving up through the Bolan Pass and occupying Quetta. Canning declined and instead prepared to sail up the Persian Gulf and hit the Persians on home ground. London opinion, which had been unenthusiastic about Dalhousie becoming embroiled with border tribes, was even less so over getting involved in Persia over Herat. In October, 1856, the *Times* ran a long editorial declaring that the city was of no importance and then dealing with the alleged Russian menace:

> But here comes in the terrible apprehension—the tail of the comet that is one day to sweep us off the face of all creation. Though Herat is surrounded by deserts on all four sides, yet it is only about 500 miles from the Caspian Sea which the Russians have only to cross and they are within two months march of Herat; and at Herat they have only to fight their way through to Kabul and they are at us in India.

In the same month, the Persians took the city and

* One of his last moves was, in 1856, to annex the troublesome province of Oudh and inspire a wit to produce the following for *Punch:*

"Peccavi! I've Scinde", cried Lord Ellen, so proud
Dalhousie, more modest said "Vovi, I've Oude."

For the benefit of those who, like myself, have weak Latin "Vovi" is "I have vowed." If the joke is not immediately apparent, try it aloud a couple of times.

Canning promptly sent five thousand men up the Persian Gulf and ashore at Bushire. The *Times* grumbled and urged its readers to see if they could even find Herat on the map, since

> perhaps ten years hence everybody will be in mourning and the theaters will be empty and . . . country balls will be countermanded, and a gloom worse than the worst November fog will hang over the metropolis because, having captured Herat and stationed a large army there, and put a Clubhouse General of old age, the gout and several other disorders in command, the army has been driven out into the snows of winter or the heat of summer and disappeared.

The worst the *Times* foresaw never quite came to pass, but thirty years hence there would not be an Englishman in public life who was not acutely aware of the location of Herat and the fact that the Russians were drawing yearly closer to it. Incredible amounts of paper were consumed debating whether the city was or was not "the key to India" and, if so, what ought to be done about it. For the moment, however, there was only a dull campaign in Persia which ran into more trouble from the weather than it did from Persians. Bombay, from which most of the troops were drawn, found it mildly fruitful in "promotions, commands, staff appointments and contracts," but Calcutta, on the other side of India and hence rather out of it, dismissed the affair with "every war breaks the monotony which is the curse of India, as of all aristocratic societies."

The war-let did make a change in relations with Afghanistan. On the first day of 1857, John Lawrence and Dost Mohammed met north of Peshawar to negotiate a new treaty. The Dost made his camp at the mouth of the Khyber, and as he rode down to meet Lawrence, the British lined the route for more than a mile with seven thousand troops—with an eye to instilling "a salutary feeling of awe." The Dost did not record his feelings, but the Afridis sniped away enthusiastically and killed one lieutenant.

The new treaty went a good deal further than the old one. The Dost was to receive a lakh of rupees ($50,000) a month to keep his troops in the field against the Persians, and for the first time since the Afghan War there would be British officers in Afghanistan. A three-man mission under Harry Lumsden was to go to Kandahar to keep an eye on how the lakh of rupees per month was spent. Lawrence would have preferred to have them at Kabul, but the Dost said he could not answer for their safety there and Lawrence gave in. Lord Lytton would have done well to have listened to the same advice from the Dost's son twenty years later.

The Persian expedition wound up its duties in March; the resulting treaty turned Herat over to the Afghans. The following period of peace and quiet was brief even by Indian standards. On March 29 a sepoy named Mangal Pandy of the 34th Native Infantry sabered his adjutant, a Lieutenant Baugh, and achieved immortality; in the mutiny of the Bengal army that followed, the British called all the mutineers Pandys. Canning had been close to the mark when he told the Court of Directors at the farewell dinner they had tendered him before he left for India, "We must not forget that in the sky of India, serene as it is, a small cloud may arise, at first no bigger than a man's hand, but which, growing bigger and bigger, may at last threaten to overwhelm us with ruin."

During April the cloud was allowed to grow bigger and bigger, in spite of the fact that it was common knowledge that the sepoys had severe religious objections to the cartridge for the new Enfield rifle which was being issued as a replacement for the old, short-ranged Brown Bess. The cartridge was said to be greased with either cow fat—offensive to the Hindu—or pig fat—offensive to the Mohammedan. In early May, eighty-five troopers of the 3d Cavalry, stationed east of Delhi at Meerut, refused to drill with the new cartridge and were promptly court-martialed and sentenced to ten years' hard labor apiece. The next day—Sunday, May 10—what came to be known in India as "the Devil's Wind" started to blow in earnest. The rest of the 3d attacked the jail and set their mates free; all three regiments on the station then joined in murdering any Europeans they could lay their hands on. There were two thousand European troops at Meerut— more than enough to have coped with the outbreak—but their commander was the customary antique and by the time he had his people organized, the sepoys had completed their burning and killing and marched off to Delhi. The Europeans there were massacred, three sepoy regiments sent to help went over to the mutineers, and the aged King of Delhi hauled an old silver throne out of storage and proclaimed himself king of all India.

When the news reached the frontier, Herbert Edwardes—still at Peshawar—managed to make light of it in a letter to Lumsden at Kandahar and said, "It is all very well of you ambitious youths ... to go off to Kandahar and expect CB-ships and promotions for the pluck of it. But next time you go, please take the native army with you. . . . These mild and inoffensive Hindus have been trying to drive the English into their ships." Edwardes's tone might be flip, but the situation in the northwest was bad and he knew it. There were 11,000 European troops. The Piffers had now risen to 14,000 men and they were chiefly Mohammedan bordermen who could be counted fairly safe in a mutiny of Hindus. There were, however, 36,000 Hindu sepoy infantry.

When the news reached Lahore on May 12, John Lawrence was away at Simla, trying to shake off the agonies of neuralgia, but his second, Robert Montgomery, acted on his own. He told the local brigadier that the four sepoy regiments at Lahore had to be disarmed at once even though there was only a portion of one European regiment—the 81st—and twelve pieces of artillery to do the job. The brigadier hemmed and hawed, Montgomery insisted, and next morning close to 3,000 sepoys were paraded before 500 Europeans and told to lay down their arms. The European infantry stepped back to reveal the twelve cannon drawn up behind them and the order "Eighty-first, load!" was given. They loaded, there was a moment of silence which must have seemed an eternity for the men involved, and then the sepoys laid down their muskets and sabers. The capital of the Punjab was, for the moment, safe, and John Lawrence, who had a fondness for figures of speech involving playing cards, beamed on his men and called them "pukka trumps."

At Peshawar, Edwardes disarmed as many regiments as he could lay hands on—often over the objections of their own officers. "They had implicit confidence in their men—they had!" he wrote Lumsden. "We were youngsters who knew nothing of war. . . . The officers of the 5th Light Cavalry gave in their own swords and in some instances I believe spurs; and all were injured innocents." When the 55th Native Infantry spotted the dust of a column coming in its direction, it guessed what was up and ran into the border hills. "Poor Colonel Spottiswode committed suicide—unable to bear it!"

To keep an eye on Indian regiments too far from
Europeans to be disarmed, Edwardes proposed to Lawrence the formation of a "moveable column," which
was to "punch the head of any station that says knife!"
Lawrence took the suggestion, assigned two European
regiments and two of Piffers to the force, and put Neville
Chamberlain in command. He then set about telling the
Commander-in-Chief of India, how to run his war. There
was absolutely no authority for the Chief Commissioner of
the Punjab giving orders to the C-in-C, but Iron John took
a dim view of the Chief and the "wretched, pottering
fellows" around him. General George Anson was a man
with virtually no practical military experience and was
probably glad to take any advice he could get.*

By the book, Anson's orders should have come from
Canning, but Canning was at Calcutta, Anson was at
Ambala on the southern edge of the Punjab, and all
between was mutineer country. What communication
there was had to come by ship all the way around the tip
of India and up through Bombay.

Lawrence was emphatic from the first that the whole
thing would be won or lost at Delhi. Almost his first words
on the subject were, "The city of Delhi and the magazine
should be recovered at once." To do the job, he proposed
to supplement the European force at Meerut with another
sent down from Ambala. "If Delhi fall at once, all will go
well." Lawrence said it again and again. When Anson
seemed to be dawdling at Ambala and talked about en-
trenchments, legend has Lawrence stinging him with
"Clubs, not spades are trumps!" Poor Anson marched out
only to be carried off by the cholera, and his successor,
Reed, arrived at Delhi to find that his force was barely
strong enough to hold a ridge north of the city against the
rebels who came out "every other day with a skirmish and
a general action once a week on bhang and opium days."

To help, Lawrence started stripping the Punjab of men.
First came the Guides, who marched 580 miles in twenty-
two days during the blazing heat of an Indian May and
went into action the day they arrived.

Lawrence considerably underestimated the difficulties of
storming Delhi, and throughout the mutiny he never

* London appointed a number of improbable officers to India, but
Anson was special. He had not been on active duty since Waterloo,
and even a fond biographer has to settle for saying that he played
excellent whist.

stopped lamenting the regular military. "I do assure you that some of our commanders are worse enemies than the mutineers themselves," he wrote in one letter, and others are peppered with epithets like "that ass." On the hunch that a frontier officer might ginger up the regulars, he first sent Neville Chamberlain down, and then, in July, the whole moveable column under the remarkable John Nicholson. Variously known as "the northern tornado" and "the autocrat of all the Russias," Nicholson was a man only a John Lawrence would have put up with. "Turbulent and imperious," always in trouble with authority, he promised his chief to behave himself and promptly tried to steal an extra battery of artillery to take to Delhi with him. Lawrence sent him off anyway and chortled that Delhi "ought to fall within the next fortnight. . . . In Chamberlain and John Nicholson I rest my main hope." Edwardes seconded him: "Chamberlain and Nicholson are worth armies. . . . Amid the ruins of the Regular army these two Irregular pillars stand boldly up against the sky—and I hope the Tom Noddies may study their architecture." In actual fact, Chamberlain took a disabling wound shortly after reaching Delhi, and although Nicholson did prodigies—including cutting off a sepoy column and taking thirteen guns the day after the moveable column arrived—Delhi would hold until September and even then prove a tough nut to crack.

Lawrence had stripped the Punjab of troops to a degree which was beginning to alarm even the men closest to him. When the moveable column went, Edwardes wrote Lumsden, "Since I wrote last to you the clouds blackened terribly and Brigadier Wilson, commanding the army at Delhi, began to threaten a retreat. Sir John once more began pouring re-inforcements from the Punjab." A bit later it was Lawrence has "rather overdone himself" in the matter of troops to Delhi and finally the cry, "Anchor, Hardy, anchor!"*

There were a great many atrocities committed by both sides during the mutiny, although those committed by Indians have received a good deal more publicity. In the Punjab—although Lawrence was committed to what might be called practical mercy, he wanted to "open the door for the escape of the least guilty"—there were atroc-

---

* The line is originally Nelson's at Trafalgar. He asked Hardy how many enemy ships had been sunk and when Hardy replied that it was a complete victory, the dying Admiral gasped, "Anchor, Hardy, anchor."

ity stories; the most famous was the extermination of the 26th Native Infantry.

The 26th had mutinied; it had murdered its commanding officer with an axe, and Lawrence was so short for men that the best he had to send after them was an officer named Cooper and a force of Indian policemen. Cooper did his job—out of 600 mutineers, the great part drowned trying to cross the Ravi River and the remaining 240 were executed. The number of executions might have seemed on the excessive side, but the whole thing would probably have gone unnoticed had Cooper not published his own account of the affair in what Lawrence ever after referred to as "that nauseous dispatch." Having described how the 240 men were brought to the police station for execution and how a dry well in which to dispose of the bodies was located, Cooper proceeds to revel:

> Ten by ten the Sepoys were called forth . . . they were pinioned, linked together and marched to execution. . . . Every phase of deportment was manifested by the doomed men . . . astonishment, rage, frantic despair, the most stoic calmness. . . . About a hundred and fifty having been executed, one of the executioners swooned away—he was the oldest of the firing party—and a little respite was allowed. Then proceeding, the number had arrived at 237 when the District officer was informed that the remainder refused to come out of the bastion where they had been imprisoned temporarily. Expecting a rush and resistance, preparations were made against escape. But little expectation was entertained of the real and awful fate which had fallen on the remainder of the mutineers. . . . The doors were opened and behold! They were nearly all dead. . . . Forty-five bodies, dead from fright, exhaustion fatigue, heat and partial suffocation were dragged into the light and consigned . . . into one common pit. There is a well at Cawnpore,* but there is also one at Ujnalla.

As Canning put it, "I hope that Mr. Cooper will be judged by his acts done under stern necessity rather than his own narrative of them."

---

* Where rebels threw European women and children down a well.

During the dark days of June and July, Lawrence had been thinking ahead, and since he did a good deal of it in letters to Edwardes, he finally put it flatly to him that they should consider "what should be done, in the event of disaster at Delhi." As he saw it, the Piffers could hardly be expected to remain loyal, and treaty or no, Dost Mohammed would certainly be tempted to another try for Peshawar. Lawrence's answer was to make a virtue of necessity, invite the Dost to take Peshawar, and then try to hold the rest of Punjab with European troops. Edwardes was against the plan and Canning scotched it for good with the ringing order, "Hold on to Peshawar to the last," but the willingness of Lawrence to give ground on the frontier foreshadows the future. As Governor-General, he was the father of "masterly inactivity" in the northwest and the *bête noir* of the forward school.

In any event, there was no disaster at Delhi. On September 14 the artillery battered the gates and three columns, one led by Nicholson, swept ahead. Edwardes crowed, "Well done, our man!" and only found out later that Nicholson was carried back mortally wounded and that the whole assault had bogged down into inconclusive street fighting by British troops thoroughly drunk from the city's wine shops. Commanding General Archdale Wilson came close to panic and talked of pulling everybody back, but Nicholson on his deathbed muttered, "Thank God, I still have enough strength to shoot that man." Wilson got his nerve back, Delhi fell, and if the mutiny was not over, the end was clearly in sight. Edwardes wrote Lumsden, "We have rolled back the tide of rebellion with our own resources—by the strength of the Punjab—without a man, or a round of ammunition or a rupee from Calcutta, or England. It is much to be *humbly-proud* of . . ."

VI

Masterly Inactivity and the Forward School

With the end of the mutiny came the end of the rule of the Honorable East India Company. The old Board of Control went out the window and in its place stood a Secretary of State for India. To the title Governor-General, Canning now added Viceroy. To the army, the change meant no relief from the cumbersome three-presidency system with three separate armies, but it did mean a vast increase in the number of European troops. The pre-mutiny force had stood at 45,000 Europeans and 250,000 Indians. A few years later, the figure was 75,000 Europeans and only 140,000 Indians. For the first twenty years after the mutiny there was very little for either of them to do. Fifteen frontier expeditions went out, but only one involved serious casualties and thirteen of the fifteen produced less than one hundred dead and wounded.

This is not to say that interest in the northwest declined. In 1864 John Lawrence came back to India, this time as Governor-General—the first commoner to hold the post in almost a hundred years. He was barely off the boat when two events turned every British eye in India toward the frontier. The Russians picked up the Central Asian projects which had been interrupted by the Crimean War and moved south to take over Tashkent. In Afghanistan, Dost Mohammed died and it required no seer to predict a bloody civil war between his sons before one secured the throne. Some of the more active imaginations in London and India saw the Russians pouring down through Central Asia, taking advantage of the Afghan troubles to establish themselves there, and then marching down to India.

Lawrence thought it all pure Russophobia. He intended to stay out of Afghanistan, he did not want to send British

177

officers there as observers, and he did not intend to occupy any Afghan territory along the frontier. Any of these measures would only "engender irritation, defiance and hatred in the minds of the Afghans." As for Russia, it was his firm belief that it "would be impolitic and unwise to decrease any of the difficulties which would be entailed on Russia if that power seriously thought of invading India, as we should decrease them if we left our own frontier and met her halfway in a difficult country and possibly in the midst of a hostile population." Rather than go rampaging about Afghanistan, it was always Lawrence's opinion that in the—to him, unlikely—event of a real Russian threat to Afghanistan the matter would best be handled by a firm pronouncement from London; he thought it might take the form of a threat to send the English fleet into the Baltic.

Lawrence was not without supporters. The Secretary of State for India wrote him, "I am altogether against trying to set up a permanent influence, as it is called, at Kabul," and again, "I entirely approve of your conduct as to the Kabul Amir. Perfect neutrality is the rule I should act upon." There was, however, a large, vocal opposition which at about this time was given a title—"the Forward School." There was nothing really new about the grouping. Palmerston, Auckland, and Macnaghten had all been Forward Schoolers, and after the first failure in Afghanistan the breed never really died out; in 1856, to take a random example, a pamphleteer writes, "We have a garden which is India; the walls are the fortified towns of Tartary and Afghanistan; let the Russians once seize them and our garden is theirs."

The Forward School picked up a concrete goal in 1854 when John Jacob, commanding on the frontier in the Bolan Pass area, sent one of his young men with ten cavalrymen riding up through the pass to the town of Quetta "just to see what it looked like." Jacob wanted to occupy it; it would secure the Bolan and from there the British could operate on the flank of anyone trying to move down the Khyber. The idea didn't sell, but four years later Sir Bartle Frere, the Commissioner for Sind, was still pushing: "The value of Quetta," he wrote, "is probably quite as well known in Paris and St. Petersburg as here. . . . My *immediate* apprehension is, not that we may see a Russian General above the Bolan, but simply that if we go to sleep and neglect to secure Quetta, we may any day—when Dost Mohammed dies, or the next triennial Afghan revolution comes round—hear that Quetta has been seized by some adventurer, who may or may not be a friend of ours."

The reference to Paris reflects Frere's rather novel concern that the French as well as the Russians had designs on Afghanistan, but this quirk aside, he was an intelligent man and his views were sensible enough. As he wrote Canning in 1860, "I do not look on the Russian advance into Central Asia as any evil and I know a time must come when the limit of our legitimate influence will touch the limits of theirs. This may be done in peace, and I think the sooner the better. But I would like it to be, if possible, far from our own frontier."

In short, it was the old Palmerston position, and the difference between Lawrence and Frere came down to Lawrence's feeling that it was wisest to let the Russians struggle through Afghanistan and let them incur the wrath of the inhabitants. It doubtless gave Frere confidence that the Sind school always felt it knew how to deal with tribesmen far better than the Punjab school and that, given the opportunity, the Sind men could make the Afghans as docile as their Beluchis.

Frere might not regard the Russian advance into Asia as any evil, but a great many other people did. By November, 1864, Prince Alexander Gorchakov, the Czar's Foreign Minister, felt it necessary to issue a statement explaining Russia's position, and a very neat piece of diplomatic writing it was.

> The position of Russia in Central Asia is that of all civilized states which are brought into contact with half-savage nomad populations possessing no fixed social organization.
>
> In such cases, the more civilized state is forced in the interest of the security of its frontier and its commercial relations, to exercise a certain ascendancy over their turbulent and undesirable neighbors.

After enlarging on the enormities of uncivilized neighbors a while longer, Gorchakov went on to note sympathetically that many other nations had had similar problems—the French in Morocco, the United States with the red Indians, the British in India. Russia's recent advances had only been a minor frontier adjustment. He then closed on a heartening note:

It is needless for me to lay stress on the interest which Russia evidently has not to increase her territory and, above all to avoid raising complications on her frontiers, which can but delay and paralyze her domestic development. Very frequently of late years the civilization of these countries, which are her neighbors on the Continent of Asia, has been assigned to Russia as her special mission.

Since this was more or less what Britain had been saying about her role in India, there wasn't much available in the way of a retort. In India, some of the more ardent Forward men raised the cry "Occupy Quetta," but Lawrence stood firm and London backed him up with instructions that he was not to move forward without "precise instructions" from home.

Within six months after Gorchakov's paper, the Russians were edging south again, and in 1868 they took advantage of a silly piece of bravado on the part of the Khan of Bokhara to annex that khanate. This is not to make Gorchakov out a liar. The new Russian province of Turkestan was governed by a very able, very ambitious general named Constantine Kaufmann, and it was just as far from St. Petersburg as Calcutta was from London. A great part of the time, Turkestan made its own policy.

The fall of Bokhara roused the Forward School, and the most important result of the rousing was the *Memorandum on the Central Asian Question* by Sir Henry Rawlinson. Sir Henry was an authority who carried weight. During the Afghan War he had served as Macnaghten's assistant, and his reports from Kandahar showed a much stronger grip on reality than his chief's did from Kabul. By 1868 he was back in England and a member of Parliament. He had, in fact, at first intended to offer his observations in a speech in Commons, but on the day he was scheduled to speak that body got itself bogged down in the Irish University question and Rawlinson put himself on paper instead.

He started with the perfectly accurate assumption that the Russians would keep moving south and eventually wind up on the northern border of Afghanistan. Such a position, he felt, would entitle her "in naive estimate to challenge our Asiatic supremacy, the disquieting effect will be prodigious. . . . The approach of a rival European power betokens change, and to the active, gambling, reckless spirit of Asiatics, change is always exciting and agreeable." He also pointed out that the ability to put pressure on India would give Russia leverage on Britain in any European matter.

Having marshaled all this, he asked if Britain was any longer justified in pursuing a policy of masterly inactivity. His answer to himself was the most detailed forward program so far offered. He wanted to recognize Sher Ali, one of the Dost's warring sons, and give him a subsidy, arms, and a British mission to Kabul. Quetta was to be occupied and a railway built from Lahore to Peshawar in order to get troops up to the border in a hurry if necessary.* He conceded that some Afghans might not be terribly keen about the proposals and then dismissed them with ". . . it is now a matter for serious consideration whether in submitting to continued exclusion from Kabul we are not sacrificing substantial interests to an undue regard for Afghan feeling."

The *Times* considered all this and raised the question, "Shall we some day or other have to fight with Russia for the possession of India. . . . Ought we not to secure, while we can, the control, command or possession of Afghanistan? The stride made by the Czar's forces in Bokhara is looked upon as a warning not to be mistaken." The *Times*'s own answer was a firm no. Invasion of Afghanistan might be popular in India because it would mean not only "active employment for a military population, but chance of promotion, glory and gain." The *Times*, however, was not to be tempted by promotion, glory, or gain. In its eyes, the real danger lay in rushing out to meet the anticipated danger halfway.

In January, 1869, John Lawrence—forty years of Indian service behind him—took the traditional post at the top of the steps at Government House and waited for Richard Bourke, Lord Mayo, to climb the steps and replace him. No one thought a great deal of Mayo. By common consent he was a decent enough man with a capacity for hard work, but his background was almost entirely in Irish affairs, and opinion held that he was not a

---

* Rawlinson had a similarly elaborate program for Persia, including support for the Shah's desire for a naval force on the Persian Gulf in spite of "the singular maritime inaptitude of the Persians."

thrusting man, but one more likely to follow policies than create them.

Accordingly, it must have come as a surprise when Mayo, scarcely off the boat, set about making arrangements to meet Sher Ali. As he wrote a friend, he wanted to fringe India with "strong, independent, friendly, though not altogether neutral states." He claimed not to fear the Russians—if they came, they could be destroyed in one campaign and they knew it. In April the meeting came about amid the fields of tents and lines of soldiery normal to an Indian durbar. The Amir got a handsome gift of money, but he did not get a firm promise of military aid against the Russians and he did not get—this is perhaps even more important—a firm promise of British aid against his brothers, with whom he had been feuding with varying success for the past five years. Sher Ali's people felt that this was a more or less open invitation to the brothers to revolt and represented a hope on the part of the British that "our family shall exterminate one another." For the moment, however, both the border and Central Asia were quiet. In all of 1869 there was only one small version of what the *Times* called "those tedious hill campaigns which have been so prodigal with both money and life." Prince Gorchakov assured London once more that Russia felt Afghanistan quite outside her sphere of influence, and a British diplomat went off to St. Petersburg unofficially to try to get a specific agreement on just where Afghanistan's northern border was.

The new negotiations went on for four years; during that time, the debate over Russia in Central Asia churned on and then boiled to a climax in the fall of 1872, when the Russians sent a smallish expedition against Khiva. Its commander got careless and allowed his force to march along without any scouts out; the Khivans pounced on him and killed almost all his horse and camel transport. Back went the Russians, but there was little doubt in London or Calcutta that Kaufmann would send another expedition. Jingo journalists were already predicting this was only one more move in the series by which Russia would eventually get to Herat, "the key to India." In Russia there was a good deal of pained comment that anyone should object to what Russia was doing. The official *Gazette* noted that any time Russia took steps in Central Asia "foreign papers have been in the habit of imputing to her aggressive designs alleged to be directed against the British possessions in the East Indies." A little later, the same paper

asked whether the British would ask Russian permission
when the time came to get tough with Kabul. It did con-
cede that its own military did from time to time get out of
hand: ". . . not a few expeditions were undertaken in
times past not because they were indispensable for military
or other public purposes, but in order to supply officers and
men with opportunities for distinction and advancement."
The language is hardly distinguishable from the *Times*
discussing Indian feelings about a war in Afghanistan. In
the case of Khiva, however, the *Gazette* assured its readers
that genuine interests were at stake.

The St. Petersburg *Vedomosti* did mention that getting
Russian troops close to India might make for useful leverage in the event of further Anglo-Russian troubles in
Europe. The *Journal* in the same city colored the Russian
case a little—much in the manner of the British reflecting
on the morals of the Sikh Maharani—by retailing a story
about the Khan of Khiva going into a rage when he heard
of the advance and "slaying with his own hands" one of
his attendants.

In the British press there were predictions of a Russian
invasion of India and letters to the editor, signed "A
Frontier Officer" and the like, threatening that the Afghans were coming even if the Russians weren't. The first
public hint that it was all nonsense and that negotiations
were in progress came in December, when a Berlin correspondent reported that St. Petersburg rumor had it that
the British ambassador, Lord Augustus Loftus, had assured Gorchakov that Britain would not stand in Russia's
way at Khiva so long as she did not menace Afghanistan
or any of the territory between Afghanistan and Khiva
claimed by Sher Ali. The Russian response was to admit
that a new expedition against Khiva was in preparation,
but that it was a small one, that it was intended only to
punish acts of brigandage, and that "not only was it far
from the intention of the Emperor to take possession of
Khiva, but positive orders had been prepared to prevent
it, and directions given that the conditions imposed should
be such as would not in any way lead to the prolonged
occupation of Khiva." Colonial powers were quite used to
one another saying one thing and doing something else.
The *Times* said it would be very nice if what the Russians
said was true but felt it necessary to add that nothing a
diplomat says really binds government for the future or in
the event of changed conditions. The editorial agreed that
it would be a splendid thing for Anglo-Russian relations if

Kaufmann's troops did quit Khiva once proper chastisement had been handed out, but it didn't really sound as if
it expected them to.

On February 12, 1873, the fruits of the negotiations
were presented to the public. Gladstone's government
offered the correspondence to Parliament, and what it
seemed to add up to was that the northern boundary of
Afghanistan had been agreed upon by Russia and Britain
and that Russia had agreed to keep on her side of it.
When the news reached Sher Ali, he was furious about his
boundaries being settled over his head, and the British had
to propitiate him with fifty thousand pounds and five
thousand Enfield rifles.

Once the two high contracting powers got to thinking
about the arrangement neither was particularly happy
with it. In London, the *Times* muttered that ". . . after this
first feeling of satisfaction, the public can hardly fail to
ask a further question. . . . What is the importance of
determining the northern boundaries of Afghanistan? . . .
Are we to be understood, in short, as having practically
partitioned Asia and consigned the whole region north of
Afghanistan to Russia?" The reaction in India wasn't any
better. "Any fixed line up to which the Russians may thus
be invited to come and beyond which our action will be
fettered" was "out of the question."

In Russia, the unofficial organ of the Russian Foreign
Office started by complaining that the British meant to
exercise an exclusive influence in Afghanistan. It then
went on: "England evidently wants to place Russia under
her tutelage. In whatever direction we may move, we
must be prepared to receive an English Note and undergo
the infliction of a diplomatic campaign. . . . This sort of
treatment no independent Power will submit to."

On March 19—just as Kaufmann was marching off for
Khiva with 12,000 men and forty guns—the *Times* responded with ladylike exasperation to the *Gazette* by
noting that "we almost despair of convincing any foreigner that a policy of colonization differs essentially from a
policy of conquest, or that a nation may have an acquisi-
tive propensity without being aggressive." The distinction
was too fine for the Russians. The St. Petersburg *Golos*—
the mouthpiece of the Russian War Office—took up the
fight and in rapid succession first called for the subjugation
of Khiva, then undertook to prove that annexation was
inevitable, and finally trumpeted, "Let us announce openly
and boldly that our troops will never turn their backs [on

Khiva] whatever our detractors may have to say. Russia is neither Burma nor Kashmir and need not shrink from avowing her deeds. She is quite competent to determine without foreign assistance where her frontiers are to be and protect them if necessary."

Tempers got worse. The *Times* replied that the British too "have interests in Asia to protect, and we also are strong enough to protect them." From here on the debate began to degenerate into a brawl. The *Gazette* said that the intent to evacuate Khiva could not be taken as a "solemn promise" and added that if the British didn't like what the Russians were doing in Asia, well, the Russians didn't like the size of the British navy any better. The *Times* snapped back that Khiva was a pretty poor conquest anyway. While the Shah of Persia was visiting Britain, the St. Petersburg *Mir* set a low for the whole business with an editorial which talked about "Bloody Albion" and, in some confusion of national animals, went on about the "perfidious and cruel" British tiger. The *Times* treated the matter as virtually beneath reply and simply urged Englishmen to ". . . treat the Shah with all possible courtesy undeterred by the jealous criticism of any foreign press."

In St. Petersburg, Augustus Loftus expressed regrets about the tone of the Russian press but had to admit that the articles in the British press had also produced "some soreness."

On June 27, 1873, word reached London that Kaufmann had taken Khiva with little or no difficulty. Once there he of course stayed, and no one was really particularly surprised. Loftus asked about the assurances on evacuation, but the best the Russians were able to come up with was a rather lame excuse that the Czar had forgotten just what assurances he had given and a promise that nothing of the sort would happen again. Loftus was inclined to be philosophical about it. So long as conquests by Russian officers in Central Asia were rewarded by the order of St. George, this sort of thing was bound to happen. Loftus's solution was to quiet them down by giving them the Order before they went out.

In January, 1874, Gladstone dissolved his government, went to the country, and took a sound thumping which brought the Conservatives back into power with Benjamin Disraeli at the helm and Robert Arthur Talbot Gascoyne-

Cecil, 3d Marquis of Salisbury, as Secretary of State for India. Salisbury was one of the bluest bloods in England—the family had been prominent since Henry VIII. He detested Disraeli personally and considered him a foreigner because he was Jewish, but on the Afghan question they held tolerably close views. Both wanted more British presence there and Salisbury urged the position on Lord Northbrook, now Governor-General, who had succeeded the unfortunate Lord Mayo after he had been stabbed to death while on an inspection tour. He explained to Northbrook that he did not expect the Russians to attack India, but he did think they might encourage the Afghans to make trouble—hence a British representative at Kabul was desirable. He was under heavy pressure from Forward men on his own Indian Council. In 1874, Bartle Frere circulated a strong letter to the Council members in which he envisioned an unpleasant day when the Russians might "drill the Amir's troops, cast his cannon, coin his rupees and physic him and his subjects."

Even John Lawrence conceded in a reply to Frere that the approach of Russia to India was "fraught with future trouble and danger." His own solution was to "watch events." As he wrote Salisbury, "The great point of the matter is, that Russia should understand that England is prepared to defend her hold on India at any cost. Nothing short of this will suffice if the march of events brings Russia to the frontier of India; but that conviction of England's resolution will, I believe, prove quite effectual." Frere's answers were in the Rawlinson line—troops into Quetta; British missions at Kabul, Herat, and Kandahar.

Salisbury was urging his Governor-General on with letters saying, "We cannot leave the keys of the gate in the hands of a warder of more than doubtful integrity, who insists, as an indispensable condition of his service, that his movements shall not be observed." Northbrook actually got it down to a conference with Sher Ali's agent at Simla and was asked what the British policy would be in the event of Russia stepping over Afghanistan's northern border. Northbrook's own inclination was to promise him money, arms, and troops, but London told him that the question was too important to be discussed at the time. Northbrook replied that if agents were forced on Sher Ali without assurances they were likely to "occasion a break," and that shortly.

Given the differences between them, one man or the other had to go. Accordingly, both Disraeli and Salisbury must have been pleased when Northbrook resigned before 1875 was out and left them free to pick their own candidate. The choice—after three other men had turned the job down—was Lord Lytton, the man who would proclaim Victoria Empress of India. In his instructions to Lytton, Disraeli called the state of affairs in Central Asia "critical" and observed that "sentiments of irritation and alarm at the advancing power of Russia ... find frequent expression through the English press."* Lytton's instructions were firm; he was to take "decided measures for counteracting the danger of the Russian advance in Central Asia and in particular for re-establishing our influence in Afghanistan."

To do the reestablishing, he was empowered to offer an increased and regular subsidy to the Amir, a promise of British support for his favorite son in the event of the Amir's death, and a pledge of "material aid" in case of Russian aggression. Salisbury's aims were actually modest enough. As he told Disraeli, he was worried about the lack of information from Afghanistan; he wanted agents at Herat and Kandahar, but was quite willing to forgo one at Kabul as he judged the place "too fanatical." Lytton was more ambitious. He was a disciple of Bartle Frere's, and the two men actually crossed paths at Suez as Lytton went out to India. Frere took the opportunity to press his views, and what they were are quite clear from a letter he had written Salisbury from India only a few weeks earlier. He wanted an ambassador assigned to the Amir even if he couldn't go to Kabul but had to operate at a distance— much as Claude Wade had with the Sikhs in the days of Runjeet Singh. When the Amir and the ambassador did meet, Frere wanted enough soldiery present to make a distinct military impression, but he warned against sending officers who were "bullies and swaggerers" and added, "There are plenty of English officers who do not dislike Afghans or natives generally, and who can be trusted to treat them, as gentlemen should, without flattery or nonsense." He was adamant about offering the Amir any "humbug" about the peaceable nature of Russian designs in Afghanistan and wanted the ambassador to

* Helped along by a Russian Rawlinson-Frere type, M.A. Terentyef, who published *Russia and England in Central Asia*, which speculated on Russian aid for a second Bengal Mutiny and on Russian pressure in India once Britain and Russia came to blows over Turkey again.

be altogether frank about the fact that Britain's interest in the country stemmed from its usefulness as a buffer against Russia. On the other hand, the Amir was not to be given an overweening sense of his own importance, but rather shown clearly that his position was that of "an earthen pot between two iron ones." Whether Salisbury forwarded a copy of his letter to Lytton or whether Frere used the same figure of speech when they met at Suez, the phrase made a profound impression on Lytton and he used it in one of his less delicate comments on Kabul.

The earthen pot was to be assured that the British desired no territory, but only the presence of observers to keep an eye on the Russians up north. Lytton himself would have liked to have occupied Quetta, but the Russians had already heard enough on the subject to send notes objecting.

In addition to the three specific concessions Lytton had been empowered to make to Sher Ali, he also had a very loose clause in his instructions should the Amir turn him down. It said that he could reconsider "from a new point of view the policy to be pursued in reference to Afghanistan." Before trying the new point of view, however, Lytton tried the ambassadorial system. He took over as Governor-General in April, 1876, and almost immediately began negotiations designed to have Sir Lewis Pelly, a cousin of Rawlinson's, invited to Kabul to discuss "matters of common interest." Sher Ali considered the project dangerous to the life of the envoy and, although he didn't say so, probably thought it likely to be an incitement to some of his own domestic enemies. He countered by offering to send his own ambassador down to India for talks. Lytton said no and Sher Ali tried again. Either an Afghan agent would meet Pelly on the frontier or an Indian national maintained by the British at Kabul would come down and report to the Governor-General. Lytton picked the latter course, and in October there were two fruitless interviews at Simla which consisted of nothing more than Lytton demanding British officers in Afghanistan and backing his demand with a threat to proceed on the frontier "without regard to Afghan interests." In short, he was sliding over to the "new point of view" section of his instructions. From London, Salisbury had reaffirmed his free hand in a letter which contained the phrase ". . . you do not address advice to a billiard player at the moment he is about to strike."

In due course, Sher Ali sent his Prime Minister, a sick

old man, down to Peshawar, where he and Pelly wrangled away until March, 1877, when the Prime Minister died and Lytton told Pelly not to receive a new envoy from Kabul even though he knew one was on the way. Lytton was no longer on his own; there were a number of new pieces on the chess board. Russia had been working itself up to another war with Turkey, Disraeli called a conference at Constantinople to head it off and failed, and no one doubted that it was only a matter of days before Russian troops started to move. Once they moved, Salisbury made a guess to Lytton that "they may think it judicious to keep our hands full, which a little pressure at Kabul will, they hope, do." He did not, however, look for serious trouble; the Russians were little more than "the size of the patch they occupy on the map," and there was nothing in their real power to explain "the abject terror which deprives so many Anglo-Indians and so many of our military party of their natural sleep."

His confidence was not shared in India. After the closedown of the Peshawar conferences, Lytton wrenched a treaty from the Khan of Khelat which permitted him to occupy Quetta. In April '77, Russia and Turkey finally did go to war. Lytton's next proposal was to occupy Kabul, Ghazni, and Jalalabad and establish advance posts as far forward as Kandahar, Herat, and Balkh. Salisbury made an effort to soothe him. "If I took your gloomy view," he wrote, "I should commence immediate enquiries as to the most painless form of suicide." It seemed to him that Lytton listened too much to his soldiers, and it was Salisbury's contention that they were dangerous advisors on military policy. "No lesson seems to be so deeply inculcated by the experience of life," he informed his Governor-General, "as that you never should trust experts. If you believe the doctors, nothing is wholesome; if you believe the theologians, nothing is innocent; if you believe the soldiers, nothing is safe."

Salisbury was as worried as anyone else about the Russians winning too much from the Turks and taking control of the Straits, but his terrors did not extend to General Kaufmann leading a march on Calcutta. In June, he went before the House of Lords and tried to put the dangers on the northwest frontier into some sort of perspective. "I cannot help thinking," he said, "that in discussions of this kind a great deal of misapprehension arises from the popular use of maps on a small scale. As with such maps you are able to put a thumb on India and a finger on Russia, some persons at once think that the political situation is alarming and that India must be looked to. If the noble Lord would use a larger map ... he would find that the distance between Russia and British India is not to be measured by the finger and thumb, but by the rule."

As the Russians went about trouncing the Turks, however, the militancy in London began to match the spirit in India. The word "jingo," in fact, derives from a music hall song of the period: "We don't want to fight, but, by jingo if we must . . ." Victoria herself told Disraeli, "What the Queen wishes to repeat again and to insist on is that the Emperor be told distinctly though confidentially that we will not allow him to go to Constantinople." Nevertheless, the Emperor's troops kept moving that way until the ironclads of the British Mediterranean fleet were sent through the Dardanelles and into the Golden Horn. Through the early months of 1878 the ships sat on one side of Constantinople and the Russian troops on the other. In March Parliament voted six million pounds war credits, and in April Salisbury ordered seven thousand Indian troops to embark for Malta.

The number of troops wasn't likely to be much help if war did come, but India judged rightly that it was quite large enough to produce new Russian pressure in the northwest. For the past year Russian scouting parties had been nosing along the frontier, and now they moved troops to the northern border of Afghanistan. Rumors coming down to India put the number as high as 80,000; actually there were only 15,000, and Lytton's intelligence on them seems to have been remarkably good. At one point they were moved two hundred miles, and he not only knew of the move but had considerable detail on how badly they had suffered from the heat.

Actually, the major Russian effort to "create a diversion by way of Afghanistan" (as they phrased it) was going to be diplomatic. In the same month that troops were ordered to Malta, St. Petersburg determined to send a mission to Kabul to see if they could get a treaty. The officer in charge was General Stolietoff; there were six junior officers and an escort of twenty-two Cossacks. When Sher Ali heard they were coming, he seems to have perceived the consequences to himself quite clearly. He wrote urging them not to send the mission, made the same representation about being unable to guarantee its safety, and said he wouldn't receive them if they did come.

Stolietoff kept right on coming. Feelers went down to India for British assistance, but Lytton put out the word that British attitude was to be "vigilantly, but imperturbably passive."

By the time Stolietoff actually reached Kabul in July, however, things had taken a considerable turn. Salisbury, now promoted Foreign Minister, had assembled the great powers at the Congress of Berlin, the Russian treaty with the Turks had been revised to the satisfaction of everybody except the Russians, and the threat of war had vanished. Kaufmann had to tell Stolietoff "not to go generally as far as would have been advisable if war with England had threatened." Salisbury and Disraeli came back to London in triumph and the Prime Minister told a cheering crowd, "Gentlemen, we bring you peace and, I think I may say, peace with honour."

Lytton didn't see it that way at all. In an angry letter home, he pointed out that the year before "We were told ... that our warnings were witless; our anxieties nightmares; our calculations, the crude excursions of an untutored fancy; our conclusions, airy fabrics, raised ... from a foundation which, while we were building on it, had already vanished from the region of fact." One can almost feel him pausing for breath before sailing into his next. *"Now* the Russian outposts are actually 150 miles nearer than they were *then. Now* the Russian officers and troops have been received with honour at Kabul within 150 miles of our frontier and of our largest military garrison. And this is a distance which even on the large scale maps recommended to us looks very small indeed."

Lytton knew exactly what he proposed to do about it. He was going to send his own mission to Sher Ali—a man he was currently characterizing as "not only a savage, but a savage with a touch of insanity"—and there was to be no nonsense about dynastic guarantes or a subsidy. If the Amir would not receive the mission, accept a second permanent one at Herat, and turn over control of all Afghanistan's foreign affairs to India, Lytton proposed to occupy the Kurram Valley and Kandahar. Salisbury assured Lytton that Augustus Loftus was asking questions in St. Petersburg about the Russian Kabul mission and told him to do nothing until the questions were answered. Lytton was out of patience. In September the Kabul mission began to assemble under General Neville Chamberlain, and since Chamberlain himself thought the Amir no more likely to comply with the demands than "to be expected to turn Christian and apply for a bishopric" an army began to assemble for the necessary follow-up.

To make sure the Home Government didn't pull the rug out from under him, Lytton announced the mission and an angry note went from Disraeli to the Indian Office:

> I have read with some alarm the V-Roy's telegram. It appears that Lord Lytton cd* not have been kept au fait to the communications that have taken place and are taking place betw. HM's Government and that of Russia on the subject of Afghanistan. . . . As far as they have proceeded and as far as I can judge the explains of the Russian Govt. are satisfactory. . . . What injurious effect Lytton's policy, ostentatiously, indiscreetly, but evidently officially announced in the Calcutta correspondence of the *Times* of yesterday may produce, I cannot presume to say.

Calcutta felt a good deal more assured about the meeting. The *Times* was informed by its man there that the mission "forms but a single move in an extensive concerted scheme for the protection of India." In other words, there would appear to have been a good deal more in the wind than anyone would discuss for publication.

On September 22 a portion of the mission proceeded into the Khyber. Neville Chamberlain felt so certain that it would be turned back by the border guards at Ali Masjid that only a handful of men under a more junior officer were sent in order that—if necessary—rebuff could be made to appear less serious. Major Louis Cavagnari drew the assignment and was stopped as expected. Of Faiz Mahomed Khan who commanded the guard he inquired, "Will you oppose the passage of the mission by force?" The commander assured him that he would and added, "You have had a straight answer."

As Salisbury remarked, "We are in the mess and must get out of it; my counsel is to minimize both the action and the splash." Disraeli had a good deal more to say. "He was told to wait until we have received the answer from Russia to our remonstrances. I was very strong with him on this. . . . He disobeyed us. I was assured by Lord Salisbury that under no circumstances was the Khyber Pass to be attempted. He was told to send the Mission to Kandahar. He has sent it by the Khyber and received a

---

* Disraeli was fond of this sort of shorthand.

snub, wh. it may cost us much to wipe away." The Prime Minister then put his finger on the crux of the matter with the observation that "when V'Roys and Comms-in-Chief disobey orders, they ought to be sure of success in their mutiny."

The Russian press speculated joyously on the British lion breaking his teeth on the rocks of Afghanistan. Continental papers predicted that if Britain moved into the country the Russians would move on Merv.*

Far from being contrite about his mutiny, Lytton was begging London for permission to commence hostilities immediately. Specifically, he wanted to issue a manifesto (he might have remembered Auckland and been more careful about Simla Manifestos), chase the Afghans out of the Khyber, occupy the Kurram Valley, and advance from Quetta to Kandahar. London was not so precipitous. Salisbury saw nothing but trouble in trying to force the Khyber and even more in going to Kabul. His advice was to go only to Kandahar, where the Amir was not particularly popular. Disraeli said flatly that the whole business was simply Lytton's attempt to force London's hand. In all, the Amir was to have one more chance. It wasn't much of a chance. On November 2 Lytton was allowed to send an ultimatum which demanded that Sher Ali get rid of Stolietoff, called the rejection of the British mission an "act of enmity and indignity to the Empress of India," and demanded a full apology for the same in writing. Further, the Amir was to get ready to receive a permanent mission, and "Unless these conditions are accepted fully and plainly by you and your acceptance received by me not later than November 20, I shall be compelled to consider your intentions as hostile and to treat you as a declared enemy of the British Government."

No one really expected the ultimatum to be accepted, but it might serve to make a war which was not altogether popular a little more so. The antiwar party had found a powerful voice in John Lawrence, who first raised all the obvious objections in two long letters to the *Times*: If Sher Ali was dethroned, who was to be put in his place? If some new Shah Shujah could be located and enthroned, how was he to be kept there except by a permanent British occupation at vast expense? In short, how were the

---

* The Irish enjoyed the discomfort of their old enemies in London. One editorial said, "There can hardly be in the whole world one manly heart that will not be moved to admiration of the Amir's patriotism and courage."

troubles of the first Afghan War to be avoided? Lawrence then accepted the chairmanship of an Afghan Committee which took the position that the government had no right to go to war when Parliament was out of session and unable to vote on the matter. One of his coworkers, the Duke of Argyll, even undertook to explain or at least to mitigate Sher Ali's reception of the Russian mission. He had been disappointed in the Ambala conference, he was fearful of the British using Afghanistan as a base against Russia, his reception of the Russians "need not have had a very serious interpretation put on it."

At Kabul, the unfortunate Amir knew a serious interpretation was being put on it and wrote Kaufmann for Russian aid. With the Treaty of Berlin signed, Kaufmann apparently calculated that getting tangled with the British in Afghanistan was more than even his slack superiors at St. Petersburg would tolerate and said no.

Viceregal feeling can best be gaged by the comment of one of Lytton's aides, who said, "Our principal anxiety now is lest the Amir should send an apology or the Home Government suddenly interfere."

In India at that time the Northwestern Railway came to an end at Jhelum—southeast of Peshawar—and here trains were putting off stores far faster than the short-handed supply officers were able to deal with them. Mules, ponies, and donkeys sent up for use as transport died for want of somebody to attend to them. For miles along the track, grain and other perishables had been dumped to spoil or to be stolen by enterprising villagers. From Jhelum north, everything moved by bullock carts—chiefly leased from a reluctant local peasantry—and the Grand Trunk Road was choked with them as infantry and cavalry regiments tried to move up through the confusion.

The force was to move out in three columns the minute the November 20 deadline expired. The most easterly, under Sir Samuel Browne with 15,000 men, was to force the Khyber. The center, 6,500 men under Frederick Roberts, was to occupy the Kurram Valley and then move on north to the Shutagardan Pass commanding Kabul. In the west Sir Donald Stewart and twelve thousand men were to go by the old Bolan Pass route, reinforce the Quetta garrison, and occupy Kandahar. The overall object was not only to chastise the Amir but to provide India with something Disraeli had just thought of—a "scientific frontier." Even the Prime Minister's supporters wished he had refrained from the suggestion that there might be a little territorial aggrandizement involved in the operation.

At 3 A.M. on November 21 the first troops were already over the border. In fairness, there was something more involved than hurrying to the fray; the columns had only a few weeks to get the job done before snows closed the passes for the winter. It was an infinitely better equipped army than the one that had gone north in 1838. Instead of Brown Bess muskets it had breach-loading rifles, and though the cavalry and the lancers still carried weapons of another age these were now supplemented by carbines. The Afghans had a few Enfields of their own, but the basic weapons were still the jezail and the long Afghan knife. The one notable improvement was a properly handled artillery. The guns themselves were no great shakes, but the gunners handled themselves so well that a number of British officers entertained the suspicion that they had been trained by the Russians. Actually, it seems far more likely that they were trained by men who fled over the border after the mutiny of the Bengal army in 1857.

Although Sher Ali had a force estimated at fifty thousand infantry and ten thousand cavalry,* the campaign of 1878 produced only one action of the sort designed to get generals KCB's and promotions. Sam Browne's column advanced into the Khyber as far as Ali Masjid, paused before the great rock rising 350 feet from the bottom of the pass and crowned by a fort, and spent the rest of the day keeping out of the way of extremely accurate artillery fire. During the day and night that followed, however, a detachment of Guides infantry, the 1st Sikhs, and the Leicestershire Regiment scrambled and stumbled over "the most curious pile of mountains ever traversed" on the east of the pass. The dawn of November 22 found them thoroughly winded, but far enough into the hills to descend on the Afghan rear. The Afghans pulled out; Sam Browne paused long enough to make sure they really had left and, amid considerable sniping, marched through the Pass to Sale's old camp at Jalalabad.

In the west, Stewart's force retraced the steps of the 1838 expedition north from Sukkur and found the country just as inhospitable as their predecessors had. "A melancholy waste" was one comment, and the pass itself became known as "the slayer of camels" as the poor animals died

---

* Almost certainly very high; Roberts consistently reported more men ahead than were really there.

from lack of forage and the bullocks literally tore their feet off pulling the heavy guns. As before, the guns wound up being manhandled through. To make things worse, the temperature stood around zero for much of the time and the Indian troops suffered badly and the camp followers worse. Stewart cursed his supply department for not sending them off better clothed and wrote his wife, "I am not very clear about the rights and wrongs of this war, but we could not over look the rejection of our mission, though whether it was wise to send a mission in the way it was done is quite another question. There does not seem to be much chance of a scrimmage in this part of the world, and I am sorry for it, on account of the troops have undergone so much hard work. . . ."

The only general to get the action Stewart so badly craved was Roberts. Frederick Roberts, known to officers and enlisted men as "Bobs," was the son of General Abraham Roberts, who had commanded Shah Shujah's troops at Kabul in the last war and gotten himself sent down country by insisting too strongly to his superiors that they were of no use whatsoever as a fighting unit. The son inherited the father's independence of mind. One critic conceded him great energy but considered that his "constitutional daring and his contempt for an uncivilized foe predisposed him to rash resolves and hasty action." The remarkable Sir Charles MacGregor considered that he was "not up to the mark and will break down when a crisis comes." On the other hand, MacGregor rarely had a good word for anybody and this comment is one of his milder efforts. When operating with full steam up, he could dismiss three officers in a single sentence as "a shallow lazy fellow," "an affected ass," and "a bumptuous ass."

Roberts was a spare, bantamy little man with a funny droopy moustache but very hard eyes. On November 21 he hustled his force into the Kurram Valley—sixty miles long and three to twelve miles wide—and from the first the hard eyes were fixed on the Peiwar Kotal, the pass leading up and out of the northern end of the Kurram. The top of the pass was 3,800 feet above the valley floor, and here, if Roberts's spies had it right, the Amir's force would make its stand. By the afternoon of November 28 Roberts was close enough to rush part of the 29th Punjabis to the foot of the pass in hopes of grabbing some cannon his spies said the enemy had left there. Instead of guns, they found stiff fire from the top of the pass and had to fall back, bringing the information that the only path up was so narrow that troops would have to make the ascent in single file or struggle through the pine woods on either side, inevitably losing formation in the process.

Roberts made camp to think it over, the Afghan artillery promptly shelled the campsite briskly, and Roberts fell back to get out of range. As one officer pointed out, if the Afghan gunners had waited a little longer—until the troops were so fully unpacked that they couldn't move out quickly—the shelling might have done serious damage.

Roberts looked the ground over for two days and decided to flank the position out. He would lead the bulk of his force, some 2,200 men, around his own right flank. A smaller force would hold the camp and feint straight ahead while a still smaller unit would swing wide around the left as a distraction. At ten o'clock on the night of December 1, Roberts led the men out. It was windy, cold, and very, very dark. The assault units were the 2nd and 29th Punjabis, the 5th Gurkhas, and the 72nd Highlanders. Behind each regiment came its ammunition mules and the stretcher-bearers. All the men were quite aware that if they didn't reach the high ground to the right of the Peiwar Kotal before daylight they were likely to need the stretcher-bearers badly.

The column lost time when part of it took a wrong turn and had to retrace its steps, then lost some more as they found the dry bed of a mountain stream by which they were ascending tougher going than anyone had expected. It was rocky, and as one man said, "About the most trying stuff to walk over I have ever seen." First light was just coming on; the column was still not at the top and suddenly there was a rifle shot, then another from a Pathan company of the 29th. Roberts assumed that the shots were an attempt to give a warning to the Pathans on the Afghan side. If so, it failed, but Roberts pulled the 29th back and put the Highlanders and the Gurkhas into the lead. He had his surprise. As dawn broke, there was light fire from a barrier of fallen trees above them, but most of the garrison must still have been asleep, because the Scots and the little Nepalese dodged forward through the pine trees to carry the barrier and then moved on to take two more like it. By eight in the morning the force was firmly in position on the plateau—and in no position to go anywhere. There was a deep, steep gulley which no one had anticipated between Roberts and the Peiwar Kotal, and there were Afghans on the far side in force.

The early fighting had left the Highlanders and the

Gurkhas scattered; all Roberts had left until they reassembled were the suspect Punjabis. The Sikh companies looked ready for work, but the Pathans seemed sullen so the Sikhs were sent forward by themselves. Twice they charged, and all they had to show for it were heavy casualties, including a dead commanding officer. The Afghans then came on themselves and twice got within thirty yards of the British position before being beaten back; the whole business was beginning to look like a bad day's work until Roberts's Chief Engineer found a spot from which the four mountain guns the force had with it could be brought to bear on the main Afghan position. They went to work about one o'clock. By three, Roberts was able to move his men forward again; the Afghans had pulled down off the Kotal.*

The cost of the action was minor for the British—twenty dead and eighty-three wounded. One more death was added when the first man of the 29th Punjabis to fire during the flanking movement was judged by a Court of Inquiry to have attempted a warning and sentenced to death. The second man pleaded that he'd fired only because he thought the fighting had started and got off with seven years. Meanwhile, Roberts marched north to the Shutagardan Pass, found it undefended, and from the top of the pass observed that he could move quickly onto Kabul. His orders forbade it; he brought his men back into the Kurram Valley to spend the winter. It was not a particularly comfortable winter. "Letter writing was a difficulty as the ink froze in the bottles," one man wrote, "and washing was out of the question, as sponges and water were alike blocks of ice."

In the west, Stewart was pushing along in spite of an alarming number of desertions. A good many of his men had been recruited at the last moment to fill out regiments under circumstances which he himself said smacked of the press gang. Others were in such poor physical condition as to have been scarcely worth pressing in the first place. In spite of all, he entered Kandahar on January 8, 1879, after covering four hundred miles in six weeks. The troops were greatly impressed with the massive mud walls, very high and in some places forty feet thick, but less so with what was behind them: "Trees, spectators, beggars and ruins." Two of the spectators promptly tried to assassinate

* In his own account of the affair, Roberts suggests a figure of 18,000 Afghans on the Kotal. Actually, there were about 4,000.

two British lieutenants and Stewart wrote his daughter, "There are a lot of Ghazis* about the place, but I have told the troops they must look after themselves, as I am not going to let them bully us, or frighten us into *not* going about the town or wherever we like." Shortly after he wrote another letter, the first sentence of which pretty well sums up the troubles the British had had and continued to have in Afghanistan: "I am in a difficulty to know what to do with the country now we have got it."

The Khyber, the Kurram Valley, Kandahar—all the immediate objectives had been gained, but it was apparent even to the people back home that the campaign had not been a particularly neatly handled affair. The *Times* said editorially that there had been shortcomings, neglect, and mismanagement and that some officers were not fit for their duties. They also published a letter from an officer in the Khyber force which went into more detail. "The Indian commissariat was at one time supposed to be the best in the world." he began. "If it is so still, all I can say is God help the others. . . . Like the Bourbons our commissariate seems incapable of learning or forgetting anything." As he wrote, supplies were not getting through to Ali Masjid, only nine miles from the base at Peshawar.

A more eccentric complaint came from an officer who wrote that "the great defect I observe in all our late wars is the childish fear generals have of losing any of their men." For his part, there had not been enough fighting and the solution he offered was to advance with much smaller forces—thus making the affair more even, thus encouraging the Afghans to stand and fight.

If the military situation had at least the appearance of stability, the political did not. On December 10 Sher Ali announced that he would proceed to St. Petersburg, visit his friend the Czar, and try to have an international conference assembled to hear his case against the British. Three days later he headed north, leaving behind the pronouncement that his "lion devouring warriors" had won a number of victories. To take his place at Kabul, he released his son Yakub Khan from the prison into which he had clapped him six years earlier.

The Russians did not like having the British in Afghanistan and indeed were already contemplating measures to counter it, but support of Sher Ali was further than they cared to go. As the *Journal* of St. Petersburg said, "The

---

* Religious zealots or fanatics, depending on the point of view.

Amir will receive all sympathy and hospitality, but the idea of mediation is an illusion." He didn't even get the hospitality; St. Petersburg told him not to come and Kaufmann told him bluntly that his only hope was to make the best terms he could with the British. In February, 1879, Sher Ali died and about the only monument to commemorate him was a piece of self-righteous verse produced by a British Indian official. In part, this horror went:

> And yet when I think of Sher Ali, as he lies in his
> sepulchre low
> How he died betrayed, heartbroken, 'twixt infidel
> friend and foe
> Driven from his throne by the English, and scorned
> by the Russians, his guest
> I am well content with the vengeance, and I see God
> works for the best.

Negotiations between Yakub Khan, Sher Ali's son and the new Amir, and the British—with Louis Cavagnari handling the British side—went on all winter and they went slowly. Lytton wanted the new Amir to give up control of the Khyber and Michni passes, all of the Kurram Valley up to the Shutagardan Pass, and some ground north of Quetta; turn the management of his foreign relations over to the British; and receive a permanent British mission. Yakub Khan would agree only to the British mission and sat back to see what a waiting game would get him. In early March the military, which had never wanted to negotiate anyway, was alerted for a further advance. The *Times* said of the soldiers, "The reluctance ... to treat with the Amir is doubtless due in part to the still greater reluctance to forego the intended march on Kabul." Roberts put the military's position on the grounds that the "Afghans had not had the sense of defeat sufficiently driven into them."

Lytton was in a difficult spot. He was under so much pressure from London not to go further that his secretary told Roberts flatly that the Viceroy had no choice in the matter. Moreover, he had three forces over the border, but they were all in country which could barely feed its own people, let alone occupying forces. Finally, the border tribes along the lines of communication were edgy. As Stewart reported, "The people here say they can't fight us, but they don't hesitate to give out that they will worry us in every way they can." He had already made up his own mind about any permanent occupation of Kandahar—the British could not supply an army there for any length of time and neither could the Russians. It was "a wretched country."

Yakub Khan's situation was not much more comfortable. If he gave in too readily his own people would turn on him; if he remained adamant too long, Lytton was almost certain to get permission to move on Kabul and get it over with. To make things worse, from across his northern border there came discomfitting rumors that Abdur Rahman, a grandson of Dost Mohammed who had been living under Russian protection, was about to move on Kabul, raising the northern Afghan tribes as he came. By May, Yakub decided his chances were better with the British than they were with Abdur Rahman and decided to negotiate.

He came down the passes and the British made the meeting place Gandamak, where the last dozen or so men of the Kabul force had died in 1840. The bones of some of them were still to be seen when the rocks which served to cover the graves the Avenging Army had made were kicked aside. On May 8 Cavagnari rode out to meet the Amir with an escort of fifty of the 10th Royal Hussars— the "Shiny Tenth"*—and 50 sowars of Guides Cavalry. The two men rode back into Gandamak with troops lining both sides of the road and then spent the next two weeks haggling while Yakub tried to get the treaty terms eased. In the end, he got a little and then had to give a little. The British were to keep all the territories Lytton wanted, but the Amir would be permitted to keep the revenues from them plus an outright grant of six lakhs of rupees. On the other hand, Yakub had to submit to a stipulation likely to do him serious harm with his own people. There was cholera in the Punjab that spring; Peshawar, an unhealthy hole at best, was a charnal house. In all, there were 26,000 cholera deaths in 1879 as against 215 the year before. The Amir was simply told that while the plague was on, the troops would not be brought back to the plains as had been planned when the British mission started for Kabul.

So the war was over or appeared to be and no one was

---

* "Shiny Tenth" is a corruption of "China Tenth" and has nothing to do with service in that country. Rather, the regiment had at one time been such a favorite of the Prince Regent's that it had to be handled with special care—hence "China Tenth."

particularly happy about it. The *Times* called the treaty honorable, but there was a curiously mild, cautious tone about the statement. Some of the soldiers frankly regretted the lack of more fighting and the chance for promotion. Others, like Stewart, worried about the future. "I wonder what the people at home will say," he wrote. "I think we have taken too much country and have made some very stupid blunders in detail, which will lead to grief hereafter." John Lawrence saw that hereafter with gloomy precision. Of the treaty itself he said that he feared it would end in nothing "but evil for us," and of the Cavagnari mission to Kabul he predicted flatly and accurately "they will all be murdered, every one of them."

Major Sir Pierre Louis Napoleon Cavagnari was a veteran frontier political officer. He had been born in France of a French-Italian father and an Irish mother, and there were a variety of opinions about him. To one man, he was of "rash and restless disposition of overbearing temper, consumed by the thirst for personal distinction." To another, "Cavi" was "about the finest fellow in India." Perhaps the most balanced judgment came from Neville Chamberlain, who had been with him on the first attempt to send a mission to Kabul. He thought:

> Cavagnari did very well with me and we got on admirably together. He is a clever fellow, with great will, and untiring energy—more of the Nicholson style than any man I know; he is inclined to be hasty and imperious, and more likely to control those he is brought into contact with through his force of character and through fear than from any personal attachment. I should say he is more the man for facing an emergency than one to entrust with a position requiring delicacy and very calm judgement. I think he has very strong fixed ideas, and that his action would be to make events lead up to his views. If he were left at Kabul as our agent, I should fear his not keeping us out of difficulties. . . . We shall need there a man who will see everything, and be content with only reporting to Government what is indispensable it should know.

Cavagnari himself was not wildly sanguine about the prospects. He estimated his chances of getting back alive as four to one against. On July 15 he passed through Roberts's camp in the Kurram and the general too had forebodings. He accompanied the envoy to the crest of the Shutagardan; just before they parted Cavagnari noticed a magpie, a bird considered an ill omen, and begged Roberts not to mention it to his wife. Shortly after, they shook hands, turned away in their opposite directions, and then, on impulse, turned around, shook hands again, and parted for good.

On July 24 Cavagnari entered Kabul with a civil officer, a doctor, and a military escort of seventy-five men from the Guides under Lt. Walter Hamilton. He felt well received and even reported that the local band "made an attempt at 'God Save The Queen.'" A few days later, however, he was reporting that some of the Afghan troops were mutinous and that he was advised not to go outside his residence near the Bala Hissar. Ordinarily an ebullient man, his dispatches began to take a morbid turn and contain lines like "If my death places the red line on the Hindu Kush, I don't mind" and "They can only kill the three or four of us here and our deaths will be avenged."

CHAPTER

VII

... And Back Again

If the British disliked the Russian advance into Central Asia, they can scarcely have imagined that the Russians would be any more pleased with their own. As far back as January, a St. Petersburg paper put it in terms that sound exactly like the British press:

> They will then attempt to extend their influence to Kashgar, Persia and in general to all Central Asian countries bordering on us and then for us will rise a direct danger to our interests in Asia and to our moral influence even in Turkestan. . . . We must attentively observe and take swift measures in order to parry the blow being prepared for us by the English policy in Asia.

By July, when Cavagnari left for Kabul, there were rumors about the measures the Russians were preparing to take; it was to be an expedition against the Tekke Turkomans which would bring them within 350 miles of Merv. The Marquis of Dufferin and Ava—successor to Augustus Loftus as ambassador to St. Petersburg—was instructed to make inquiries. He did so, but he was a realistic man and while he listened to "soothing assurances" it was his opinion that diplomacy was likely to do very little, since both Britain and Russia intended to "consult their own interests with very little regard for the other."

During the '60's and early '70's, the Russians had been working their way down both coasts of the Caspian. In 1869, a fort was built at Krasnovodsk. By 1873, they were down to Chikishlaw and in 1877 the Krasnovodsk garrison was moved there to commence probing eastward toward the Merv oasis. In the matter of the Turkomen tribesmen in between, Kaufmann's orders were precise; they were "to give over the Turkomen settlements, and their families, to complete destruction." It was a good deal easier said than done—the country between the Caspian and Merv is desert and the Tekke Turkomen are excellent fighters. The Russians had already had two expeditions mauled when a third was prepared early in 1879 while the British wintered in Afghanistan. Its departure was delayed when a Tekke raid carried off a number of its camels, but by June it was ready and the force—eighteen thousand men—marched out in August led by a general named Lomakin whose double misfortune it was to be stupid and unlucky. He had commanded the two previous excursions in this direction, but seems to have gained little from the experience.

The object of the advance was Geok Tepe. Today, irrigation has made it the center of a thriving agricultural area, but in 1879 it was a formidable mud fort in the middle of a desert where the only forage for animals was scrub plants able to resist drought. Lomakin knew he would have to move quickly to get the job done before his baggage animals wore out. He made a base camp about a day's march from the fortress and then made an unhappy distribution of his men. Out of a force of 18,000, he went forward with only 3,790. The explanation offered is that the remainder were necessary to guard the baggage. Moreover, a good part of what he took with him was cavalry, which is of small use assaulting mud walls thirty-five feet thick at the base. Off they marched, according to a Russian account, with the buglers playing "inspiriting tunes," the regimental choirs singing, and the officers dreaming of the conquest of Merv.

The cavalry saw the first action of the day when the Tekkes opened the eastern gate of the fort in hopes of getting their women and children out toward Merv and the cavalry was called upon to drive them back inside the walls. Lomakin's artillery then went to work on the walls. Around four in the afternoon, the women and children again tried to make a run for it and again were sabered or driven back inside. Shortly after five, the decision was made to assault. The artillery had made no breech in walls fifteen feet high and it is difficult to imagine what the general expected his infantry to do. In fact, they fell back after losing one man out of every three in a furious struggle, and as night fell, their commander—expecting to be overwhelmed at any moment by a Tekke assault in the dark—started to lead his army, 80 percent of which had yet to see action, back to the Caspian. It had four hundred miles to go and it almost starved before it straggled back in to Chikishlaw in November.

While Lomakin marched to Geok Tepe, Cavagnari observed at Kabul and did not particularly care for what he saw. The city was full of Afghan troops, half mutinous because they had not been paid in months, and the authority of Yakub Khan seemed extremely shaky. Cavagnari wanted to bolster him by getting Lytton to give him enough money to pay his troops, but Lytton said no. Rather it was his notion that Cavagnari should hold out the money as a carrot to be handed over as soon as Yakub made assorted governmental reforms Lytton thought desirable.

The mission itself was living inside the Bala Hissar in a collection of mud and lath buildings—one for the British officers, another for the men, others for stables. They were not loopholed for defense and, considering that the mission was supposedly under the protection of the Amir, scarcely could be. Their roofs were commanded by higher buildings on all sides.

On August 25 Ambrose Kelly, the medical officer, wrote his father that "Kabul, at present, is not in a very quiet state," and Cavagnari had a warning from a retired Indian army soldier living in the city that trouble was coming. About eight in the morning on September 3, it came. The unpaid soldiers had been told to go to the Bala Hissar for their money. When they found they were to get only a month's pay, there was anger and a general movement on the British quarters. Some say the cry was "Go to the British Embassy and demand pay; there's lots of money there," others that it was simply "Let us kill the enemy, then the Amir." Whatever the words, they began stoning the mission; on the testimony of the only member of the Guides to escape, the Guides infantry on guard duty opened fire on orders from no one higher up than the noncommissioned officer commanding the guard. The Afghan troops fell back to their own camp for arms and ammunition and were back about ten o'clock, an armed mob under no particular command.

Lieutenant Hamilton tried to fight his men from behind the low parapet on the residency roof, but the fire from higher buildings was too much for them and by noon they were driven inside the residency—half the Guides dead or wounded, Cavagnari wounded, and the building beginning to burn. Three messengers were sent to Yakub for aid; the first two were killed and none of the men in the residency lived long enough to know that the third did make it and eventually got back to India to tell their story.

The Afghans pounded the residency with two cannon. Hamilton took Kelly, Cavagnari's assistant Jenkyns, and twelve Guides for a try at them. They drove the Afghans off the guns, but were unable to pull them back into the Residency; the Afghans charged back and retook the guns while Hamilton retired with six Guides dead and Kelly mortally wounded. Leaving only a few Guides to provide covering fire, Hamilton and Jenkyns took the men out again. This time it was Jenkyns who was dropped before they even reached the guns. Again they were unable to pull the guns away, and as they fell back, the burning residency started to collapse. Cavagnari died in the flames if he was not already dead of his wound; Hamilton and the handful he had left took refuge in a small brick building which had served as a bath house. From here, he led a forlorn sally, this time trying to bring one gun in. According to an eye witness, he killed five men before he went down. He was hacked a good deal, but in the euphemism of the day was "not dishonoured." There were a few Guides left under a Sikh noncommissioned officer; they fought to the end and the late summer sun was setting before the last of them was dead. The mission had lasted five weeks and six days; the story of its end went down the line, and as the telegraph at Simla began its da-dit, da-dit the first words to come in were the ominous ones "Clear the line."

Roberts was at Simla when the news arrived on September 5; by the afternoon of the next day he was on his way to take command of what troops could be pulled together in the Kurram Valley and denominated the Kabul Field Force. By the end of the month he had two brigades of infantry, one of cavalry—7,500 men in all— and was ready to move to the crest of the Shutagardan and then down into Kabul.

This time there was no reluctance in London. Victoria had wired Disraeli that she wanted ". . . no hanging back, or fear to be found fault with, must deter us from strong and prompt measures. . . . Pray urge this on the Viceroy." Disraeli was of a somewhat more mixed mind. To Salisbury he said, "This is a shaker," to the Queen he noted that it was fortunate that Parliament was not sitting to

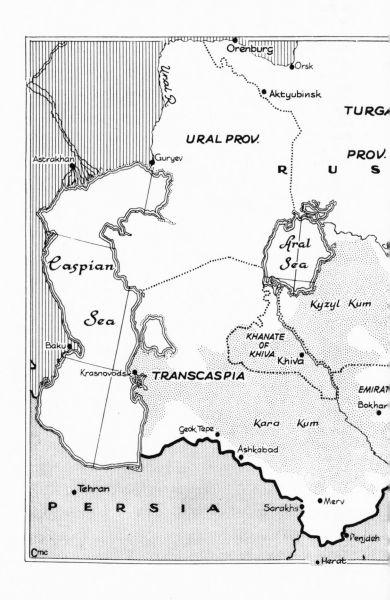

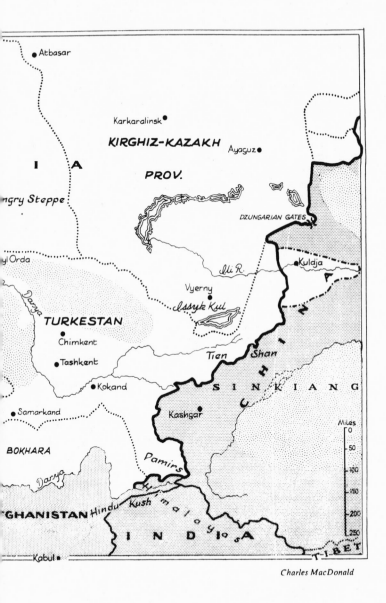

Charles MacDonald

vote against the measures about to be taken. About Lytton, though, he was beginning to have the most severe doubts. He had a letter from Lytton commenting on his various generals, and the Prime Minister's comments on the comments were heavily sarcastic:

> Except Roberts, who he believes is highly gifted, and certainly is a strategist, there seems no one much to rely on; Stewart respectable; Massey promising. . . . As for General Sam Browne, according to Lytton, he ought to have been tried by court martial and he goes thro' them all with analogous remarks. And these are the men whom, only a few months or weeks ago, he recommended for all these distinctions. I begin to think he ought to be tried by a court martial himself.

Certainly Lytton's announcement of the disaster had a feeble sound. "We now have to weave a fresh and, I fear, a wider web from undoubtedly weaker material. . . . I feel most keenly how heavy must be the weight with which this sore and sudden blow will fall upon Her Majesty's Government," he wrote. He then went on to butter up the Prime Minister a little: "On the other hand, however, the great advantages of our new frontier [he did not say "scientific"] will be revealed in the comparative alacrity and freedom from serious danger with which its possession enables us to reach Kabul in a crisis."

His instructions to Roberts were a good deal less mealy-mouthed and ought to be borne in mind in considering Roberts's subsequent proceedings in Kabul. His chief told him that the massacre of the mission was something for which the entire Afghan nation was to be held "collectively responsible."

Shortage of transport was Roberts's biggest headache, and the man on whom rested the ultimate responsibility for getting it was Colonel Charles MacGregor, his chief of staff. MacGregor was, as usual, fuming.* For one thing, he had hoped for an infantry brigade, but ". . . the Chief or Lumsden, or both put a spoke into my wheel, damn them, I owe them one." For another, he was, in his view, surrounded by incompetents. One was a "lounger

---

* MacGregor apparently saved his fuming for his diary. Mortimer Durand, who knew him well, considered him "grave and silent." In addition to other eccentricities, MacGregor claimed to descend from Rob Roy and was forever collecting MacGregors from Scots regiments with an eye to assembling them all back in the Highlands on ground he intended to buy some day.

about town," another should "have been shelved," and the whole Commissariat Office was "weak fussy gentlemanly."

About the coming action, on the other hand, he was most hopeful. "Bobs is very sanguine about advance," he wrote in his diary, "thinks they will fight, it will be a great thing for him, he will be made a Baronet at least." Mulling this a few days, he thought about himself and made another entry: "This may be a big business and if so I ought to be a KCB or a KCSI at least."

Even after renting five hundred brewery carts, MacGregor never did find enough transport, and from first to last Roberts improvised. His chief device was to send half the troops ahead with all the transport, encamp, and then send transport back for the second half. It divided his forces and made them twice as vulnerable if attacked, but he got away with it.

By September 27 the force was at the top of the Shutagardan, and the next day Yakub Khan came into camp explaining that he had fled Kabul to get away from his own mutinous troops. Roberts, who thought him an "insignificant looking" young man with a "very shifty eye," promptly put him under heavy guard—ostensibly as a sign of honor.

On October 5 the advanced brigade of the force was only twelve miles from Kabul and there was only one obstacle between them and the city. The heights of Charasai rose one to two thousand feet above the plain, the only way through them was a narrow gorge, and on the heights a mixed force of Afghan regulars and tribesmen was ready to make a fight of it. A more careful man than Roberts would have waited for his second brigade to come up, but he judged that delay simply encouraged the enemy and attacked the next morning. With only moderate artillery support, the 72nd Highlanders and the 5th Gurkhas went straight up the ridge, and if the Afghan artillery had been handled nearly as well as it had been earlier, both regiments would have paid for Roberts's impetuousness. As it was, it was simply not an Afghan day. By 3:45 in the afternoon, Roberts had the ridge with only eighteen killed and seventy wounded; the next day he was camped outside Kabul, preparing to make a formal entrance.

The Amir, Yakub Khan, had no desire to return to his throne. He resigned, announcing that he would rather be a grass cutter in the English camp than rule Afghanistan.

Roberts was thus in the uncomfortable position of begging Yakub to reconsider his decision. Without any Amir of Kabul, he had no one in whose name to rule and no one with whom to make a peace treaty. They compromised. Roberts messaged Simla for instructions and the Amir agreed to keep his title until a reply came through.

October 12 was the day of the formal entry into Kabul (*sans* the Amir, who sent his son instead), and they went in with the band "playing like mad" and troops lining the road from the camp to the city. One arrangement had been overlooked—no one had had the main gate of the Bala Hissar unlocked; but after a little delay, Roberts entered, the British flag was run up, the band played *God Save the Queen* and Roberts proceeded to the Hall of Audience to deliver his proclamation. Though it had been toned down by Mortimer Durand, who considered the original "utterly wrong in tone," it was still bellicose enough for MacGregor to call it a "most ridiculous proclamation breathing death to every one, an altogether childish and silly production."

Roberts started off by saying that because of the desire of the "great British Government" to "temper justice with mercy" he was not going to level the city. Having thus reassured his audience, he went on—in line with Lytton's instructions—to say that some portions of the city would be destroyed and the entire population fined. Rewards were offered to anyone turning in men implicated in the Cavagnari massacre, and anyone who had fought against the British during the advance on Kabul was to be punished on the grounds that they were in rebellion against the Amir.

To investigate, Roberts appointed two Courts—one under MacGregor with the particular object of investigating whether the Amir had been implicated in the Cavagnari massacre, and the other a Military Court to determine who had taken part in the affair and who had fought against the British. The second court MacGregor, admittedly a man of strong opinions, considered to be composed of two idiots and one lazy man. In the matter of the Amir, he was more positive: "Morty is very much concerned about the Amir and says he is being treated badly and condemned without a hearing. I think there is quite enough proof to make us suspect him and if we suspect him we should quod [jail] him."

In all, forty-nine men were executed for being involved in the massacre, and the evidence against some of them was so flimsy that it became a catchword in Kabul that any evidence was good enough to hang an Afghan. In one case, a correspondent from the Allahabad *Pioneer* wrote by way of justification that "the man's general demeanor and known character were all against him. A more ruffianly face could scarcely be found in the whole of Afghanistan."

To the credit of British India, there were important voices on the other side. The Bombay *Review* asked, "Is it according to the usages of war to treat as felons men who resist invasion?" and forecast accurately that "our campaign of retribution is sowing a harvest of hatred." The influential *Friend of India* said, "We fear that General Roberts has done us a serious national injury, by lowering our reputation for justice in the eyes of Europe." Even Neville Chamberlain, a veteran member of the military establishment, saw nothing but trouble ahead. "It is impossible to destroy a whole male population," he wrote a friend, "nor can any civilized government think of punishing the innocent with the guilty. . . . I shall be much surprised if your general is not constantly being called upon to suppress insurrection somewhere or another."

It took Roberts himself less than a month to see the senselessness of the policy, and on November 12 he issued an amnesty proclamation which announced that he was now in possession of information which tended to show that many of the Afghans who fought against the British had done so in the belief that the Amir was a prisoner in the British camp. Therefore, they were not in revolt against the Amir, therefore, on behalf of the British Government, Roberts was happy to proclaim a free and complete amnesty for anyone not involved in the massacre.

Besides, he had a great many other things to worry about. Durand had written even before the end of October that he himself was concerned about "our want of hold on the country." Intelligence was weak, there was no government (Yakub would sign anything with his own name, but nothing as Amir), and a highly regarded priest, Muskh-i-Alam, was successfully preaching holy war to the Ghilzais and the tribes of the Kurram. Nor was Roberts making his position with the tribes any stronger by burning those villages whose tribesmen he considered slow in providing supplies. MacGregor thought the burnings a poor idea, the more so since it reminded him of the way the English used to burn Highland villages in the old days. Durand went even further, saying:

> I think this sort of thing is wrong and impolitic. It causes deep and lasting resentment and it will not quiet the country. . . . There will never be wanting a few reckless fellows who find the temptation to snipe at small bodies of our men quite irresistible. It is only natural. Were England conquered by Afghans I should feel quite the same. "Oh, damn Jones' haystack, lets have a shy" and then the unhappy Jones should suffer while I sat and smiled on the summit of a neighboring hill.

Finally—and only briefly to be sure—there was a rumor that the Russians were coming with twenty thousand men. The whole business probably started with a particularly nasty editorial in the St. Petersburg *Gazette* which foresaw a British victory in Afghanistan unless "another factor" appeared on the scene. The *Gazette* then proceeded to spell out the new entrant.

> This factor is Russia, that nation in whose ledger is written a long list of attacks, injustice and insults poured upon us from the Crimean campaign* even to this day. Russia is the country which a mortal enemy . . . has hemmed in by an insupportable chain of intrigue, force and pretensions from the Amur . . . to the Bosphorus. . . . We do not want the English in Asia; while we are pursuing our national duties and interests she will always be there as our adversary until the question is settled—We or she? If 20,000 well equipped Russians were sent, that would form the first stage of the ejection of the English from Asia, then our endless eastern frontier would be rid of a dangerous neighbor.

The rumor died as quickly as it had started and Roberts turned his attention to the tribal problem. On November 1 he moved his troops into the Sherpur cantonments north of the city; these were a good deal more defensible than those the British had occupied in 1840. Sher Ali had built them for his own army, and British engineers had added proper winter quarters. In early

---

* It is interesting to note that the *Gazette* considered the Crimea a lost campaign rather than a lost war.

December Muskh-i-Alam's tribesmen began to assemble
on the heights around Kabul and Roberts set out to cut
them up before they became properly organized. His first
sortie went out on December 10 and got a deal more
than it had bargained for. The plan called for two
columns to move west from Kabul, one attacking an
Afghan force moving down from the north and driving it
onto the other column which had come round to its rear.
The Afghans slipped out of the trap and very nearly got
between the British and Kabul with only a small cavalry
force and four pieces of light artillery barring the way.
Some ten thousand Afghan infantry were coming on with
their mullahs out in front bearing red and white banners,
and the fire from the four artillery pieces was having no
perceptible effect on them. The 9th Lancers and the 14th
Bengal Lancers* were ordered to charge. They did and
Durand saw "what I hope I may never see again." The
charge was made over broken ground unsuitable for
cavalry; the two regiments came out "a shapeless mass,"
fled the field, and left the four pieces of artillery to the
Afghans. The 9th was rallied for one more try, but it
went no better than the first and a number of unhorsed
cavalrymen were left to straggle off the field as best they
could in high boots and with their sword scabbards banging between their legs. Roberts had ordered the gates of
Kabul closed when the other column sent out to perform
the original entrapment finally caught up with the Afghan
rear and slowed the assault. Next, the 72nd Highlanders,
hurried out from cantonments, came up, and the Afghan
charge petered out. As they fell back, MacGregor picked
up a scratch force of Sikhs and Gurkhas and retrieved the
four abandoned guns, a feat on which he never ceased to
congratulate himself. His first diary entry on the subject
calls it "a happy thought"; a second says, "I may be a
peer yet," and later he notes with joy that the London
papers have reported the feat ". . . this is very lucky, the
Queen may see it and give me the cross." In time, he
began to anticipate the honorary dinners which would be
tendered him when he returned home and even started to
work up a speech which began, "Ladies and gentlemen, I
have had the honor and luck of being engaged a few

---

* The 9th was known as "the Delhi Spearmen" because of the
vigor with which they chased fugitives after the fall of Delhi in '57.
The 14th had walked to Afghanistan using their horses to carry
baggage rather than be left behind when transport ran short.

times against the enemies of her Majesty, but I must confess I never was in such a funk as when I discovered the intention . . . to propose my health. . . . We soldiers are very unaccustomed to expressing our thoughts in the form of a speech."

For the moment, however, there was no time for speeches. The force was safely back in cantonments and the Afghans did not have Kabul, but Roberts himself called the affair a reverse. He telegraphed Jalalabad to push a brigade up nearer Kabul and added that if the telegraph line was cut, it was to be considered a bad sign and the extra brigade should be sent all the way forward.

From the tenth to the fourteenth, Roberts pushed his luck to the limit, sending troops out from Sherpur in an effort to push the Afghans off the hills. He wasn't successful, and if Afghan tactics had been just a bit better he might very well have had one or more units cut off and chopped up. By noon of the fourteenth the hoards of Afghans reminded one young signal officer of the crowds at Epsom on Derby Day, and Roberts decided that the time had come to pull back into Sherpur and let the enemy come to him. When the news got back to London, the *Times* remarked approvingly that "General Roberts has done well to restrain the gallant impetuosity of which he had given so many instances and retire to a safe position."

The position was a strong one. Three sides of the camp had fifteen-foot walls and the fourth side was the Bemaru Heights, along which a series of trenches had been dug. It was larger than Roberts would have preferred—2,200 yards long by 1,200 wide—but supplied with enough food and ammunition to hold its own for four months. Roberts had little doubt that the assault would come shortly or not at all. If for no other reason, there was no Afghan supply system capable of keeping a force estimated at thirty thousand men in the field for any length of time.

On December 22 spies said the attack was set for 6 A.M. the next morning. At 4 A.M. the British went to their posts; punctually at six a signal fire blazed on the heights and, with a rattle of musketry badly aimed in the dark, the assault began. Besides the sound of the firing, what the men who were in Sherpur seem to have remembered best is the strange slapping sound of thousands of Afghan sandals as the attackers came running forward over the snow. As a fight, it didn't amount to much. The Afghan soldiery was in no way prepared to go against troops with superior weapons in decently organized positions, and though Roberts made the mistake of leaving a few buildings around the cantonment standing for cover, the garrison was never really badly pressed. Bemaru Heights got the most pressure, but the attacks were badly coordinated—two or three hundred men rushing forward at a time in the greenish light thrown by British star shells—and when, around ten in the morning, Roberts sent four guns through the pass in the heights the whole business began to come apart. The Afghans fell back before the guns, the cavalry was turned loose in pursuit, and what followed did no credit to the occupying forces. Stragglers were hunted down; three lancers were assigned to each, and when the man was finally run down he was killed. The British losses had been 11 dead and 46 wounded; the Afghan casualties were estimated at around 3,000. Next morning, the extra brigade from the south came up and the Sherpur cantonments were clearly safe.

If the victory made for a merry Christmas at Sherpur, it did not get back to England in time for the holiday. The *Times* called it "an unusually hard Christmas," and the Archbishop of Canterbury asked that the troops be remembered in everyone's Christmas prayers. Even when the good news came through on December 29 there was a singular lack of rejoicing, and the New Year's editorials talked a good deal more about getting back to the lines of the Treaty of Gandamak than they did about further adventures. Lord Lytton might make a New Year's speech about holding all the territory gained in Afghanistan, but in the opinion of the *Times*, what Britain wanted was "repose." Even at Kabul, Durand thought that a "little carelessness or ill luck might at any time bring about a disaster. Afghan fighting men are not to be despised when they greatly outnumber you. I have always undervalued them until now, and overvalued the power of superior arms and discipline and overvalued also the European soldier." At Kandahar, Stewart too did not care for the look of the future and wrote his wife, "I must say the people who said that when once we gave up our own frontier there was no telling where we are to stop, seem to have prophesied rightly."

Roberts summed up the problem thus: "What was to be done with Afghanistan now we have got it? and Who could be set up as Ruler with any chance of being able to hold his own?" Actually, there were other questions. Should the country be put under one ruler or broken up into small states? Should the Afghans or the Persians have Herat? As Salisbury said, "The question—shall we lean on the Persian or the Afghan leg—is still perplexing." He was not particularly optimistic either way. As he said, "It is a fallacy to assume that within our lifetime any stable arrangement can be arrived at in the East. The utmost we can do is to provide halting places where the process of change can rest awhile. But what we have to do is rather to assume the probability of change, and so shape our precautions so that it shall effect no vital interest of ours."

It was Lytton's notion that the best way to provide resting places was to divide Afghanistan into small states, one governed from Kabul, another from Kandahar, and the third—Herat—to be turned over to the Persians. A seemingly suitable candidate was available to rule at Kandahar, but there seemed no one capable of doing the job at Kabul. At this moment, a most unlikely prospect from the British point of view appeared north of the Hindu Kush.

Abdur Rahman was a grandson of Dost Mohammed. As a young man, he had fought in the civil war which followed the Dost's death, and in 1869, his faction beaten, he fled north to become a pensioner of the Russians. Now, ten years later, the Russians had given him $12,500 plus a few hundred muskets and urged him south to try for the throne.

In 1880, he was about forty years old,* of medium height, and starting to grow heavy. Mortimer Durand thought him a sort of Afghan Henry VIII: "Brave . . . able . . . cruel and sensual." A later Viceroy of India called him "cruel, vindictive, overweeningly proud, but of inflexible purpose, fearless heart and indomitable energy." There is a suspicion, however, that he put on a hard front when dealing with the British. His autobiography has glints of humor in it, and Lepel Griffin, who handled the negotiations leading to his accession to the throne, found him pleasant, intelligent, and courteous.

Lytton was desperately in need of somebody. For one thing, he feared a general Afghan rising. For another, London was extremely unhappy about the cost of the adventure, which was now in the neighborhood of ten million pounds. Finally, Britain was on the verge of a general election and an unresolved Afghan situation was the last thing the Disraeli government wanted to take into the campaign. Lytton's anxieties are quite apparent in a

* His exact date of birth is unknown.

letter to Stewart shortly before the Kandahar force was marched up to Kabul with orders to deal with malcontents around Ghazni on the way. Abdur Rahman, he felt, represented the "last chance of effecting an easy settlement of durable relations with Northern Afghanistan." In other words, a war started to forestall Russian influence at Kabul was now to be settled by the installation of a Russian pensioner in the same location.

The British had scarcely more than the word of Abdur Rahman's mother that he was well disposed toward them, but given the straits Lytton was in he wired London: "Necessary to find without delay some Native authority to which we can restore northern Afghanistan without risk of immediate anarchy on our evacuation of Kabul. . . . No prospect of finding in the country any man strong enough for this purpose. I therefore advocate early public recognition of Abdur Rahman." On March 15, 1880, London sent its approval, and all that remained to be done was to persuade perhaps the most astute statesman the British had to deal with during their time in India to take the job.

Mr. Lepel Griffin, a civil officer from the Punjab, was sent to Kabul to do the persuading, and he began with a letter to Abdur Rahman, then sitting north of the Hindu Kush and collecting followers. "It has become known that you have entered Afghanistan," said Griffin, "and consequently this letter is sent to you . . . in order that you may submit to the British officers at Kabul any representation you may desire to make to the British Government with regard to your object in entering Afghanistan." Mr. Griffin had very little time in which to operate if he was to bail out the Disraeli government. He arrived at Kabul on March 19 and the elections were set for the last day of that month.

Abdur Rahman replied that he hoped to see Afghanistan living in "ease and tranquillity" and under "the honourable protection" of both Britain and Russia. Griffin passed the message along to Simla, and Simla exploded that joint protection by Britain and Russia could not be "entertained or discussed." On the other hand, Mr. Gladstone had become Prime Minister, and Lytton had his orders to get the troops out of Afghanistan by October at the latest; since the new claimant to the throne had delayed his answer, the first of May was only a few days away.

Griffin wanted his man to come down to Kabul and

talk things over; Abdur Rahman, the lesson of Shah Shujah in mind, had no intention of doing anything of the kind so long as the British were there to make him seem a puppet. Instead, he kept asking poor Griffin the most difficult questions. Would his territories include Kandahar? Would a British envoy on the Cavagnari model be left at Kabul? What benefits could he expect from the new connection in terms of cash and defense in case of attack?

Simla was quick to reply that he would not get Kandahar, but was a good deal less definite on the other points. As MacGregor said, "He does not mean to come in till he knows exactly what we want, and I do not believe anyone can tell him because no one knows." Fortunately for the settlement, Lytton was now replaced by Gladstone's man— George Robinson, Lord Ripon—and the new Viceroy was willing to provide Griffin with a more concrete set of answers for the Amir-to-be. He was not to have Kandahar, but he could have Herat if he could take it; no British representatives would be maintained in his country, but his foreign affairs were to be conducted entirely through the British government. On the other hand, he had a promise of British help against unprovoked aggression.

Griffin got a very prompt reply which expressed Abdur Rahman's great pleasure with the offer and then, without mentioning Kandahar, went on to say how particularly pleased he was that his boundaries were to include all the territories of his grandfather, the Dost. Since the Dost had always claimed Kandahar, there was suddenly a great deal of talk at Kabul about forgetting Abdur Rahman and calling back "the wretched Yakub Khan" from his exile in India.

Thinking it over, Ripon decided that the question of Kandahar could be gotten around, and another letter went off to Abdur Rahman simply saying that the Government of India didn't know what he meant by territories formerly held by the Dost. To Kabul went orders to pull out and leave the Afghans to form their own government if the letter didn't do the trick.

Abdur Rahman, who seems to have had a nice sense of when not to overplay a good hand, said no more about Kandahar and accepted an invitation to send three of his representatives into Kabul. There, in durbar on July 22, it was announced that the "Viceroy of India and the Government of Her Most Gracious Majesty the Queen Empress are pleased to announce that they publically recognize Sirdar* Abdur Rahman Khan, grandson of the illustrious Amir, Dost Mohammed Khan, as Amir of Kabul." On Ripon's very precise instructions the word was "recognized" and not "proclaimed"; the Queen Empress's government had had all they wanted of trying to erect monarchs in Afghanistan. As an official noted in his diary, "The Government are very nervous about the measure and are afraid of committing themselves too much."

Apparently the thing was over. Griffin and the Amir haggled over how much aid in money and arms he was to receive, and the troops prepared to march back to India. Then, on July 28, news came from Kandahar which Stewart called "the worst misfortune which can happen to us" and which caused the Secretary of State for India to report to Parliament thus: "I regret to say I have received news of a most serious character from India. Primrose telegraphs today from Kandahar 'Terrible disaster, General Burrows' force annihilated. We are going into the citadel.' "

Primrose commanded the force which had replaced Stewart at Kandahar. It was a weakish unit at best; the Indian regiments were from the Bombay army and generally considered inferior to those of the Bengal army, and neither General Primrose nor his unfortunate subordinate Brigadier Burrows was a particularly gifted leader.

As early as December, 1879, there had been bazaar gossip in Kandahar that Ayub Khan (a son of Sher Ali), who ruled at Herat, was boasting that he intended to drive the British and their puppet the Wali of Kandahar out of that city. Nothing came of it until the following June when Ayub, anxious to grab as much as he could for himself before Abdur Rahman was firmly on the throne, set out for Kandahar. The Wali, who had very little faith in his own troops—quite rightly as it turned out—asked Primrose for help. Primrose gave him a brigade under Burrows—two regiments of Bombay troops and one of Europeans, the 66th Foot, known as "the Brave Boys of Berks."

A Lieutenant Maclaine who was part of the force had some doubts, but was glad of anything that broke the monotony of the Kandahar cantonments. As they marched out on July 3 he made a diary entry: "So we're off. Hurrah! ... The brigade, though not very strong ... is

* Roughly, "general."

quite enough for anything we are likely to meet." A few days later he expressed some further misgivings: "If the enemy approach it is to be hoped we will not mix with or put any trust in the Wali's troops."

On July 15 the Wali's men did exactly what Maclaine feared and deserted to Ayub in a body; Burrows had 2,476 men to oppose a force estimated at 12,000 and superior in artillery. Twelve days—during which time Primrose could have brought the rest of the division out from Kandahar to the assistance of his outmanned and outgunned brigade—passed. On July 27 Burrows allowed himself to bump into Ayub rather than make his fight on ground suited for defense, and the matter was all over in a few hours. A Lieutenant Lener of the 66th wrote his family a confused but graphic description of the rout:

> It is a great disaster—colours, band instruments and all our baggage and ammunition falling into the hands of the enemy who surrounded us and must have numbered 13,000 or more. . . . They covered the entire plain and had 34 guns to our 8. Fighting began at 11 by day. Heat and thirst terrible. Thrice I fell exhausted after our line had been broken, then we retreated in a panic. My captain was killed. I hobbled between two Sepoys at first and then was put on a trooper's horse behind him and, thoroughly exhausted, ultimately on a gun. We were pursued all through the night. . . . The first volley of the 66th stopped them, but our natives broke and then a panic ensued. I thought our retreat was cut off.*

What happened—in less subjective terms—is that Burrows let himself be caught in the open, and for the first three hours of the action his infantry lay on a steaming plain while a thoroughly unequal artillery duel went on between Burrows's twelve guns and Ayub's thirty. Around noon, the Afghan infantry charged and were driven back; when they repeated the effort at 2 P.M., however, the British artillery had run out of ammunition and the infantry began to give way. Burrows tried to get his cavalry to charge across the front to give the infantry time to reform, but the charge never materialized. The cavalry had been standing under artillery fire for five hours and they were badly rattled. An experienced officer might have rallied them, but by one of the marvels of misman-

* Letter to the London *Times*.

agement produced by the seniority system, they were
commanded on the occasion by an infantry officer whose
previous experience had chiefly been with the Indian police.

It was fashionable after the battle to blame the whole
thing on the collapse of the two Bombay regiments. In
fact, two companies of Jacob's Rifles did falter early
under the shelling, but the rest of the regiment was firm
until the end. The 1st Bombay Grenadiers have it proudly
on their regimental record that they left the field in good
order. Contrary to what young Lener thought, the pursuit
was not particularly vigorous; if it had been, the annihila-
tion first reported might have become a fact. The facts
were bad enough—Burrows had over a thousand killed
and wounded and his force scattered all over the fifty
miles from Maiwand to Kandahar. Among the survivors
was a small white terrier named Bobby—a mascot of the
66th. Victoria later decorated him with the Afghan medal
and he eventually wound up stuffed in the 66th's regimental depot.

At Kabul, Simla, and London there was general agreement that the disaster had to be retrieved, but there
agreement ended. London wanted to send troops all the
way from Britain to relieve Primrose and the force sealed
up in Kandahar. Simla wanted to send troops from Quetta, but there simply weren't enough men there to do the
job. At Kabul, where there were rumors that Ayub must
have been assisted by Russian officers, both Stewart and
Roberts thought their men ought to be sent. On August 3
Ripon made up his mind; Roberts was to lead a force of
ten thousand men to Kandahar, and Stewart was to retire
to India with the rest via the Khyber. Lepel Griffin finally
met Abdur Rahman face to face, and though the inter-
view was marred by the Amir's laryngitis, he agreed to
assist Roberts by sending a party of his own officers in
advance to spread the word that the Amir was simply
sending an infidel force out of the country by way of
Kandahar and to threaten drastic reprisals against any
Afghan who molested them. British diary entries of the
time are full of remarks about what a good fellow the
Amir was being; it does not seem to have occurred to any
of the writers that the Amir must have been delighted to
have the British deal with Ayub and save him the trouble
of doing so later.

For once a British force in India was going to march
stripped down. Roberts allowed his officers one mule each
for baggage—a far cry from the caravans that had gone

up the Bolan Pass forty years earlier. On August 10 they set out for Kandahar. Four days later Stewart marched south for India and the Amir Abdur Rahman entered Kabul. The *Times* reminded its readers that it would take Roberts four weeks to get to Kandahar and conceded that until he did "the public mind will be held in an attitude of somewhat painful suspense."

Bobs did not keep them waiting quite the full four weeks. Thanks in large part to the Amir's advance men, who cleared the way so that they got through without so much as a skirmish, he reached his destination on August 31—having covered 318 miles in twenty-three days. Each day of the march, the rouse was sounded by 2:45 in the morning, the camp was struck, the load was blown at 3:40, and at 4:20 the head of the column was in motion. Roberts gave them a ten-minute break each hour and a twenty-minute halt at 8 A.M. for breakfast. It was a very decent performance, but in spite of all the fanfare, certainly no more impressive than Stewart's march from Kandahar to Kabul in April, which took thirty-two days but involved a good deal of fighting on the way, including a major action near Ghazni. Roberts himself felt that "the March," as it came to be known, was an overrated performance and considered his advance on Kabul in '79 "in every particular more dangerous, more difficult." A jubilant newspaper correspondent with the force, however, thought it was all very grand and told his readers that it proved "the soundness of the stock from which the British officer is drawn and the merits of a manly English education."

A story current at the time had Primrose so cowed that he refused to raise the Union Jack over Kandahar for fear of drawing enemy fire. Roberts was quite the contrary. He knew he had an army superior to anything Ayub could put in the field and he gave it only one night's rest before putting it to work. At 6 A.M. on September 1 it was deployed north of the city facing the Afghan forces who had taken position in and around the Baba Wali Kotal. Primrose's forces were told to demonstrate toward the Kotal, but as at the Peiwar Kotal, Roberts had no intention of going straight ahead. One brigade of infantry, with the 92nd Highlanders* and the 2nd Gurkhas leading, fought through the Guni Mulla village around the

* The 92nd was part of the famous "stirrup charge" at Waterloo when they went at the French hanging onto the stirrups of the Royal Scots Greys.

edge of the hills while a second brigade with the 72nd
Highlanders and the 2nd Sikhs swung wider until both
brigades linked up at Pir Paimal village.

So far the work had been light, but the Afghans swung
around their guns on the Kotal and made a stiff fight of it
until a final charge burst into their gun line. Sepoy Inder-
bir Lama of the 2nd Gurkhas was first man through,
pronounced the guns captured in the name of his regiment, and, to clinch it, rammed his cap down the muzzle
of one of them. Ayub Khan fled toward Herat, his army
dissolved, and Roberts had his victory with only minor
casualties—fifty-eight dead plus the unfortunate Lieutenant Maclaine, who had been captured at Maiwand and
had his throat cut when the Afghan retreat began.

CHAPTER

VIII

... And Forward Again

Roberts went home to England to be lionized, Primrose went home in disgrace, and the battle over the retention of Kandahar began in earnest. The *Times* editorialized against it—"We have learned long ago that Afghanistan is beyond the range of our dominion"—and promptly got a rocket from Colonel George Malleson, a prominent writer on Asian affairs, which began, "Sir, if instead of pursuing a policy of half measures the British Government had two years ago boldly announced its intention of claiming the inheritance of the Moguls and carrying the borders of the Indian Empire to the Oxus, such a misfortune as that which has recently occurred in Afghanistan would have been impossible."

The *Times* promptly replied, "Kandahar, as Colonel Malleson insists, is not safe by itself. We must add Herat and we must add further such other positions as may make Herat safe. Persia must come next. . . . However far we go there will always be an equally good reason for moving on further."

Very few people wanted to go quite so far as Malleson; Kandahar was the nub of the matter. The Patriotic Society urged its retention. A letter writer signing himself Kandahari speculated on the arrival of Russian agents in the city the moment the British left. Yet another writer wanted to hold on to it in order to educate the locals. On the other side of the question, an Anglo-Indian wrote to say that only the military wanted the city and that because "of unreasoning fear of Russian advances." Bosworth Smith, John Lawrence's biographer, took a predictably Laurentian view and moved to let it go "in view of the random expeditions into Central Asia the proposed retention involves."

In India, one letter writer said plaintively, "Is Kandahar to be given up? It is the only trophy we hold of this

226

disastrous and costly war." Lepel Griffin came down to Simla and got himself into very hot water by making a speech which was reported thus: "As to the talk about annexation he could only thank God that the destinies of the country were not yet entrusted to crack brained enthusiasts who fancied it high and Imperial policy for the Government to drag its coat through Asia for a barbarian to trample upon." The correspondent felt that "Mr. Griffin showed a want of tact and taste in this sweeping denunciation of a policy which has the approval of nearly the whole Anglo-Indian community." Even in India, however, doubts were being expressed. The Wali was clearly incapable of governing the city. The cost of occupying it was ruinous. Why not, the argument ran, ease the Wali out and turn it over to Abdur Rahman? Everything except the timing became more or less official when in the Speech from the Throne in January, 1881, the Queen Empress said, "It is not my intention that the occupation of Kandahar shall be permanently maintained."

The statement had not been extracted from Victoria without a good deal of effort. In May, 1880, she had told Gladstone flatly, "In making your statement respecting Afghanistan pray do not commit yourself to retrogressive steps—Remember the Punjab where we reinstated the young sovereign and afterwards annexed it." A month later she went into a full-dress temper when her Prime Minister suggested some arrangement with the advancing Russians to define spheres of influence in Central Asia. Relying heavily on italics, she wrote him, "With respect to Russia & the renewal of a more friendly understanding with her—the Queen *most strongly* deprecates any such notion. *She* is our *real enemy & Rival*—the only one perhaps . . . we have. But she *is so, that* the Queen *knows & beware* of trusting her fair words."

By September there was definite news of the Russians building a railway from the Caspian for another try at Geok Tepe, and a *Times* correspondent in India reported that "there is a general disposition in India to find in the unconcealed desire of the present government to abandon Kandahar an explanation for . . . signs of renewed Russian activity in Central Asia." Gladstone persevered nonetheless, and his struggle with Victoria went on till the day before the delivery of the Speech from the Throne. On January 5 she sent Gladstone a wire which said, "I think a positive declaration of not retaining Kandahar most dangerous. Anything short of a positive declaration I would consent to." A few hours later, a second wire went out: "I strongly object to the stipulation about Kandahar. ... Cannot this be omitted from the Speech?" Gladstone replied that Parliament had to be told, and besides, the announcement was very vague about when the withdrawal would take place.

What was bothering the Queen Empress was the new expedition against Geok Tepe. London knew that the fortress was now under siege, and by the end of January, word came through that it had fallen. To make matters worse, it had fallen to a force commanded by General Mikhail Dimitrievich Skobelev, who was generally credited in Britain with being the chief author of a plan drawn up in 1877—when Britain and Russia were at loggerheads over Turkey—for the invasion of India. He also had some thought-provoking phrases attributed to him, including, "It will be in the end our duty to organize masses of Asiatic cavalry as a vanguard [for the invasion of India], under the banner of blood and rapine, thereby reviving the time of Tamerlane." Nor were his personal mannerisms likely to endear him to a British audience. A heavily perfumed and becurled man, he fancied a theatrical get-up which included all-white uniforms and white horses.

To the unfortunate Turkomen—who called him "Bloody Eyes"—he can scarcely have been more reassuring, since he was on record that "I hold it as a principle that in Asia the duration of peace is in direct proportion to the slaughter you inflict upon the enemy." Against the Tekkes, he was as good as his word. He advanced with only 7,000 men—a much easier force to supply than the ponderous one which had come before—but brought sixty guns to batter the walls of the fortress. Inside, there were 35,000 Tekkes, including women and children. Skobelev pushed his siege lines so close that his men could hear conversations on the walls, then breached them with his guns and sent his troops forward with a "no quarter" order. Some 8,000 men, women, and children were killed trying to escape; another 6,500 were killed inside the fortress, which was then given over to four days of looting.

Victoria had the personal assurance of the Czar that the expedition would not be allowed to develop into a further advance on the Merv oasis—only 250 miles north of Herat—and politicians worried on the subject were accused of "Mervousness" by those who weren't. The ambassador to Moscow, however, had an admission from a Russian politician that once you turned a general loose in Central Asia it was exceedingly difficult to know where he was going to stop. Skobelev did not disappoint; he was moving eastward and had gotten to within 180 miles of Merv when St. Petersburg decided he was pushing things too far and relieved him.

He came home as ordered, but his statement did very little to clear the air:

> To my mind the whole Central Asia question is as clear as daylight. If it does not enable us in a comparatively short time to take seriously in hand the Eastern Question, in other words, to dominate the Bosphorus, the hide is not worth the tanning. . . . Without a serious demonstration in the direction of India, in all probability on the side of Kandahar, a war on the Balkan Peninsula is not to be thought of.

In short, just what the more thoughtful British Forward Policy men had been maintaining all along.

For the moment, though, the Russian momentum was done. Alexander II was assassinated by those whom it was popular at the time to call nihilists. His successor had the same internal discontent to cope with, and his budget people were making serious protests against military expenditures. A temporary calm fell over Central Asia, and in April, 1881, the British left Kandahar and marched south through the Bolan Pass. The Second Afghan War was over.

Clearly, the Russians at Geok Tepe were not going to sit permanently out in the middle of the Turkoman desert, and Merv, one of the many places pronounced to be the key to India, was the most likely next step. In 1881 there was talk in both London and Simla of giving them the place by treaty if they promised ever so faithfully not to go any farther. This was followed by some thinking, best described as mutton-headed, which called for giving the enfeebled Persians Merv in return for their help against Russia. Ripon quite rightly called the notion one so far off the mark that the retention of Kandahar would have been the "perfection of wisdom" by comparison. Nevertheless, the idea attracted enough people so that in 1882 a rather attractive Russian offer to work out a Turkestan-Afghanistan boundary settlement which would have left Merv to the Afghans was rejected on the grounds that treaties with the Russians were not worth the paper they were written on. Indeed, Russophobia had reached a point where the extravagant Charles MacGregor was proposing a coalition of Britain, Germany, Austria, Turkey, Persia, Turkestan, China, and Afghanistan to partition that country.

Russian survey parties edged toward Herat, Russian agents were at Merv, and in early 1883 Gladstone's Foreign Minister, Granville, was nervously writing Victoria that "there is no doubt of the Russians moving and feeling their way toward the border of Afghanistan. The question remains how this can best be met. It is doubtful whether any understanding with Russia would be really efficacious and it seems certain that the Russians do not desire to come to an understanding." He did think, however, that it might be worth reopening the question of the Afghan frontier, since "the Government of India have been authorized to renew to the Amir in very explicit terms the assurances that if he is attacked by Russia, he may rely on your Majesty's support."

Nothing came of it; Merv continued to hang like a plum, and in early 1884 the Russians grabbed it. The British were bogged down in the Sudan, where Gordon was about to be besieged in Khartoum, and as a St. Petersburg correspondent reported, the Russians were "well alive" to the fact. They had been negotiating for some time with one Merv faction while sending small expeditions against the other, who were termed "Merv maurauders." Finally, in February, the Czar was pleased to announce that he accepted the proffered allegiance of Merv. No one was terribly surprised. As the *Times* said, "No one could have been so foolish as to expect after the decisive victory at Geok Tepe that Russia would long be kept out of Merv." The editorialist added, however, that Russia should go no farther and that some "clear and decisive convention" between the two governments seemed called for.

In India, the army did get a go-ahead for its railway to Quetta project—even though it was told to call it simply "roadbuilding"—and even the new Commander-in-Chief, Sir Donald Stewart, expected to see Russian advances stopped by a joint boundary commission. Simla proposed the plan to London, and London proposed it to St. Petersburg; though the Russian War Office was loathe to stop moving ahead, the Czar and his Foreign Minister de Giers accepted in spite of them. The specter of nearly a century—the cossack and the sepoy meeting in Central Asia—was about to become a reality, but in the event, there would be only a few hundred of them escorting General Sir Peter Lumsden appearing for Britain and General Zelenoi appearing for Russia. Only a very few people foresaw that before the matter was settled, the two nations would be on the verge of war over a speck on the map—Penjdeh, a place notable for nothing whatever except that in the opinion of at least one British officer its carpet weaving was rather above the neighborhood average.

To draw a boundary in a near desert inhabited by a handful of nomadic sheepherders is a tricky business at best, and it seems to have occurred to both sides fairly early on that the more real estate one was actually sitting on, the better settlement one was likely to get. One of the cooler heads in Gladstone's government, Charles Dilke, could write a year earlier, "We already foresaw that the struggle would be over Penjdeh," because, "below Penjdeh, the Afghans would not appear to have ever extended their authority." In other words Penjdeh was the furthest that the Amir's writ could even be made to appear to run.

In early May the Russians occupied Sarakhs. No one claimed that Sarakhs was Afghan; in fact if anyone besides the Russians had a claim it was the Persians. London was disposed to make light of the affair and talk about the "accommodating temper" of both governments. The Indian press felt a little less comfortable, and one paper noted that the event "increased the uneasiness" felt in India since the occupation of Merv. Then, on May 12, there was a newspaper report that "Colonel Alikhanoff visited Pul-i-khisti,* which is well within the Afghan frontier in order to inquire into the state of affairs at Penjdeh, where there is an Afghan outpost, and that it is believed that the Russians will build a fort at Pul-i-khisti without regarding any Afghan protests."

Regardless of the authenticity of the report, the name Alikhanoff—a Muslim born Makant Ali Khan in the Caucasus—was enough to make Indian frontiersmen look for further Russian advance. The red-bearded "stormy petrel of the frontier" was a legend—a somewhat romantic one perhaps—but the hard facts were impressive

---

* At the risk of taking the romance out of Central Asian geography, Pul-i-khisti means simply "brick bridge." It will henceforth be called "the bridge."

enough. He had first come to prominence in the Khiva campaign, risen rapidly, then been broken back to the ranks for dueling only to rise again in the Turkish War and then handle the takeover of Merv. Whether, as frontier lore had it, he crept about the border in disguise and deposited anti-British agitators in every bazaar in Turkestan is another matter.

May 18 saw a meeting at the United Service Institute in London of alarmed Forward Policy men calling for the occupation by Britain of Kandahar and even of Herat. On June 9 the *Times* made a sharp turn from its talk about "accommodating temper" and a negotiated settlement. The piece was headed "The Northern and North-Western Frontiers of Afghanistan" and it announced, "There is no doubt that before the end of the present summer steps will have been commenced for the purpose of defining the limits of Afghan jurisdiction with or without the co-operation of Russia." The belligerence increased: "The frontier will be of little avail unless the English people are determined to resent its infraction by force of arms. . . . No adjustment of the frontier in this quarter can be pronounced satisfactory that fails to convert Penjdeh into a fortified Afghan position. . . . The placing of a strong Afghan garrison will provide . . . the security."

Shortly after, the Amir, at Ripon's urging, reinforced his Penjdeh garrison—but with only five hundred men. Since five hundred men were not going to make any particular difference, the move and subsequent attitudes of the Amir give rise to a suspicion that he did not put much faith in the guarantee of British help if he got into a fight with the Russians.

For the rest of 1884 the Russians inched nearer to Penjdeh, and when Lumsden arrived in the area on October 1 to talk about boundaries he found no General Zelenoi to deal with. The general was reported ill, but the cynical regarded it as a convenient delay pending the outcome of a row between the Amir and a rebellious cousin who considered himself, probably with Russian encouragement, the ruler of Afghanistan north of the Hindu Kush. One Russian paper—admittedly a fire-eater—even said flatly that the nature of the ultimate boundary would depend on the outcome of the fight between the Amir and his cousin.

The Russians demanded that the British make the Afghans withdraw from Penjdeh, the British demanded that the Russians withdraw, and the papers on both sides did themselves very little credit by enflaming opinion. The *Times* editorials were full of bits like "no flinching" and "recruiting has never languished in this country when there was any prospect of fighting." The St. Petersburg *Vedomosti* fired back: "If it be true that our Government has refused to withdraw our advanced posts in compliance with the demands of England, we cannot help rejoicing at the fact." A Calcutta paper urged London to address the Russians in the words of Dalhousie: "If you will have war, then by God you shall have it and let it be war to the knife all the world over."

Victoria cabled the Czar that the situation was causing her *"la plus grande inquiétude,"* European papers expected war, and the American stock exchange, which had been in the doldrums, zoomed—partly on rumors, partly on good solid British War Office orders to Chicago meatpackers for canned beef. In India, an army of fifty-thousand men was assembled in the northwest for the expected advance, and Lord Dufferin, Ripon's successor, invited Abdur Rahman to a durbar at Rawalpindi for a discussion of joint measures for defense. When he arrived, the band played him in with the Gilbert and Sullivan number which goes: "He might have been a Russian, he might have been a Prussian, but in spite of all temptation to belong to other nations, he remains an Englishman."

Lumsden had told the Afghans at Penjdeh that he considered it unlikely that the Russians would attack so long as he was present, but in mid-March he moved to the main Boundary Commission camp sixty miles south and the senior British officer left behind was a captain, Charles Yate, a considerably less impressive symbol of the Queen-Empress. Lumsden's final words to the Afghans were that if they "entered into a conflict with the Russians they must do so entirely on their own responsibility and would receive no assistance from us." Considering that he knew the Afghans felt they could run the Russians back to Merv, he might have put it a little more strongly.

On March 25 the Russians advanced to Kizil Tapa—less than a mile from the Afghan position—and the Afghans retaliated by crossing the bridge to the west bank of the Khusk River. However much they might have been justified in playing tit for tat, the move was bound to further aggravate a Russian force already spoiling for a fight. Captain Yate spent the next few days trying to settle matters by negotiation, but on March 29 the Russian ultimatum demanding the Afghan retirement ran out;

just before dawn of the next morning, General Alexander Komaroff, with Alikhanoff as second-in-command, marched forward for a showdown. According to Alikhanoff's account:

> . . . I marched to the left flank of the Afghans with a body of Turkomans followed by a Cossack regiment. One half of the Cossacks were dismounted and loaded, the other half held their horses. The Afghans were mounted on stallions which were restless, one of their carbines went off by accident or design and wounded one of the horses of the Cossacks. An officer rode up and reported this to me, and I replied "Blood has been shed, we must now get to business." Upon this the Cossack cavalry screen withdrew and the dismounted Cossacks opened fire on the Afghan cavalry, which was thrown into confusion, broke and fled. The Afghan infantry fought like men, firing as they retired. Altogether the Afghans lost 800 men, many of them drowned in the flooded Khusk River, while the Russian loss was only 40 killed and wounded.

There is no comparable British account since Yate and his officers stayed in their camp five miles from the bridge throughout the fight. However, there was no getting around the fact that the sepoy and the cossack had finally collided—or, at the very least, that the cossack had collided with a nation promised aid against aggression by the British and seconded by British officers on the spot. In St. Petersburg, the British ambassador told a newspaper man that war was inevitable. The British Foreign Office prepared documents announcing a state of war. Leaves were canceled in India and in the Far East. The navy prepared to operate against Vladivostok. Halfway around the world, *The New York Times* devoted half of its first page to the story under the headline "England and Russia Sure To Fight," and the article began with the ringing sentence "It is war."

Abdur Rahman, at Rawalpindi with Dufferin, turned out to be much clearer about what was really going to happen. Mortimer Durand was sent to break the bad news and was surprised to find that the Amir took it coolly, urged Durand not to be troubled, and said that as for the casualties—including one general—there were lots of generals in Afghanistan.

Although Dufferin had been told by London that any Russian advance on Herat would be treated as a *causus belli*, Penjdeh was a different proposition. Lumsden had been told in March that the government wanted to support the Amir but hoped "to settle the difference with Russia by negotiation." When the news reached London, the *Times* carried a headline "Outbreak of Hostilities on the Afghan Frontier" and contented itself with a mild editorial demand that the Russians evacuate the valley. Its St. Petersburg man reported "a slight shock here," but no expectation of war—although the Russian press was having great fun with stories about Tate and his officers running away so fast that the cossacks couldn't protect them from the tribesmen. Even from Rawalpindi a correspondent reported, "There is a belief prevalent that war will not break out." The Rawalpindi belief reflected the fact that Abdur Rahman had gone on to tell Durand that his hold over the Penjdeh tribesmen was slight and that he'd gladly let the place go in exchange for Zulfikar Pass, which approached Herat from the north. Dufferin was pleased; he was off the hook so far as making good on the British pledge to go to war against Russian aggression in Afghanistan. As he wrote home:

> The principal object I was anxious to attain was the freeing of the hand of Her Majesty's government in relation to the delimitation of the Afghan frontier . . . after a second interview I had the satisfaction of telegraphing . . . that as far as the Amir was concerned, we might run the line almost as far south as the Russians themselves required. . . . My own military advisors do not consider that it very much matters within certain limits where the line goes, or that the Russian boundary being drawn a day or two's march nearer or further from Herat materially affects the question of the safety of the place.

As early as April 15 the Russian ambassador was assured that Britain was willing to let Penjdeh go. There was no confidence, however, that the concession would be enough. The tone of the Russian press cannot have helped matters. There were demands that Russia settle for nothing less than Herat and stern warnings to Britain about any attempt to seize the town. Gladstone put on a little more pressure by going before Parliament to ask for and get the largest war credits since the Crimea.

Suddenly there was a hint of peace in the air; it would all be settled by arbitration. Calcutta reported that the notion "aroused a feeling in this country almost of despair," but on the evening of May 4 the Foreign Secretary made it official. Replying to a question from Salisbury, he rose to say that "with regard to the second question asked by the noble Marquis" both Russia and Britain would submit to the judgement of the sovereign of a friendly state rather than see "gallant officers on either side put upon their trial."

Lumsden came home in a fury. The *Times* sulked and blamed the whole business on "half hearted measures," while the Indian press howled that "the news of the arrangement with Russia has created a feeling approaching to dismay. The settlement is ... humiliating and dangerous, ruining British prestige."

In time both sides got what ground they were standing on, and it is worth asking why the sepoy and the cossack collided and then recoiled. Perhaps the best answer lies in a two-word American headline while war was still in the balance: "Bismark's Opportunity." An official Anglo-Russian detente was still twenty-two years away; but the most striking fact of life in Europe was the German victory over France in 1870, and both the British and the Russians were slowly coming around to the fact that the Great Game in Central Asia was about to be replaced by an even greater game elsewhere.

The Amir returned to Kabul wearing the Grand Cross of the Star of India, and during the final ceremonies at Rawalpindi one more chore fell on the hard-working Durand:

> ... suddenly the Duke of Connaught turned to me and said the Viceroy wished to know whether there was any objection to the Amir saying a few words to be heard by all. I said no—perforce—and was then ordered up to the dais to translate. The Amir made a speech which caused much enthusiasm and he said a certain amount more, which I carefully burked. He promised to help us against the chiefs of India, as we were going to help him in Afghanistan, and pressed me to declare this. It was a very difficult work turning a speech of this kind on the spur of the moment, but I think I succeeded. The affront to our loyal Sikh chiefs would have been unpardonable. During my

most exaulted periods a damned little musical-box bird among the presents hoisted its wings and chortled wildly.

Salisbury, who succeeded Gladstone as Prime Minister, signed the boundary agreement with the Russians in September even though he did not consider it "worth the paper it is written on." Even Sir West Ridgeway, who handled the negotiations, called it "not a good frontier either strategically, politically or ethnographically." Curiously enough, it stood up. The Russians had come as far as they were going to.

If the Russian-Afghan border was at peace, the Indian border was not; there were punitive expeditions almost every year, culminating in the campaign of 1897 when the entire border burst into flame. For what life was like most of the time, however, it is instructive to see what the historian of a Pathan battalion in the 14th Punjabis considered notable enough to put into a lengthy account of ten years' service beginning in 1890. He commences with the battalion doing garrison duty at Quetta, when the most pressing business is the necessity of discharging two newly raised companies of Achakzai tribesmen for refusing to do pick and shovel work. The crisis was shortly followed by another of similar moment:

A little later there was some difficulty enlisting buglers. A certain number of lads had enlisted for this purpose, but when it came to the point of actually becoming baja-wallahs, they seemed to think the duty was one which could only be done by men of lower grade. In short, they were not anxious to get on with it. One day these lads paraded and Ridgway reported their disinclination to Dillon, who was physically a very powerful man. The latter thereupon went up to No 1 of the front rank and put the question to him. On receiving "No" for a reply, the man received a severe clout on the side of the face. The question was repeated, "No" was again the answer and a second clout was given, this time on the other side of the head. This happily brought acquiescence not only from the "clout-ee" himself, but also from the remainder of the parade.

There were more serious trials ahead. First there was a plague of locusts and then an attack of cholera, which killed fifty including Mrs. Dillon. After this, there was nothing serious to record for quite a period; the battalion worried about the problem of moving its billiard table from Quetta to a new station, dealt with a sentry "a bit loose in the head," underwent a mild earthquake, settled a fight between its troops and the local Sikh police, and worried about sending a contingent of Pathans to a Scots regiment for training as bagpipers. At a new station near the border, the enlisted men fell to smuggling rifles to tribesmen on the other side who would pay up to $250 apiece for them. One man shot another in a gambling dispute, and the shooter, condemned to hanging, objected to being hung by the low-caste hangman:

> On hearing this, Graves said, "Very well, ask the company if anyone will undertake the task." There were no volunteers. "Well," said the commandant to Ridgway, "I want to grant his last request and as there are only you and me left, I think you had better carry out the execution." This was, as the modern saying goes, a new one on the Adjutant, and after saluting, he mounted the scaffold and after some instruction by the pukka executioner as to the manner of adjusting the rope and Momim [the condemned], who was steady as a rock, had said a few words of warning to his comrades, acknowledging the justice of his sentence, the cap was snapped over his head. The rope was placed around his neck and the signal given for the block to fall. To Ridgway's infinite relief Momim died instantly, for the former in his agitation had fastened his hands in front of him instead of behind.

Three officers were shot by a berserk sentry while playing billiards; the battalion moved to Rawalpindi, then to Mian Mir; cholera struck again; a gramophone was purchased ... and on and on and it was 1904 before they finally saw a little action during a campaign into Tibet.

The life was not unpleasant. A French traveler who visited the Peshawar cantonments wrote that it

> ... resembles all the cantonments which I had already seen. The same broad avenues, the same allotment of the ground into large sections, the same white bungalows lost in vast gardens, the same scrupulous comfort in the fitting up of the club and officers' mess,

the same dog carts with the same little ponies followed
by the same little fox terrier galloping in the dust of
the carriage and everywhere the same impeccably
correct gentlemen with the same bronzed complex-
ions, the same eyeglasses, the same shaped mous-
taches, the same beige jackets, white flannel trousers
and tennis shoes. Whoever has seen one English cantonment has seen all.

Things were not, however, all cantonment life. The
railroad to Quetta was being pushed up to New Chaman,
right on the Afghan border, and the Amir said it was
"pushing a knife into my vitals." To upset him further,
there was continual talk of extending the line all the way
to Kandahar and a persistent rumor that the British were
anxious to redefine the Afghan-Indian frontier. The Amir
quite rightly suspected that the redefining was going to
cost him territory.

Simla wanted to redefine because it thought—correctly—
that a good deal of the tribal raiding on the border went
on with the encouragement of the Amir and even with
guns and ammunition supplied by him. Everyone conceded that he could not stop the raids completely even if he
wanted to, but the notion got around that they might be
reduced by declaring the tribal area a sort of buffer state
in which the Amir was not supposed to meddle. The
British would be allowed in only to chastise tribes for
raiding on the plains. Abdur Rahman warned Lansdowne,
the new Viceroy, that "if you should cut them out of my
dominions, they will neither be of any use to you nor to
me. You will always be engaged in fighting or trouble
with them and they will always be plundering."
Lansdowne, who considered the Amir "a cantankerous
and suspicious old savage" and was forever nagging him
about the somewhat drastic punishment he handed out to
his enemies, wouldn't listen, and in 1893 sent Mortimer
Durand to Kabul to make a new treaty. Abdur Rahman
gave in without much argument, apparently reasoning
that his influence over the tribes was about the same,
boundary or no boundary, and Durand sweetened the pot
by increasing his annual subsidy by an additional $300,-
000. At the time, the Durand Line was acclaimed a
considerable achievement and even elicited congratula-
tions from Victoria. In retrospect, it seems the greatest
single cause of the great Pathan rising which came only
four years later.

In the tangle of mountainous mini-states to the east of Afghanistan lived a number of eccentrically titled rulers including the Thun of Hunza, the Akhund of Swat, and—more eccentric than all—the Mehtar of Chitral. A man of "fiendlike temper" who divided his time between slaughtering his subjects for their property and selling them into slavery, he was nonetheless satisfactory to the British. He accepted their subsidy, permitted them to keep a Bengali newswriter at his court, and did not make overtures to the Russians, who were poking about farther north in the Pamirs. The nearest British presence was 120 miles due east at Gilgit—although mileage is misleading when speaking of an area in which going from almost any place to anyplace else involves crossing a mountain pass of some 12,000 or 13,000 feet.

In 1892 the old Mehtar had died and the struggle for succession had gone as follows. The outstanding candidates were two of his sons, one a homosexual incompetent, the other a lout. After some scuffling during which the British stood neutral, the lout got the throne, only to be shot off it by a half brother, Sher Afzul. British neutrality ceased. Sher Afzul had been staying with Abdur Rahman at Kabul, and rightly or wrongly, to British eyes it appeared that the Amir was trying to put his own man across the Durand Line, where he had been told he could not go. Surgeon-Major George Robertson, the resident at Gilgit, marched to Chitral with the old Mehtar's deviate son; Sher Afzul fled back to Kabul, and Robertson put his man on the throne. As an indication of local conditions, the Bengali newswriter told Robertson that the customary salute for distinguished visitors would be omitted because there was suspicion that the saluting party might load live ammunition and shoot to kill.

Leaving the new Mehtar with two British officers and fifty Sikhs, Robertson departed. The new man lasted a year and then, in late 1894, was assassinated by another half brother. Once more Robertson started out from Gilgit to set things straight, and on the way he got bad news: Chitral had been invaded from the south by Umra Khan, a border chief in "a state of irritation" over the work of the Durand boundary commission. By the time Robertson actually got to Chitral there was another new face; Sher Afzul had hurried on from Kabul for another try at the Mehtarship. Abdur Rahman had given the most solemn assurances that he would not be allowed into Chitral again, and when the British remonstrated with the

Amir he replied that Sher Afzul had gotten out of Kabul
without his knowledge. A number of veteran frontier
officers observed that nobody got out of Kabul without
the Amir's knowledge.

Sher Afzul and Umra Khan patched up a treaty de-
signed to get the British out, and on March 1, 1895,
Robertson found himself besieged in the rickety fort at
Chitral. He remained so for fifty days.

In the fort, there were 83 veteran Sikhs, 257 half-
trained Kashmiri riflemen, and 52 Chitralis of dubious
loyalty. The British officers were Captain Colin Campbell,
Captain C. V. F. Townshend,* Lieutenants Harley, Gur-
don, and Baird and Surgeon-Captain Whitchurch. The siege
was only three days old when the little officer-force was
reduced by two. A reconnaissance went out to test Sher
Afzul's strength and got itself bushwhacked; before it
could get back to the fort, Baird was mortally wounded
and Campbell so badly hit that he was never an active
member of the defense.

Not the least of Robertson's concerns was the fort
itself. It was big enough—eighty yards square with walls
twenty-five feet high and a tower on each corner—but the
walls were chiefly 4 by 4 timbers in mud mortar and the
towers were pine. Robertson feared that it would take
very little to get the lot blazing. Moreover, there was high
ground on all four sides of the fort and anyone exposing
himself during daylight was likely to have tribesmen banging away at him with perfectly good modern rifles. The
supply situation was more cheerful. Rifle ammunition was
adequate, the food would stretch to three months, and
water could be had from the Chitral River via a covered
way which protected the water carriers.

On March 5 messages came in under a flag of truce
demanding that Sher Afzul be recognized as Mehtar and
the British get out. Robertson stalled and spread rumors
that he was running out of food. As a morale booster, he
told fourteen of his Sikhs that they were up for the Order
of Merit for gallantry during the fight to get into the fort;
by his own admission, there probably weren't fourteen
who really deserved it, but he was in a poor position to
quibble.

Each night, the Chitralis pushed their barricades closer

---

* Charles Townshend commanded during the even more famous
siege of Kut during British Mesopotamian operations during World
War I. The second time, his luck ran out and he wound up sur-
rendering to the Turks.

and the besieged prepared fireballs—pine chips stuffed into canvas bags and the whole soaked with kerosene—to be pitched out to illuminate the landscape in the event of a night attack. Through March, though, there was no general assault, casualties from sniping were light, and the worst the besieged had to bear was the news that two small relief forces from Mastuj had been badly cut up. Nonetheless, Robertson felt his people considered their "prospects a little cloudy" and he determined to give them a lift by producing a proper flag. There was red and white cloth to be had, a blue turban provided the missing color, and an empty tobacco tin had a picture of the Union Jack on it to give the Sikh tailor something to work from. Anxious to display his own creativity, the tailor added a pair of crossed swords to the center of the design. Robertson firmly believed that thereafter everything went better: "It cheered our hearts and stiffened our backs."

He was further encouraged in a curious way. During one of the parleys with Sher Afzul, who still hoped to persuade him to pack up and march home, the remark was made that no troops were on the way from Gilgit. Robertson was delighted; he reasoned thus: the remark was gratuitous, "Chitralis stick to the truth so tenaciously that it is impossible to get it from them," hence a relief force must be coming. He was right. Colonel J. G. Kelly was coming from Gilgit with a smallish outfit and three brigades from Peshawar moved north on April 1.

The middle period of the siege is of no great military or political interest, but it does afford some interesting sidelights on how proper Victorian officers conducted themselves in a tight spot on the frontier. When it came time to slaughter officers' ponies for meat, the work was done in private so no officer would know that on a particular evening he was eating his own pony. The chief table talk—aside from the prospects of Surgeon Whitchurch marrying when they got back to civilization—was the quality of the meals served at the Savoy in London. Their own meals were washed down with the only liquor available, a rum of "a particularly coarse flavor and odor."

On the night of April 6, as last light came on, the garrison could see an unusual amount of movement in the enemy's barricades south of the fort. Then everything was quiet and Robertson turned in around 2 A.M. He awoke to heavy rifle fire and it seemed apparent that a general attack was beginning. While he discussed with Townshend where the weight of it was likely to fall, word came of something he had feared far worse. Under cover of the rifle distraction, a Chitrali party had crept up to the south side of the fort and, with a strong wind out of the south to help them along, set fire to one of the towers. As he ran to the spot, Robertson noted that he had recourse to "expletives." The noise was astonishing in the mountain dark; there was the fierce rushing sound of flames, the cracking as boards snapped in the heat, the rattle of rifle fire with the triumphant cries of the riflemen, and somehow over it all the high-pitched praying of their mullahs (tribal priests) as they urged their flocks forward. The men in the fort stood it all remarkably well considering the half trained state of the Kashmiris; two lines formed up—one passing water along to the fire, the other passing dirt in blankets. A good rush from the attackers might have caved the whole thing in, but they contented themselves with knocking down as many of the firemen as they could from long range. Just before dawn one of the bullets caught Robertson in the left shoulder, and as a surgeon, his first thought was of all the nasty shoulder wounds he'd seen in hospitals. He went to his quarters, prodded the wound to see if a bone had been hit, and finally concluded that a Snider bullet "never made more fuss with less result." Next day, he was making his usual rounds.

The force had been under siege for five weeks. They were tired, worn from a bad diet, and above all subject to a depression that even rumors of a relief force could not dispel. Then, at the end of the sixth week, a sentry reported the sound of a pick working underground just outside the walls. For a day, it stopped, then resumed; when Robertson went to listen there was a steady thud of pick work with an occasional ring as iron struck stone. They were being mined; they lacked the equipment to counter-mine, and there was nothing for it but a sortie.

In the annals of British India, the phrase "forlorn hope" is tossed around fairly loosely. Certainly the sortie at Chitral was a minor affair—the forlorn hope consisted of forty Sikhs and sixty Kashmiris, the whole led by an Irish lieutenant named Harley. Their task was to sally from the fort, dash across some seventy yards of open ground to a small building from which the mine was being dug, then dispose of the defenders, blow up the mine tunnel, and get back before a counterattack descended on them. The garrison lacked an engineer, who would normally have directed the technical side of the operation, but recourse was had to a book on the subject; suitable bags were filled with gunpowder, as was a long, narrow canvas tube which would do as a fuse since the real thing was lacking.

The attack moved off at four in the afternoon of April 17. A door in the walls was opened; it was so narrow that the men could only pass out two or three at a time, but the Pathans and Chitralis were nodding and Harley had them formed up and halfway across the open ground before there was a volley that cost him three men. Before another could be gotten off they were into the building with the bayonet. The defenders fled, but the Sikhs had a battle madness on them and went on to bayonet thirty-five Chitrali laborers as they were pulled one at a time from the tunnel. Harley put in his powder bags, lit the makeshift fuse, and then watched in dismay as a last Chitrali trying to get out of the shaft kicked the fuse to pieces. He was trying to light what was left of it when an explosion knocked him over. The tunnel was blown and the sortie party sprinted back to the fort through rifle fire.

At dusk the next day there was shouting by the sentries on the walls that the besiegers had departed and that the relief force from Gilgit was a mere two marches away. Robertson was cautious; it was decided to wait until the next morning to send out a party to look things over. Nevertheless, the last seven cigarettes were doled out, a head-wracking punch was concocted from the remaining rum, and no one bothered to go to bed.

At dawn, scouts found the besiegers gone, and at 2 P.M. on April 20 the advance guard of Kelly's relief could be seen in the distance—bugles playing. Even Robertson confessed that for the moment the sight and sound made him "emotional." When Kelly's men marched in and the seven-week siege was over, what he felt was fatigue:

I felt, by anticipation, what it must be to attain a great age and feel a listlessness about all things. They declare that we five standing there in front of the ruined outwork were white-faced and strangely quiet. Perhaps nothing short of a Pathan battle-cry and the sharp clatter of rifle fire could have really roused us; for the long sustained stimulus of danger and responsibility was gone; and only tiredness, a tiredness of brain and eyes and body, remained.

Everyone conceded that the affair was a minor siege and the relief should have ended the matter. The facts were not quite so tidy. For one thing, the relief force marching north from Peshawar had to go through Swat, and although a proclamation was duly issued announcing that the British had no hostile intentions, the Swatis made them fight twice before they got through—and the Swatis were generally considered peaceable sorts compared to Pathans.

There was then a debate as to whether to keep a permanent garrison in Chitral or go back to the old Indian newswriter. The garrison view prevailed and a half battalion was assigned. Since even half battalions must be supplied and since the tortuous route via Gilgit was not to be trusted, a new road running up from Peshawar was put through. Part of the road went through the territory of the Khan of Dir—a tame khan—but the rest went through the country of the already irritable Swatis. If the force at Chitral meant that there had to be a road, then the road meant that there had to be another force to protect it. A brigade was posted at the top of the Malakand Pass and a small force at Chakdara to watch the bridge over the Swat River. In all, the Swatis had a good deal to be unhappy about, but as one writer said, "The Swatis are not really a warlike race."

As 1897 came in, England was all a-tiptoe for the celebration of Victoria's sixty years on the throne, the Diamond Jubilee. In India the situation was somewhat less happy. It turned out to be a famine year, an earthquake year, and, in the Bombay area, a plague year. Moreover, the Indian nationalist movement had become troublesome enough for an Indian editor to be transported for life because he had published a pamphlet entitled "Preparations for Becoming Independent."

The frontier, however, seemed quiet enough in June when Mr. Gee, the local political agent, started up the Tochi Valley. He had a twin mission. He was to establish a new outpost farther into Waziri country on the British side of the Durand Line and he was to extract from the Waziris a fine for a previous misdeed. It seems to have been anticipated that the Waziris might be reluctant to pay up, because Gee went off with a heavy escort—three hundred men and six officers, the lot commanded by Lieutenant Colonel Bunny.

On June 10 they arrived at the village of Maizar, were

cordially greeted by the locals, sat down to dine, and suddenly found themselves under well-planned fire from a force of five hundred Waziris which rapidly grew to one thousand. Before they fought their way out, they had over fifty casualties; of their six officers three, including Colonel Bunny, were dead and the other three wounded. For the moment, it looked a little thing and the *Times* simply remarked that the Waziris "are a pretty bad sort of Pathan" and suggested that the necessary retribution "will not be carried out entirely with rosewater."

Actually, it was the beginning of a very big thing—the biggest tribal rising either before or since and one under simultaneous suspicion of being encouraged both from India and by the Amir of Kabul. In London, people prepared for Jubilee Day, June 22. The *Times* announced a special Jubilee edition with "the whole edition printed in England on English made paper," and there were full-page ads offering Jubilee tributes from the likes of Pears' Soap and the Schweppes tonic-water people. On the frontier, two brigades were forming up to go back and deal with Maizar, and then, on the day before Jubilee, the Peshawar Deputy Commissioner's clerk was shot by a ghazi. An Indian correspondent wrote, "There has been evidence for some time past of a spread of fanaticism along the whole of the Northwest frontier."

Next day, Victoria sent her Jubilee message to the Empire: "From my heart I thank my beloved people, May God Bless Them—V, R & I." In India, some of the beloved people responded by attacking Europeans in Poona in the name of Hinduism, and in Calcutta, the Muslims stoned Europeans while the Hindus stood by quietly. Before it was over, troops had to be called out to supplement the police. In the Tochi Valley, the two brigades assigned to Maizar were bogged down in rains, floods, and heavy sniping. When they did reach their destination the place was abandoned, but they "destroyed the defenses of Maizar." The phrase was the standard euphemism for London consumption to describe the blowing up of a village. It was justified on the grounds that there were people in England unduly finicky about being sufficiently strict with the tribes, and besides, it was literally true, since in a tribal village every house was more or less designed as a small fort. On the same day the news got back to London, there were signs of more trouble under the headline "Rising in The Swat Valley."

There are a number of explanations offered for the

Pathan rising of '97 and they probably all contain elements of truth. The most popular at the time was that it was the work of the mullahs, who felt their influence threatened as the revived Forward Policy pushed British influence into tribal country. The Maizar affair was attributed to Mullah Powindah, who had been and would be a devilment to the British for a long time. Another school of thought blamed the whole thing on Abdur Rahman. The truth is probably a combination of the two. The tribes disliked British political agents moving in on them. The *Times* might look to the day when the Pathans would become "loyal soldiers, peaceful husbandmen and industrious traders," but the Pathans did not. From the Amir's point of view the British were crowding him, and he was always confronted by the very real problem of the tribesmen rising against him. If the tribes were encouraged, provided with rifles, and perhaps even supplemented by a few Afghan regulars, it served a double purpose. It kept the tribesmen occupied and it kept the British occupied. It gave the Amir what one shrewd Amir watcher called "a prickly frontier."

By July, 1897, the brigade on the Malakand Pass had made itself comfortable. The weather was hot but the country quite lovely, with plane trees on the slopes, pines higher up, and swarms of blue and green butterflies to brighten the landscape. The Guides' post at Mardan, thirty-two miles south, was the nearest British society available, but the officers on the Malakand managed a few of the amenities, including polo.

From a military standpoint the brigade's situation was less good. The camps of the regiments were all in a sort of cup or crater commanded by higher ground on all sides. The area had not been prepared for defense, although the brigade's political officer had warned repeatedly that a priest known as the Mad Mullah was gathering a force in upper Swat.

On the afternoon of July 26 most of the officers were playing polo, and neither of the two roads along which an attack from upper Swat would have to come were outposted. The political officer's sources were first-rate. They told him the attack was coming and coming that night. He went straightaway to Brigadier Meiklejohn and persuaded him to ask that the Guides be sent up from Mardan, but that was about the extent of the Brigadier's precautions. When the Mad Mullah and his tribesmen hit at about ten o'clock, some of the officers were still in polo kit. A narrow cut in the road—only five yards wide—where a few men might have held off many was almost the Mullah's for the taking until twenty men from the 45th Sikhs managed to get there first in what was literally a footrace against oncoming tribesmen. Their colonel brought them panting into action and got them firing with the front rank kneeling and the second standing; they managed to hold on until the rest of the regiment came up. With rifle fire echoing off the walls of the pass and rocks rumbling as the tribesmen rolled them down from higher up, they fought it out until 2 A.M. before the Mullah's men pulled back.

A second force coming down the other road broke into the camp so thoroughly that the Brigadier himself, sword in hand, led the counterattack, and it was 4 A.M. before the area was cleared and the enemy fell back to content himself with sniping during the daylight hours.

When the news got back to London, there seems to have been very little realization that something more than the traditional border fuss was brewing. The *Times* regretted that "yet another proof has been given of the wave of fanaticism" along the frontier and regretted the necessary retaliation, but observed philosophically, "That is a lesson which we have been obliged to teach savage peoples in many parts of the world." The rest of the editorial had a rather peevish tone because the attack had come at ten o'clock instead of in the small hours of the morning, when Pathans were supposed to attack.

On July 27 the Guides came up to join the defense and that night the tribes—Swatis, Utman Khels, Mamunds—came on again, fighting their way right up to the little trenches thrown up around the camp and dying on the bayonets. It was the same on the night of the twenty-eighth, and the night of the twenty-ninth was expected to be the climax. The day was Jumurat—the day when the Prophet watches with special care over those who die for the faith. The tribesmen came on, lit up both by a full moon and by bonfires which the British had set outside their lines to silhouette their targets. The rifle fire was too much for them, the Mad Mullah was wounded, the whole force drew off, and a squadron of Bengal Lancers rode out to cut up the retreat. The British had 194 casualties, the tribes about 2,700.

During the same period a slim force of two hundred men at Chakdara stood off an estimated twelve thousand tribesmen, but the defense had two Maxim guns and the tribesmen persisted in charging straight at them over open ground.

The fire continued to spread. On August 1 the brigades in the Tochi Valley had their communications posts rushed and there were rumors of a much bigger attack. On August 7 Hadda Mullah raided toward Peshawar with Mamunds and, it was said, some Afghan regulars. The Amir felt it necessary to order his subjects not to join Hadda Mullah and to instruct his governor in Khost to punish any Afghans caught raiding the Tochi expedition. In mid-August came the rumor that the Afridis and the Orakzais were plotting a joint rising. On the eighteenth, rumor had the Afridis marching on the Khyber. By the twenty-third, it was no longer a rumor; they had attacked Ali Masjid and Fort Maude and the next day both of them fell. The success was predictable enough. The Khyber Rifles held both posts; the Khyber Rifles were recruited from the Afridis. In the pinch, they simply put up a token resistance and then went over to their fellow tribesmen. A few more days and the Orakzais were attacking police posts and, farther west, a person or persons unknown cut the telegraph line through the Bolan Pass in several places.

Obviously such a rising had to be chastised, and as early as July 30, the Malakand Field Force—6,800 infantry and 700 cavalry—was formed near Peshawar. Hurrying after the force was an earnest young war correspondent representing *The Pioneer* and *The Daily Telegraph.* The young man's name was Winston Churchill and he was already quite a good writer.

His first jaunt was with a political officer into the Jandol Valley (Umra Khan country), where the political officer was to instruct the khans to turn in their rifles as penance for their part in the attack on Malakand Pass. The young Churchill, who attributed to the Pathans "the ferocity of the Zulu" combined with "the craft of the Redskin and the marksmanship of the Boer," was much impressed by the first khan who came out to greet them.

His dress was imposing, a waistcoat of gorgeous crimson, thickly covered with gold lace, displayed flowing sleeves of white linen, buttoned at the wrist. Long loose baggy linen trousers fastened above the ankle, and curiously pointed shoes clothed his nether limbs. This striking costume was completed by a small skull cap, richly embroidered, and an ornamental sabre.

A few days later he joined a brigade which was to enter the valley of the Mamund tribe. The Mamunds were doubly guilty. They had taken part in the attack on the Malakand and they had joined in Hadda Mullah's raid. A prudent officer might have found this sufficient evidence of Mamund belligerency, but Brigadier Jeffreys did not draw the conclusion. His orders were to burn down or blow up all the Mamund villages, and to get on with the job more quickly he split his force into three columns. They marched at dawn and before long the columns were too far apart to support one another quickly if the Mamunds chose to resist.

The westerly column, composed chiefly of men from the 38th Dogras, decided that the village assigned it was a good deal too formidable to be assaulted without artillery and promptly marched back to brigade base camp. The center column consisted of the 35th Sikhs, a squadron of the 11th Bengal Lancers, and a section of the Buffs* plus Churchill, equipped with a long seaman's spy glass for watching the action. About seven in the morning they sighted some Mamunds, squatting in their blue or white robes with their rifles held upright beside them, on a smallish conical hill against the mountains at the end of the valley.

The Sikhs were ordered to take the hill, then to go on to burn the village farther up the slopes. Up the hill they went, the blue and white figures moved farther back up the slopes, and shortly the Sikhs were into the village and busily preparing it for burning. By 8 A.M. they were about ready to do the job when suddenly the slopes above were alive with blue and white figures who came bounding down, keeping up a heavy fire with good rifles and waving wicked looking Pathan knives. Through his telescope, Churchill saw a lieutenant go down and "a tall man in dirty white linen pounced upon him with a curved sword. It was a terrible sight." A Sikh rifleman "sprang into the air, and falling, began to bleed with strange and terrible rapidity from his mouth and chest." A rout seemed in the making, but someone—Churchill never found out who— told the bugler to sound the charge and the badly pressed Sikhs somehow formed and went forward again.

* Properly The Royal East Kent Regiment. The nickname derives from the buff facings on their dress uniform.

Satisfied that the tribesmen had retired, Jeffreys sent his men back to the village to finish burning it and to recover the body of the lieutenant. They did so, but it all took too long and the day not only wore on, but a thunderstorm came up almost black as night. By the time they began to retire, the enemy was hanging on their flanks in the dark, exhausted men who hadn't eaten since their morning biscuit were falling out of ranks, and tribesmen were sprinting into the column to cut men down. Jeffreys simply had not learned what more experienced frontier soldiers knew by heart—the hardest part of a punitive expedition is getting out after the work is done. Most of the column straggled into camp and then stood-to all night expecting a rush in the rainy dark. Jeffreys stayed out with twelve stragglers from the Buffs and two companies of Sikhs to see that the guns got in safely. In the dark, the Sikhs got separated and the Mamunds jumped Jeffreys and the Buffs; they would surely have gone under if the Sikhs hadn't heard the firing and hurried back to help.

Next morning, Jeffreys marched his column out properly concentrated. As they approached the first village, Churchill watched the sappers blow up an outlying tower. "A great cloud of thick brown-red dust sprang suddenly into the air, bulging out in all directions. The tower broke in half and toppled over." The artillery peppered the Mamunds higher up, the village was properly burned and the retirement properly covered. Before they left, Churchill had a look at a dead Mamund sniper and noted that "he had been an ugly man originally but now that the bones of his jaw and face were broken in pieces by the bullet he was hideous to look upon. His only garment was a ragged blue linen cloak fastened at the waist." The sight did not inspire pity; rather it reminded him of the lieutenant killed two days before and some lines of Kipling's:

> Two thousand pounds of education
> Dropped to a ten rupee jezail.

In all, six villages were dealt with in the next few days. The young correspondent began to perk up a bit, think less of dead lieutenants and more of "brisk little skirmishes" and "villages selected for chastisement." On September 21 the Mamunds sued for peace and the force was further heartened by a message from the Queen Empress expressing sympathy over their losses. "The cynic and the socialist may sneer," said Churchill, but "the

patriot, who examines with anxious care those forces
which tend to the cohesion and disruption of great com-
munities, will observe how much the influence of loyal
sentiment promotes the solidarity of the empire."

The Mamunds were told that if they wanted peace they
would have to turn in twenty-one rifles taken from the
Sikhs in the action of September 16. They balked. Twelve
more villages and some thirty forts were promptly demolished, and the rifles came in. Churchill reflected that
perhaps never before had twenty-one rifles been bought
with so much blood and money.

Farther west, a second expedition was forming to go
into the Tirah Valley to deal with the Afridis and
Orakzais. It was the largest force—35,000 men and 20,-
000 camp followers—ever assembled for purely frontier
duty. Its artillery was good; its infantry was equipped
with magazine rifles and carried the dumdum bullet. The
dumdum, named for the Indian infantry station where it
was manufactured, expanded on contact with bone and
was designed, in the expressive word of Webster's Dic-
tionary, for "man-stopping." In fact, a study of the literature of the campaign produces only one complaint about
weapons. The lancers wanted some sort of blockage about
one third of the way up the lance, since, without it, the
impaled Pathan had an awkward habit of wriggling all the
way up in his death throes and having a whack at the
lancer with his knife. In some few cases, the whack got
home.

The British superiority was so overwhelming that the
campaign is not a particularly interesting one. Indeed the
only incident which caught public imagination at the time
was the storming of the Dargai Pass by the Gordon
Highlanders. Formed for the assault, they were addressed
by their colonel thus: "Men of the Gordon Highlanders,
the General says that position must be taken at all costs.
The Gordon Highlanders will take it." And they did—
played in by a wounded piper who, after being knocked
over, propped himself against a rock and went on piping.
Less attention was paid to the fact that the Gordons had
to be withdrawn the same day because they couldn't be
supplied properly and the whole job done over again the
following day.

There is a record of the day-to-day grit of border
fighting. The author, if not destined for quite so much
fame as Churchill, would eventually be General Sir

Horace Smith-Dorrien and the commander of Sir John French's Second Corps during the early months of World War I. When the Tirah expedition started, he was simply an officer in the Sherwood Foresters and on leave in London at that. On reading that his battalion had been ordered across the frontier, he went to France, took a train from Calais to Brindisi, then walked aboard an India-bound freighter without a ticket. Nineteen days after leaving London, he joined his men at the foot of Sampangha Pass. In a matter of not more than minutes, he was ordered out with half the battalion to sieze advanced positions. Smith-Dorrien had never been on the frontier before, and his introduction was not made easier by the appearance of his brigadier. In his own words:

> We were lying down in the position we had secured, but I had to stand up to salute him. He gave me a warm greeting, hooked his arm in mine and insisted on walking up and down discussing the art of war, in spite of my protests that we provided the sole mark for the enemy to aim at. It was some time before I could manoeuvre him into a position of safety. Why neither of us was hit I do not know, but I came to the conclusion that a too brave General might not be a pleasant companion.

A few bits from his diary over the next two months:

> I was sent to raid villages toward the Bara Valley. . . . We only saw twenty-four of the enemy, and captured one hundred mule loads of grain etc. . . .
> Very cold at night, swarms of transport passing up. The enemy cut into an ammunition column, killed five men of the Queen's. . . . Our foraging parties fired on from two sides. I started coffee-shop for the men. . . .
> At night camp-fire, successful singing. . . . A little sniping. Ice every night. . . .
> Took J. Bowman's company out this afternoon to raid villages near camp; stayed too late, enemy crept up under trees. . . . We had to make undignified retreat. . . .
> Ordered out . . . to reconnoitre a fresh valley. Very pretty day. Enemy rather truculent, a good deal of firing. . . . Retirement very pretty and well carried out. . . .

Saw the Waram Valley below us full of villages. Waited for guns and then moved down a fair but rough path into valley. We had great fun, firing and skirmishing. Afridis in small numbers, but wonderfully active. . . . Soon the valley was one big bonfire. . . .

Rained all day and snowed only a few feet above us. Hills all white. The Mess President (myself) had provided: pig's cheek, *pâté de fois gras*, Stilton and port, most comfortable mess in camp.

Christmas day. Sniping at intervals all day. . . . Private Betts was killed, Sergeant Samworth and Corporal Bill wounded. Christmas dinner; drank "Absent Friends." Expect they rather liked being absent. Sniping on and off regularly until we turned in. . . .

An awful thing had happened during the day. All the towers and villages were being blown up by the Sappers, a most interesting operation to watch. One fuse was long in action. A smart young R. E. Officer, Tonge, and a Havildar went to put it right and were both blown to bits.

Tirah force rolled on and behind it the inevitable debate began over what was to be done once the tribes had been chastised. The retiring Commander-in-Chief of India, Sir George White, set out the military position at a farewell dinner tendered him at Simla. Like most soldiers, he deplored the political officers' habit of paying the tribes to keep the peace and called it bribery. As he told the dinner, "We hear a great deal of abuse of the forward policy, but . . . by fate's inexorable decree civilization must advance and savagery recede . . . it behoves the Government of India to exercise its rule over the dangerous elements which are included in and border on this great Empire strongly . . . not by compromise (enthusiastic applause)." A good many common-sensical people, Churchill included, pointed out that the complete military occupation of the area was simply too expensive.

IX

The End of the Game

On the last day of 1897, Smith-Dorrien was in the Khyber chasing Afridis, but the cold and the howling winds had virtually ended the campaign until spring. The year-end editorial in the *Times* observed that "a combination of grave troubles in India, bravely met if not at once subdued" would be one of the items for which the Diamond Jubilee year would be remembered, and indeed the three lead headlines that day were all Indian—Famine, the Frontier, and the National Congress Party.

The new Viceroy selected to cope with these problems was George Nathaniel Curzon, one of those whose claims to fame is a little rhyme written while he was still an undergraduate at Oxford:

> My name is George Nathaniel Curzon
> I am a most superior person
> My cheek is pink, my hair is sleek
> I dine at Blenheim once a week.

He was the youngest man—thirty-nine years old—ever selected for the post and on a number of counts an unusually qualified choice. He had traveled in India, Central Asia, and the Far East, stayed at Kabul as a guest of the Amir, and published an exhaustive study of Empire problems called *Russia in Asia*. He had served as Under Secretary for India and as Under Secretary for Foreign Affairs. In spite of these impressive achievements, there were those who had their doubts. Some found him still with "many of the defects of the youthful temperament," others "flippant," and still others thought his "restlessness and conceit" likely to lead to trouble.

He was an announced Forward Policy man and even a friend writing to congratulate him added a P.S. "Let me beg as a personal favour that you will not make war on

Russia in my life-time." Another wrote, "It will amuse you to hear that I am being told by the Acute Forward Policy people . . . that now I shall have as many wars as I want!" The Russians had their own doubts, and one editorial on the appointment called him one of "the most extreme Russophobe party, who close their eyes to everything that does not seem to confirm their hardly intelligible hatred toward Russia."

Actually, the Curzon of 1898 had sounded a good deal more ferocious than he was going to act. He might talk of cossacks at the gates and contemplate an advance either to the northern frontiers of Afghanistan or the Kabul-Ghazni-Kandahar line, but what he actually proposed was modest. The tribes were to be controlled by tribal levies, and there was to be an increase in British officers to prevent—hopefully—more performances like the Khyber Rifles in '97. Indian army troops would be concentrated at a few major stations and a number of light railways and new roads pushed well forward to get them to trouble spots quickly.

When Curzon actually arrived in India, he could look toward his Afghan frontier and find it decently quiet, but a glance farther west toward Persia filled him with the grimmest forebodings. The Russians, already strong in northern Persia, were edging south, and to Curzon it seemed only a matter of time before she would have outflanked the Afghan buffer and stand on India's western border. He recommended to London the establishment of a new buffer by an agreement with Russia to divide Persia into two spheres of influence, with Britain keeping only enough to hold Russia off the frontier and away from the Persian Gulf.

For the moment, London could see very little promise in an agreement with the Russians. For one thing, London was a good deal more concerned about South Africa, where British regulars were taking a thorough thumping from Boer farmers. For another, the Russians had taken the opportunity to apply a little pressure. In February, 1900, the Foreign Office had a Memorandum from the Russian Embassy suggesting that the time had come for the establishment of direct relations between Russia and Afghanistan. The tone was friendly enough; the note hastened to add that the relations would be nonpolitical and said that the Russian government still conceded that Afghanistan was outside her sphere of influence.

Two weeks later the Amir had a similar note from the

Russian agent at Bokhara and duly passed it along to
Curzon. The Viceroy was emphatic that the Russian request should be turned down flatly if it involved any sort
of Russian agent at Kabul. A commercial agent was
bound to become a political one, with dreadful results at
Kabul and in India. Salisbury, now in his third stint as
Prime Minister, took a different tack. For one thing, he
had his hands full in South Africa. Moreover, he was
always a less bellicose man than his Viceroy, of whom he
said once, "He always wants me to negotiate with the
Russians as if I had five hundred thousand men at my
back and I have not." Finally, he was a very old, tired
man and probably senile. Orders came down that British
representatives were to avoid discussing the problem with
Russians at all, if possible, and to stall if backed into a
corner. In the way of old-fashioned diplomacy, correspondence over the matter dragged on for four years before
the outbreak of the Russo-Japanese War led the Russian
ambassador to observe that "for the moment discussion of
outstanding questions could not with advantage be continued."

Nevertheless, it could be reopened, and a good many
people thought it would be. Cecil Spring-Rice, then at the
British Embassy in St. Petersburg, summed it up: "Russia
has notified her intention of sending, when she pleases,
her Agents into Afghanistan." Arthur Godley, Under
Secretary for India, said, "If we are, as appears likely,
going to agree to the proposal sooner or later, I hope that
it will be made the occasion for getting a general understanding with Russia."

On the frontier, Curzon raised his tribal levies, an-
guished a number of officials by wrenching the tribal
areas from the control of the Punjab and establishing
them as the Northwest Frontier Province reporting directly to the Viceroy, and the tribes went right on raiding
as they always had. The butcher and bolt expeditions
went out so regularly that they became something of a
frontier joke, known as "Wilcox's Weekend Wars" after
General Sir James Wilcox who conducted them.

Then, with almost no warning, the frontier was shaken
in 1901 by the death of Abdur Rahman. The least anyone
expected was a civil war in Afghanistan with the Russians
fishing in troubled waters. Preparations were made to
push troops north from Quetta and Peshawar. Remarkably, one of the Amir's sons, Habibulla, managed the
takeover neatly; the Russians did not meddle; and all was

well until the next year, when the young man declined a Curzon invitation to come down to India for a visit.

When Salisbury wrote the Viceroy, "I am a good deal disquieted about Afghanistan," it is likely that he was partly disquieted about the Amir, but at least equally about what his Viceroy was likely to do about the Amir. On no evidence save his rejected invitation, Curzon leaped to the conclusion that Habibulla was swinging toward a Russian alliance and proposed a series of steps which gave London the willies. In his opinion, "If you allow a man and a state of his calibre to flout the British Empire, then we had better put up the shutters and close business." Rather than close business, Curzon proposed to send a letter which was very much an ultimatum and, if no satisfactory reply was received, to advance to Kandahar and beyond. To Salisbury, it must have sounded unpleasantly like Lord Lytton all over again. Curzon was firmly informed by London of "the growing dislike, if not abhorrence, of any forward move or any action likely to entail military operations."

The motives were not peaceable but financial. In 1900 the German Reichstag had voted to double the German navy. The British navy had to grow with it, and there simply wasn't enough money around for another promenade through Afghanistan. The situation was retrieved when Habibulla sent a new letter reopening negotiations. The Amir was a stubborn young man. In 1904 he received a British delegation at Kabul, but he never did come down to India to see Curzon.

In September, 1905, Teddy Roosevelt was at Portsmouth, New Hampshire, supervising a treaty ending the Russo-Japanese War, and the British ambassador at St. Petersburg was able to write home that as a result of the Russian defeat "the military and Chauvinistic party in Russia has fortunately sustained ... a shock from which it is probable that it will never recover." He saw the "liberal and constitutional party" as the party of the future. He might have added that the Czar was faced with a revolution at home, which made it doubly unlikely that he might be looking for trouble in Central Asia.

As far back as 1888, Salisbury had suggested to the Russians a settlement of the Persian rivalry; there had been a number of other feelers over the years, and now the new Liberal Party Foreign Secretary, Sir Edward Grey, spoke to the Russian ambassador about a general agreement over the outstanding questions between the two countries. By March, 1906, negotiations were far enough advanced for London to write the new Viceroy, Lord Minto, "Suppose you were coming to some sort of understanding with Russia—a hypothesis which may be many hundred miles off realization—and suppose that we held the upper hand in the negotiation, what would be the terms that you would exact from Russia as essential to the bargain?"

Minto replied that the Amir was a more dangerous enemy than Russia and said, "If we are to enter upon an entente with Russia, let us bargain with her elsewhere than in Central Asia." He was promptly rapped across the knuckles with a reply that said that there was no "if" about the entente and that Central Asia was certainly going to be part of the package. By May, there was talk in the press about an Anglo-Russian agreement over Persia, Afghanistan, and Tibet, and while Grey would reply to a questioner in Parliament that no such agreement existed, he did add that Sir Arthur Nicolson was in fact on his way to St. Petersburg to negotiate it.

The Anglo-Russian Convention of 1907 is a remarkable document. It took a year to negotiate—yet it did little more than commit to writing the facts of life as they were. Once written, it was widely disregarded and widely disliked in both countries, and nowhere in the entire document is the real subject matter—Germany—so much as mentioned.

Germany had passed Britain in steel production and it had been perfectly obvious for some time that she could handle France or Russia separately any time she was of a mind to. Russia and France had had an Entente since 1892; Britain had broken with "splendid isolation" to make a French Entente in 1904. It required only a British-Russian agreement to complete the Triple Entente —or the encirclement of Germany, depending on the angle from which one viewed it. Difficulties in handling public opinion were formidable. Friction in Central Asia aside, Britain had a treaty with Russia's recent enemy, Japan. The Japanese defeat aside, the Russians were still groggy from the 1905 revolution when troops had fired on a crowd marching to the Winter Palace and killed one thousand civilians. A good deal of Russian opinion felt that Britain had simply grabbed a moment when Russia was weak to get a treaty. On the British side of the fence, Russophobia—never far from the surface—had been given a boost when British trawlers were fired on by a nervous Russian Baltic fleet during the Russo-Japanese War. Take it all in all, the only real item the two had in common was a mutual fear of Germany, and this was the one thing they could not possibly sign a treaty about. The Czar would never have stood for it, and a good section of the Russian Foreign Office would never have stood for it. As Nicolson saw it, the discussion should be restricted to "a matter of fact agreement on the respective British and Russian interests in certain specific regions. The proceeding . . . must be thoroughly businesslike and the field in which they were to operate must be strictly defined." Under the ground rules of the old diplomacy, this gave Germany nothing to complain about—even at a time when a private in a British regiment in India saw clearly that the way the British reserve was being built up meant that a war with Germany was sure to come.

On May 29, 1906, Nicolson—slight, stooped, arthritic—presented himself to the Russian Foreign Minister, Alexander Izvolsky—short, plump to bursting, dandy. Nicolson found his man "not without vanity and ambition, nervous, somewhat timorous of responsibility," but nonetheless a man who was "sincerely anxious to come to an understanding."

Izvolsky had a number of hopes riding on an understanding. He hoped for British support in the Balkans; he hoped that Russian finances, in even worse shape than usual, would be bolstered by a British loan; he hoped that Britain might reconsider its position on the Dardanelles. Most immediately, however, his bad dream was the Imperial Ottoman Baghdad Railway Company. In plain English, the company was a concession permitting the Germans to build a railway across Turkey—or right up to the back door of Russian-dominated northern Persia. A Russian paper called the project one which "threatens Russia and Great Britain with untold evils." In sober fact, there wasn't much—short of war—either country could do to prevent the railway from being built, but if they could compose their differences they might at least stand shoulder to shoulder against further German penetration.

While the talks dawdled on through the rest of 1906, Minto in India set about mending his fences in Afghanistan against the evil day when he would have to tell the Amir that a British-Russian arrangement had been made in Central Asia without consulting him. Habibulla finally consented to come down to India for a visit—a favor never granted Curzon—and in January, 1907, togged out in western clothes and a red fez, he arrived in a fearsome downpour. One irreverent young man thought he looked like a successful pawnbroker and estimated the two thousand Afghan troops he'd brought along as an escort inferior to Portuguese infantry. The young man had never fought on the frontier.

The arrangements were opulent. The Amir was seen into camp through an arch twinkling with tiny electric lights, trees and ferns were moved into the campsite, the Amir's bed was a silver fourposter and instead of plain sheets (we have Minto's word for it) he had gold and silver embroideries—which, in a simpler age, one can only think of as having been damned scratchy. Some 32,000 troops passed in review before him and he was reminded that they represented only a fraction of the India army. The Amir seems to have had a perfectly splendid time and remarked to Lady Minto that he hoped to repeat the experience the following year—which caused the Vicereine to remark, "With a sickly smile I told him that we should look forward to that pleasure, privately praying that the Government would never allow the experiment to be repeated oftener than once in five years." By February 6, Minto himself was writing, "The Amir is still with us. I am afraid these words can hardly convey what they mean to me. Lady Minto and I are in the last stages of exhaustion."

At last they got him off and, as London approvingly wrote Minto, ". . . without one single bit of new engagement on our part." Poor Habibulla was enchanted with western ways—too much so to suit his own people, and one observer predicted that he would someday be "knocked on the head some fine morning by his brother or some other near relative." Let it be said that he was true to his commitments even during the First World War when he might have bettered himself by doing otherwise. The British in India laid great store by personal diplomacy; with Habibulla it worked.

In St. Petersburg Izvolsky and Nicolson worked to get an agreement against the opposition of a Russian military party which was by no means as defunct as had been suggested to Grey. To satisfy Simla's desire to protect India's western border, Nicolson had to get the easternmost Persian province—Seistan—declared a British sphere of influence. The Russian military, whose designs included all Persia, thought Izvolsky was giving away too much. In Afghanistan, they suspected that British officers would be sent to train the army, then lead it against Russian Central Asia. In fact, it was quite plain that the Russians spent as much time worrying about an Anglo-Indian invasion as the British did about a Russian threat. A report of their fears went to London, and Grey wrote at the bottom of it, "I am convinced that the apprehension of the Russians that we might adopt an aggressive policy against them in Central Asia is a real one on their part."

Nicolson stood firm on Seistan and attempted to be reassuring about Afghanistan. The Amir, he pointed out, had never shown the slightest desire to have British officers for his troops—in fact, quite the contrary. Moreover, a well-armed, well-drilled Afghan army was likely to be considerably more of a nuisance to India than it would be to Russia.

It was August, 1907, before the job was finally done. In Persia, Russia got a large sphere of influence in the north—where she was anyway—but not a large enough one to put her on the Persian Gulf. Central Persia was a neutral zone and Nicolson got Seistan and the country that covered the entrance to the gulf.

In Tibet, both sides agreed not to send representatives or attempt to secure concessions for themselves or their subjects. In Afghanistan, Nicolson simply got in writing three things which had been said any number of times. The Russian government confirmed that Afghanistan was outside its sphere of influence, and she agreed to conduct her relations with that country through Britain and not to send agents into the country.

The Persians were furious, the Afghans were furious, and when they both declined to concur in the convention, the British and the Russians declared it in force anyway. After all, Persia and Afghanistan were not what the convention was about. As Nicolson wrote Grey:

> Essential as a friendly Afghanistan may be to our position in India, equally essential, I submit, is a friendly Russia to our general international position, both as regards the actual situation and also in respect to that in the not distant future. If we wish, and I presume we do wish, in the interest of peace to avert the possibility of any Power assuming a position from which she could dictate to others, a close understanding with France and Russia is, I submit, an object for the attainment of which every effort should be made.

What the convention was about was not lost on the nation concerned. As Germany's man in St. Petersburg wrote home, "These plans need not necessarily be ascribed to any anti-German tendency, yet Germany is the country which is most effected by the agreement."

"Yes," wrote the Kaiser at the bottom of the dispatch, "when taken all around, it is aimed at us."

On the northwest frontier, if the specter of Russian invasion had gone away, at least for the time being, the realities had not. With a regretful eye on the costs involved, the government mounted yet another butcher and bolt expedition—this time against the Zakka Kel Afridis.

If German press comment—on official instructions—was calm to the Anglo-Russian agreement, other German reaction was less pacific. The naval building program rushed ahead, and the Kaiser told a group of his officers that he wanted "A strong navy; a strong army; and powder dry!" Britain came back with a program of super-battleships—dreadnoughts—and the public took it up with the cry "We want eight and we won't wait." The army's expeditionary force was remodeled and it was quite clear to any thoughtful person that this time it was not intended to fight Russians in Central Asia, but Germans in northern France.

If there was a war coming, the Indian flank had to be made secure. King George V was concerned about the Nationalist movement in India—the "seditious spirit" as he called it—and proposed that he himself make a trip to rally his subjects. His government noted that "this splendour would be very costly, as the last durbar only too abundantly proved," but in the end approved the visit.

His reception in Bombay in December, 1911, was cool; his staff laid it to the fact that his subjects had been expecting to see their Emperor riding on an elephant. The Delhi reception was not much better. The durbar, however, was suitably grand. There were 300,000 people encamped in 40,000 tents. This time the 10th Hussars, "the Shiny Tenth," led the parade, the golden-domed throne stood on the same spot Lytton's had, and the Iniskilling Dragoons won the polo tournament. There was a bad moment when the Gaekwar of Baroda approached His Majesty while carrying a walking stick and His Majesty recoiled in a manner suggesting that he thought the Gaekwar was about to strike him, but on the whole it went well. A *Times* correspondent was moved to say that "one felt . . . that the Durbar was not the apotheosis of tinsel Imperialism; it was the ritual of that unreasoned but increasing faith which had linked the people of a distant island with the ancient nations of the East in a common striving towards an exalted end."

The nature of the exalted end, whether the *Times* man realized it or not, had changed. The Russians were threatening to invade Persia, and even twenty years earlier the durbar message would have seemed an excellent time to tell both Russians and Persians to behave themselves—as Victoria had warned the powers beyond the northwest frontier in '77. This time, however, the message contained nothing more ringing than some small concessions to Nationalist sentiment and the announcement that Indian army troops would henceforth be entitled to wear the Victoria Cross. Between 1914 and 1918, they earned a great many of them in France and in the Middle East.

The Afghans kept their treaty with the British throughout the war in spite of considerable Turkish pressure to do otherwise. In 1919, however, they did demand control of their own foreign affairs and the British were too exhausted to say anything but yes. The border tribes behaved very much as they always had, and even today the government of Pakistan is trying to deal with their demands for the creation of an independent border state. The Russians paused while they changed governments and then came on again. The sepoy and the cossack are gone, but in Kabul today the cement factory is the product of a Russian aid program, the airfield the product of an American.

BIBLIOGRAPHY

The literature in this area is virtually endless. I have tried here to pick out some road-sign material that will get any interested reader started.

British official documents—Indian Office and Foreign Office papers—can be found in libraries under Parliament Sessional Papers. The easiest way to find a particular volume is to look under the area involved—India, Persia, Afghanistan, Central Asia. If you are able to get to London, the Indian Office material is now in the Commonwealth Office. Permission to use it is complex and you would do well to apply in advance.

An overall acknowledgment should be made to the contribution of the London *Times* to this book. In addition to its conventional reportage, it carried digests of the foreign press that can only be called gold mines. In addition, it was customary, particularly in the first half of the nineteenth century, for anyone with an interesting letter from a friend or relative to send it along for publication. Thus, Dr. Brydon's letter to his brother describing his escape is preserved in the *Times*. It was a great paper, and even after hours of wearing your eyes out on the microfilm, you still want to pick it up and hug it.

The Indian press for the period is divided into papers aimed at a British audience and into what was called "the vernacular press" aimed at an Indian readership. Unfortunately, it is just beginning to be microfilmed, and ordering photostats from India is quite expensive.

BIBLIOGRAPHY

The following are some general works that have been valuable:

Fraser-Tytler, Sir W. K. *Afghanistan*. London and New

York, Oxford University Press, 1950. A fine, balanced book by a man who knew the country firsthand.

Gleason, John. *The Genesis of Russophobia in Great Britain.* Cambridge, Harvard University Press, 1950.

Kazemsadeh, Firuz. *Russia and Britain in Persia.* New Haven, Yale University Press, 1968. A gorgeous piece of scholarship.

Krausse, Alexis. *Russia in Asia.* London, G. Richards, 1899.

Sykes, Sir Percy. *History of Afghanistan.* London, Macmillan & Co., 1940.

———. *History of Persia.* London, Routledge and Kegan Paul, 1969.

For general military background:

Jackson, Major Donovan. *India's Army.* Covers roughly the same ground in its own field that Talbot-Booth (below) does.

King, C. Cooper. *The Story of the British Army.* London, Methuen, 1897.

MacMunn, Sir George. *The Armies of India.* London, A. C. Black, 1911.

Talbot-Booth, E. C. *The British Army.* London, S. Low, Marston and Co., 1941. An excellent collection of brief regimental histories very good for details on custom, uniform, battle honors, and the like.

De Watteville, Colonel H. *The British Soldier.* New York, G. P. Putnam's Sons, 1954.

For the period up to the beginning of the First Afghan War:

Burnes, Sir Alexander. *Travels to Bokhara.* London, J. Murray, 1834.

Conolly, Arthur. *Journey to the North of India Through Russia, Persia and Affghaunistaun.* London, R. Bentley, 1834.

Corneille, Major John. *Journal of My Service in India.* London, The Folio Society, 1966. This reprint is very good on eighteenth-century British India.

Davis, H. W. C. *The Great Game In Central Asia (1800-1844).* The Proceedings of the British Academy, Volume XII. London and New York, Oxford University Press, 1927.

Elphinstone, Mounstuart. *An Account of the Kingdom of Caubul.* London, Longman, 1815.

Forster, George. *A Journey from Bengal to England.* London, R. Faulder, 1798.

Kaye, Sir John. *The Life of Metcalfe.* London, 1858.

———. *Lives of India Officers.* London, Strahan and Co., 1869.

———. *History of the War in Afghanistan.* London, W. H. Allen and Co., 1874. For years this monumental work was the dominant account of the First Afghan War. Now, however, we have the Norris book (below).

Masson, Charles. *Narrative of Various Journies in Balochistan, Afghanistan and the Panjab.* London, 1844.

Moorcroft, William, and Trebeck, George. *Travels in the

Himalayan Provinces of Hindustan and the Panjab. London, H. H. Wilson, 1841.

Norris, J. A. *The First Afghan War.* Cambridge, Cambridge University Press, 1967. Norris, obviously a brave man, has taken on Kaye footnote for footnote, and although I do not agree with all his conclusions, he has made a formidable contribution.

Pearse, Major Hugh (ed). *Memoirs of Alexander Gardner.* London, Blackwood and Sons, 1898.

Roberts, P. E. *India Under Wellesley.* London, G. Bell, 1929.

Spear, T. G. P. *The Twilight of the Mughals.* Cambridge, Cambridge University Press, 1951.

―――. *The Nabobs.* London, H. Milford, 1932.

Vigne, Godfrey. *A Personal Narrative of a Visit to Ghuzni, Kabul and Afghanistan.* London, G. Routledge, 1843.

Wellesley, Marquess of. *Dispatches.* Oxford, The Clarendon Press, 1877.

Woodruff, Philip. *The Men Who Ruled India.* London, Cape, 1953.

Additional material on the First War:

Atkinson, J. *The Expedition Into Afghanistan.* London, Allen and Co., 1842.

Barr, Lt. William. *Journal of a March from Delhi to Peshawer and from thence to Cabul.* London, 1844.

Broadfoot, Major W. *The Career of Major George Broadfoot.* London, J. Murray, 1888.

Burnes, Sir Alexander. *Cabool, Being a Personal Narrative of a Visit to That City,* London, J. Murray, 1843.

Dennie, W. *Personal Narrative of the Campaigns in Afghanistan.* Dublin, W. Curry, 1843.

Durand, Henry Mortimer. *Sir Henry Marion Durand.* London, 1883. The subject is the stormer of Ghazni; the author, his son, of Durand Line fame.

Eden, Emily. *Up the Country.* London, Oxford University Press, 1930.

Edwardes, Sir Herbert, and Merrivale, Herman. *The Life of Sir Henry Lawrence.* New York, Macmillan, 1873.

Ellenborough, E. *India under Lord Ellenborough.* London, J. Murray, 1926.

Eyre, Vincent. *Military Operations at Cabul.* London, J. Murray, 1843.

Fane, General Sir Henry. *Five Years in India.* London, H. Colbert, 1842.

Forbes, Archibald. *The Afghan Wars.* New York, Charles Scribner's Sons, 1892.

Gleig, G. B. *Sale's Brigade in Afghanistan.* London, J. Murray, 1846.

Greenwood, J. *Narrative of the Late Victorious Campaigns in Afghanistan.* London, 1844.

Gupta, H. R. *The Life and Work of Mohun Lal.* Lahore, The Minerva Book Shop, 1943.

Habberton, William. *Anglo-Russian Relations Concerning Afghanistan—1837-1907.* Urbana, University of Illinois Press, 1937.

Havelock, Captain H. *Narrative of the Campaign of Afghanistan.* London, 1840.

Hough, W. *Operations of the Army of the Indus.* London, 1841.

Imlah, Albert. *Lord Ellenborough.* Cambridge, Harvard University Press, 1939.

Kennedy, Richard E. *Narrative of the Campaign of the Army of the Indus.* London, R. Bentley, 1844.

Lal, Mohun. *The Life of Dost Mohammed Khan.* London, Longman, Brown, 1846.

Lawrence, George. *Reminiscences of Forty-Three Years in India.* London, 1874.

Low, Charles (ed). *The Journal and Correspondence of Major General Augustus Abbott.* London, R. Bentley, 1879.

Neill, John. *Recollections of Four Years Service in the East.* London, R. Bentley, 1846.

Sale, Lady Florentia. *Journal of the Disasters in Afghanistan.* New York, Harper, 1843.

Sanders, Lloyd. *Life of Palmerston.* London, W. H. Allen, 1895.

Southgate, Donald. *"The Most British Minister."* London, St. Martin's Press, 1966.

Sudley, John (ed). *The Lieven-Palmerston Correspondence.* London, John Murray, 1943.

Trotter, Captain L. J. *Auckland.* Oxford, The Clarendon Press, 1893.

Webster, Sir Charles. *The Foreign Policy of Palmerston.* London, Bell, 1951.

Following is a list of general works on the period after the First War. It will be followed by a separate list of material on the Second War.

Argyll, Duke of. *The Afghan Question—1841-1878.* London, Strahan and Co., 1879.

Edwardes, Sir Herbert. *A Year on the Punjab Frontier.* London, R. Bentley, 1851.

Edwardes, Lady. *Memorials of the Life and Letters of Sir Herbert Edwardes.* London, Paul, Trench and Co., 1896.

Falcon, Captain Robert. *Handbook on Sikhs for Regimental Officers.* Allahabad, Pioneer Press, 1896.

Forrest, G. W. *The Life of Sir Neville Chamberlain.* Edinburgh, W. Blackwood, 1899.

Ghose, Dilip Kumar. *England and Afghanistan.* Calcutta, The World Press, 1960. A good study of the second half of the century.

Gopal, S. *The Viceroyalty of Lord Ripon.* London, Oxford University Press, 1953.

Hunter, Sir William. *The Earl of Mayo.* Oxford, The Clarendon Press, 1891.

Lee-Warner, Sir William. *Dalhousie.* London, Macmillan, 1904.

Loftus, Augustus. *Diplomatic Reminiscences.* London, Cassell and Co., 1894.

Lumsden, Sir Peter. *Lumsden of the Guides.* London, J. Murray, 1899.

Lyall, Sir Alfred. *The Life of the Marquis of Dufferin and Ava.* London, J. Murray, 1905.

McMullen, Sgt. J. *Camp and Barrack Room.* London, Chapman and Hall, 1846. The best description of enlisted life. The New York Society Library has a copy.

Martineau, John. *The Life of Bartle Frere.* London, J. Murray, 1895.

Paget, W. H., and Mason, A. H. *Record of Expeditions Against the Northwest Frontier Tribes.* London, 1885. This is the major work in the field. It is hard to find in the United States, but the Library of Congress has a copy.

Parker, Charles. *Sir Robert Peel.* London, J. Murray, 1891.

Popowski, Josef. *The Rival Powers in Asia.* Westminster, A. Constable, 1883.

Rahman, Abdur. *The Life of Abdur Rahman.* London, J. Murray, 1900. By himself and very salty.

Rawlinson, Sir Henry. *Britain and Russia in the East.* London, 1875.

Singh, Khushwant. *History of the Sikhs.* Princeton, Princeton University Press, 1963.

Smith, Bosworth. *Life of Lord Lawrence.* New York, Charles Scribner's Sons, 1883.

Spalding, Captain H. (trans). *Khiva and Turkestan.* London, Chapman and Hall, 1874.

Talboys-Wheeler, James. *History of the Delhi Assemblage.* A very full account of the Proclamation of Victoria as Empress. Columbia University has a copy.

Temple, Sir Richard. *Men and Events of My Time in India.* London, J. Murray, 1882.

On the Second War:
Balfour, Lady Elizabeth. *Lord Lytton's Indian Administration.* London, Longmans and Co., 1899.

Cecil, Lady Gwendolen. *Life of Robert, Marquis of Salisbury.* London, Hodder and Stoughton, 1921.

Colquhoun, Major J. A. S. *With the Kurram Field Force.* London, W. H. Allen, 1881.

Elsmie, George. *Field Marshall Sir Donald Stewart.* Made up in large part of Stewart's very perceptive letters.

Hanna, H. B. *The Second Afghan War.* Westminster, A. Constable, 1899.

Hensman, Howard. *The Afghan War.* London, W. H. Allen, 1882.

MacGregor, Sir Charles. *Diary of the Third Afghan War.* Calcutta, 1887. Some writers count the two campaigns as separate wars.

Roberts, Field Marshal Earl. *Forty-One Years in India*. London, Macmillan, 1900.

Sykes, Sir Percy. *Sir Mortimer Durand*. London, Cassell, 1926.

Down to the Entente of 1907:

Beynon, W. G. L. *With Kelly to Chitral*. London, Edward Arnold, 1896.

Churchill, Winston. *The Story of the Malakand Field Force*. London, Longmans and Co., 1898.

Davies, C. C. *The Problem of the Northwest Frontier*. Cambridge, Cambridge University Press, 1932. Not so detailed, but in many ways an up-date of Paget and Mason.

Gooch, G. P., and Temperly, Harold (eds). *British Documents on the Origin of the War*. London, 1926. Volume IV covers the making of the 1907 Entente.

Gwynn, Stephen. *Sir Charles Dilke*. London, J. Murray, 1917.

Richards, Frank. *Old Soldier Sahib*. London, Faber and Faber, 1936. A later view from the enlisted man's side of the fence.

Robertson, Sir George. *Chitral*. London, Methuen and Co., 1898. A very good book.

Smith-Dorrien, Sir Horace. *Memories of Forty-Eight Years' Service*. New York, E. P. Dutton, 1925.

Warburton, Colonel Sir Robert. *Eighteen Years in the Khber*. London, J. Murray, 1901.

Yate, Major G. E. *Northern Afghanistan*. Edinburgh, W. Blackwood and Sons, 1887. Yate was with the Boundary Commission.

Younghusband, Sir Francis. *The Relief of Chitral*. London, Macmillan, 1895.

I would like to thank here Miss Heather Bradley of *The New York Times* London Bureau who helped to collect some of the most important parts of this research. She is, as anyone at *The Times* will tell you, beyond praise.

Index